DEEPEST VALLEY

Cedric Wright

by Paul C. Bateman, Dorothy C. Cragen, Mary DeDecker
Raymond J. Hock, E. P. Pister, and Genny Schumacher

DEEPEST VALLEY

Cedric Wright

by Paul C. Bateman, Dorothy C. Cragen, Mary DeDecker
Raymond J. Hock, E. P. Pister, and Genny Schumacher

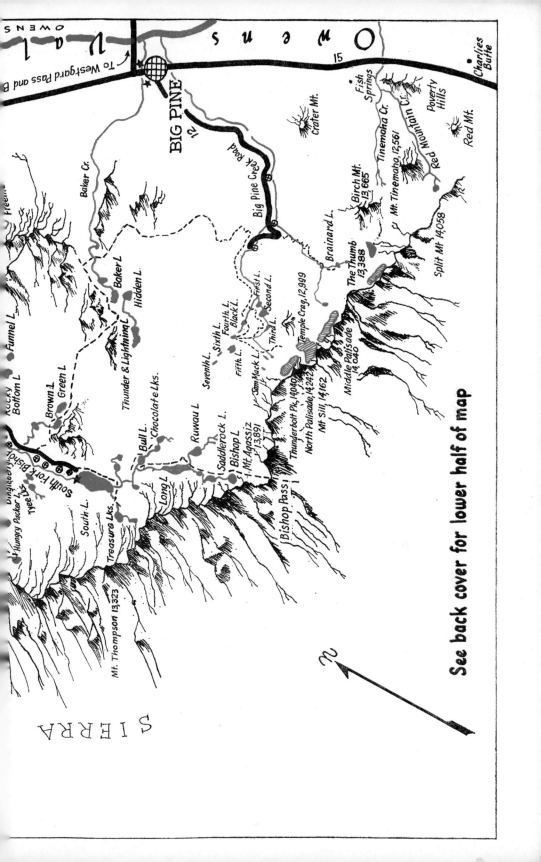

See back cover for lower half of map

The most dramatic shape a man on the moon could see, looking our way on a good summer afternoon at four o'clock P.D.T., would be Owens Valley. The Pacific Coast would be foggy, of course. The Northwest would be under a cloud, to everyone's regret. Thunderstorms would confuse the American landscape from the Rockies to the Acadian sunset. The Old World would be in the dark and South America would be too far east to catch the sun.

But there just to the right of the Pacific shines the great Sierra block, four hundred miles of it, a bright range of light—the southern climax especially, reaching from Yosemite to Mount Whitney. To the right of the bright crest is a long shadow, and to *its* right another range, narrower, but sharp and high enough itself to glisten—the White Mountain Range, subtending the less lofty Inyos.

Our book is about that four o'clock shadow, Owens Valley, two miles deep—one of the earth's great scenic resources . . .

Ansel Adams

. . . and America's

DEEPEST VALLEY

A guide to Owens Valley
its roadsides and mountain trails
Revised edition 1978

New Chapters

Inyo County files suit against Los Angeles Department of Water & Power

Precedent-setting suit seeks to limit the amount of water DWP
may pump from Owens Valley wells for its aqueduct. Outcome
will have implications for water use throughout the West. A
classic case and its issues, as interpreted by the Special Counsel
to Inyo County and the Chief Engineer of Water Works, Los
Angeles DWP. See page 201.

New road and trail information

Important changes, see page 228.

By Paul Bateman, Dorothy Cragen,
Mary DeDecker, Raymond Hock, E. P. Pister,
Paul H. Lane and Antonio Rossmann

Edited by Genny Schumacher Smith

William Kaufmann Inc.   Los Altos, California

Copyright © 1969, 1978 by Genny Smith
First edition 1962, reprinted 1963, 1966, 1969, 1972
Library of Congress Catalog Card Number: 78-50975
ISBN: 0-931378-01-X
Published by Genny Smith Books
Distributed by William Kaufmann, Inc.
One First Street, Los Altos, California 94022

Cover by Stephanie Furniss Murphy Design
Cover photographs by Ansel Adams
Winter Sunrise: The Sierra Nevada from Lone Pine
Owens Valley Road and Sierra Nevada Crest

For mail order information see end of book
Printed in the United States of America by Vail-Ballou Press

Preface

MOUNTAIN RANGES, LIKE BEAUTIFUL women, should not be compared. Each has her special fascination, each her cluster of devoted admirers. If you prize other mountains—the Tetons, the Rockies, the Cascades—we would not be so foolish as to argue with you. We would only congratulate you on having found a mountain heaven to leave your heart in.

We happen to love Owens Valley and its bordering mountains—the Inyos, the Whites, the eastern slope of the Sierra Nevada. We feel fortunate to have lived close to them for over one hundred and fifty years among us, long enough to have discovered some of their secrets, which we share with you in this guide.

Here we find adventure, fun, variety, inspiration, challenge, beauty, joy; days of wonder and peace. May you also.

Contributors: Dr. Paul Bateman, U. S. Geological Survey, Menlo Park, began his geologic studies in the Owens Valley region in 1945. The geologic material prepared by him has been authorized for publication by the Director, U. S. Geological Survey. Dorothy Cragen, Independence, is Curator of History, and President of the Eastern California Museum, and was Inyo County Superintendent of Schools for sixteen years. Mary DeDecker, botanist, Independence, with her husband and two daughters, knapsacked and jeeped most of the region, beginning in 1936, in the course of which she assembled a large collection of Inyo wildflowers. Dr. Raymond Hock, Bishop, became resident scientist at the White Mountain Research Station in 1959, studying the physiological adaptations wild animals make to environmental differences. Phil Pister, Bishop, Department of Fish and Game biologist in charge of fishery management and investigational programs, came to Inyo-Mono to live in 1954. I myself, a free-lance writer, became a summer resident at Mammoth Lakes in 1955.

Illustrators: Peggy Gray, Rovana; Esther McDermott, Susan Rinehart, Menlo Park; Ann R. Hock, Lillian Meacham, and C. Lorin Ray, Bishop.

Photographers: Ansel Adams, Cedric Wright, Philip Hyde; Tom Ross and George Bruley of Independence, William Fettkether of China Lake, Stephen Lucacik of Bishop, David Hamren of Los Angeles, Edward Jacobs of San Francisco, Fred L. Jones of Sacramento, Dorothy Petersen of Canoga Park, and Gerhard Schumacher of Bakersfield. The photograph of the Sierra Nevada from Lone Pine—the full spread in the expanded frontispiece—is from *This Is the American Earth,* by Ansel Adams and Nancy Newhall. The view of Owens Valley in the title spread is from *Words of the Earth,* by Cedric Wright.

Acknowledgments: We are grateful to the many Owens Valley people who supplied tidbits of information, lent us historical pictures and books, or helped in countless other ways.

[7]

We want to thank the following: The Bancroft Library and the Inyo County Library; Eastern California Museum; Jack Beer, Vernon Burandt, Al Crocker, and John Marshall, all of the Department of Fish and Game, Region 5; O. L. Dodd, Division of Highways, District IX; Alice Burkhart, Louis Corwin, Bob Moore, Bruce Morgan, and Art Schober, of the Eastern Sierra Packers Association; John Smith, Road Commissioner, Robert Haggerty, Sanitarian, of Inyo County; Joseph Radel, Ben Casad, Teddy Duda, George Tourtillot, and Richard Wilson, of the Inyo National Forest; Stanley Ewanoski, Sequoia National Forest; R. V. Phillips, Los Angeles Department of Water and Power; Jim Moore, U. S. Geological Survey. Dr. R. Coke Wood, Department of History and Political Science, University of the Pacific; Ruth Simpson, Associate Curator, Southwest Museum; and Dr. Philip Munz, Director Emeritus, Rancho Santa Ana Botanic Garden.

I am especially appreciative of the Sierra Club's adding this book to its long list of publications on the Sierra. Bruce M. Kilgore, editor of the Sierra Club Bulletin, and David Brower, the club's executive director, devoted many hours to seeing the book through its final stages. And the Vail-Ballou Press was extraordinarily helpful once we were finally ready.

We are also grateful to Polly Connable and Donald Moore, of China Lake; Mr. and Mrs. Tom Bramlette, Little Lake; George Brown, Mark Lacey, and Lillian Mullen, Olancha; E. R. Blitch, Bartlett; Lillian Hilderman, Keeler; John O'Keefe, Golden Trout Camp; John Aitchison and George Cook, Lone Pine; Ada Bell, A. A. Brierly, Mr. and Mrs. Val Gorman, Anna Kelley, John McCullough, and A. P. Mairs, Independence; Jim Roberts, Chuck Spencer, and Joe Steward, Big Pine; Charlotte Arcularius, Fred Brooks, Roy Boothe, Ernest Bulpitt, Mrs. W. A. Chalfant, Genevieve Arcularius Clement, Elma Yaney Crosby, Mr. and Mrs. Rollin Enfield, Ray Gray, Aubrey Lyon, Jessie Currie Miller, Claude Smith, Katherine Swall, Mildred Symons, R. A. Van Loon, Dorothy Sherwin Vellom, and Billy Young, all of Bishop; Charles Colvin, Bishop Creek; Hasse and Wesley Bunnelle, Francis Farquhar, Dorothy Doyle Morrison, Clarence Shuey, Larry and Laurie Williams, San Francisco Area; Horace Albright, Vivian Jones, Los Angeles.

If names, spellings, or mileages in this guide differ from those you find on signs and maps, this is intentional; research substantiates our versions. We have packed the guide with as much information as we could for its size. For those who would know more, a selected list of readable and authoritative books follows each section. We realize how much is yet to be discovered and known and are glad that this is so. Nevertheless, we shall welcome corrections, additions, and suggestions for later editions. Send them to the Sierra Club.

GENNY SCHUMACHER

Mammoth Lakes
June 1962

CONTENTS

With thirty photographs and seventy diagrams, maps, and other line illustrations

[10]

Vision
along the crest

IF OUR MAN ON THE moon, admiring the Sierra crest and the four o'clock shadow of Owens Valley, had a very powerful telescope, he would see everywhere, on both sides of the mountains, the enterprising works of man—fields, towns, mine tailings, stumps, reservoirs, networks of highways, and short roads leading up almost every canyon. But along the Sierra crest, all these things would be absent.

This is the High Sierra wilderness—a wilderness not because engineers couldn't build roads there, nor loggers cut trees, but a wilderness by intention. It is wild land preserved by past generations who foresaw that future generations would want some few remnants of the Old West, where all men might somehow know what virgin forest and natural beauty are. Where there is no motor noise to hide earth sounds, no scars to hide landscape, where men are willing to forego convenience in order to experience the wildness that has disappeared from all but two per cent of their land.

Along the Sierra crest, between Tioga and Walker passes, is the longest, finest, most accessible virgin country in the United States. Here one can travel by trail for more than three hundred miles in the same general direction without ever crossing a paved road or passing a settlement. No other region can make such a boast. Yet before many editions of this guide are printed, these sentences may have to be revised, for plans are well under way to cut this virgin land with at least two roads, one over Mammoth Pass and another over Olancha Pass. In the Kern Plateau, logging contracts are being let and the first of many roads being constructed. How many more roads should there be; how much less wild land?

When Joe Walker and his men trudged through Owens Valley in 1834, the western wilderness was fearsome; lost men and animals starved and perished. Today on most wilderness trails you meet dozens of people. America's wilderness has shrunk to two per cent of our land area, most of it in the west. California's wild lands included in National Parks and National Forests amount to five and two-thirds million acres. Subtracting desert lands and areas close to roads, this leaves about three million acres of mountain wilderness—three per cent of California land. It is so heavily used that some of the high-country campsites already have serious problems of wood scarcity and water pollution. Park and forest planners are thinking seriously of building sanitary facilities in heavily used areas of the back country and of restricting the size of parties and the length of their stay.

Most would agree that taming the American wilderness was admirable and desirable. But how much of the remaining two per cent should also be tamed, how much left wild? A hundred years from now, how many wilderness islands (and how large) will there be for mankind to enjoy?

[11]

No matter what agency manages them nor how they are classified, wild lands will remain wild only as long as enough people want them so and make their wishes known. Wilderness attracts not only campers and sportsmen; it also attracts the enterprising, for the dollars its development could bring the developers. It has trees to cut, canyons without roads, sites for summer and ski resorts. All may be worthwhile enterprises; all are incompatible with wilderness.

You do not open up a wilderness; you either keep it wild, or you change it—and lose it. The building of trails is the only change man can make without destroying a wilderness—provided he keeps mechanical contrivances off those trails. A road *to* a wilderness will not change it, for it stops at the edge. But a road *through* wilderness destroys the very wildness that makes wilderness unique.

There are repeated attempts to nibble away at the High Sierra wilderness; many are successful. The pressures to diminish the wild lands come in small packages—eliminate a few hundred acres here for a resort, push back a boundary half a mile there to accommodate a road. Added together, they could change the High Sierra drastically. There is every reason to believe that such pressures will continue, ever stronger and more persistent. Those who want to develop wild lands have their personal economy involved. Those who want lands kept wild count their wilderness vacations among their most cherished possessions. Feelings run deep on both sides. But if you can push through the fire and smoke, you will find that the basic issues are generally clear cut: dollars against wildness.

Every road penetrating the heart of the mountains means that much less wildness, every meadow covered with asphalt that much less beauty. What balance shall there be between wildness and development? How much development, and where? Should the Sierra be remade in the image of the Alps, with tramways, highways, railroads, and resorts throughout the mountains, or should the Sierra crest country remain a unique American wilderness resource? If we choose the former today, the question can never be asked again by a new generation. For as Wallace Stegner has written: ". . . it has never been man's gift to make wildernesses. But he can make deserts, and has."

Owens Valley

SIDE BY SIDE IN EASTern California lie a desert valley of long summers and snow-capped mountains of long winters. Just east of the Sierra Nevada's bold alpine crest rises another mighty range almost as high, the Inyo-White Mountains. The Sierra is pale gray, its slopes angular, its peaks splintered. The Inyos are tawny, their slopes and crest rounded. The highest peaks of both, Mount Whitney and White Mountain Peak, stand well over fourteen thousand feet. Between these bulky ranges, only twenty miles separating their crests, lies a long narrow trough, Owens Valley. Running its length is the Owens River, fed by short streams which rise from Sierra glaciers and tumble down deep-slashed canyons.

Here is what Mary Austin called the Land of Little Rain. Pacific clouds billowing over the Sierra crest have already dropped most of their moisture on the Coast Ranges and the Sierra's west slope, nourishing dense forests of tall redwoods and yellow pine. East of the Sierra, in its rain shadow, little forest green softens the mountains' stark outlines. What trees there are—the twisted wind-stunted whitebark and bristlecone, widely spaced lodgepole and fir—only accentuate the land's severity. The grotesque Joshua, the sparse pinyon forests speckling the higher Inyo slopes emphasize its dryness. No carpet of grass cuts the sun's glare. All is grayed—tumbleweeds bleached straw color, gray-blue haze, dead-gray brush, pale gray boulders, gray-green pinyon, tan sand. In the arid climate, earth scars heal slowly. Hills ripped open by gold seekers, gullies torn by cloudbursts look as fresh and raw as they did a hundred years ago. The work of the land-shaping forces—earthquakes, volcanoes, water, ice—is on dramatic display. The intense desert sun is brutally honest, revealing austerity as well as majesty.

Yet this country seems bleak only to the unknowing and the unseeing. It has silence and order and space. It teems with life; you need but know how to look for it. The steepness of the mountains provides a fascinating variety of vegetation and climate, meadows of alpine flowers growing a short distance from desert sage. Just a few miles from the warm Valley, the nights may be still freezing, the willows bare, the passes choked with snow. Contrasts are exhilarating. Mountain trails seem cooler because of the desert you drove through, the desert browner because of the blue lakes you just came down from.

The seasons and times of day are the keys to this land's beauty. Perhaps we can learn from its animals. Desert squirrels and rabbits know that mid-summer days are for spending in cool burrows, that dawn and dusk are the only times to travel the desert. How the colors affect you—whether, for instance, you see the sagebrush as a depressing dusty gray, or as a shining silver gray—depends not entirely on your mood, but partly on the time of day. The high summer sun masks the colors and flattens the landscape; mid-day in the sun can be too hot for you to notice anything at all. In contrast, morning breezes are cool and pungent with sage, the colors intense. When early morning shadows highlight the gashes in the mountains' bare flanks, the land comes alive. In the late afternoon when the sun drops behind the Sierra, casting the twenty-mile shadows that creep up the Inyos, you are in yet another world of pinks and purple-grays.

Deer know that by June it is time to leave for the high country, that only the cooler days beginning in late September are meant for the desert. Have you known Owens Valley and its mountains only during Julys and Augusts? Then you are still a stranger here, for the seasons bring changes unbelievable. Have you never seen this Valley of grays and tans in its brief ecstasy of spring—tinged with green, splashed recklessly with wildflowers, shrubs crowded with blossoms? And later, the Valley's poplars and oaks glowing yellow orange against a clear October sky? Each season has its glories, some brazen, some subtle. Knowing them all emphasizes their differences and makes each more exciting. Have you known the mountains only under the summer sun? Have you never seen a meadow in June, when green tips are pushing through dark moist soil? A lake half frozen, its boulder shore blanketed with smooth snowbanks, your favorite stream a network of open water and snow bridges? Have you never lingered into September to find the tan meadows white with frost, the timberline country red with the bilberry's small leaves, the aspen slopes shimmering gold?

If you would see the Owens Valley country in all its grandeur, then you must come in winter, when the stern ranges on either side of the Valley are fairylands of dazzling white peaks, joined by an arch of turquoise sky. Bare cliffs loom dark against white slopes. With a scattering of snow on their brown crest, the Inyos across the Valley echo the harmony of the Sierra's whiteness, steel gray, and shadow blue. You even may be fortunate enough to experience that rare first day after a mountain storm, when you awake to find a bright sun warming a world newly white, drab grays turned to silver, the snowline only a little above the Valley. Or those priceless days when snow banners fly, sometimes from only the highest peaks, sometimes along the entire crest. Winter is a photographer's paradise—the mountains sharply outlined, shadows from the low-angled sun accentuating every intricate ravine.

When angry clouds are building up over the crest, or gray mist is hiding the peaks and dripping down the canyons, *then* is the time for a trip to the east side of the Valley, where you can watch the battle between storm and mountains, enjoy the perfume of damp earth and wet sage. The mountains are never more colorful than when washed with rain—nor more unpredictable than when the storm clears, and the clouds that were hiding the base of the range break off and drift up-canyon. Great white mountains appear and disappear among the ragged wisps, and the Valley is a land enchanted.

Roadsides

JUST READING NAMES FROM OUR map may rouse your curiosity and whet your appetite to go exploring—Crater Mountain, Tungsten Hills, Dirty Sock, Hungry Packer Lake, Coyote Flat, the Buttermilk Country. A few are Paiute words: Coso, Haiwee, Inyo, Taboose, Tinemaha. Many features bear the names of pioneers who settled in the Valley a hundred years ago: McGee, Birchim, Baker, Diaz, Carroll, Tuttle. Since the Padres' trail never led east of the Sierra, Spanish names are few; Mexican silver miners probably left us Cerro Gordo, Olancha, Cartago.

Many of the mountains are named for people whose names mean little to us. The exploratory parties who made the first maps, faced with dozens of nameless rivers and peaks, chose to name many of them for various army officers, artists, philosophers, and scientists, then famous but now mostly unknown. A few they named for leaders of their expeditions—Walker, Owens, Kern, Wheeler. We might wish they had retained more Paiute names, which reflect the Indians' close acquaintance with their land and keen perception of its subtleties. Translations would give us, for instance, Windy Peak, Mountain of the Black Feathers, Buzzard Hawk Lake, Mountain Lion Spring. Prospectors named their claims with far more imagination: Green Monster, Flapjack, Gold Wedge, Lost Burro, Merry Christmas, Wahoo, Iron Chief, Free and Easy, Black Dream, Southern Belle. No doubt they chose some as come-ons for potential investors; others mirror their typical humor and optimism.

The Seasons

Timing your trips according to the seasons will make the difference between sheer delight and discomfort. Exact times vary each year; sources listed at the end of the chapter can tell you whether the season will be early or late. For exploring the Valley and its foothills, fall and spring days are a joy, the air crisp, the sun bone-warming. Tourists are scarce; the pick of the campsites and fishing spots are yours. In many ways August is the least attractive month for mountain camping; roadside lakes and campgrounds are crowded. Those who know the high country best often choose early and late summer. Though nights may be cold, long underwear and a down sleeping bag will keep you comfortable. Cabin rates are often lower in the off-season. In June and July it is spring in the mountains, the streams full, flowers on even the dryest slopes. In September there are weeks of Indian summer, and if you are lucky, fresh snow frosting the ridges.

Mountain Driving

In this guide we take you only on safe roads that most cars can make easily. Some of the canyon roads are much steeper than they seem, however; to avoid boiling, shift down to low gears before you think you need to. On narrow roads, remember that *uphill* traffic has the right of way. When you are driving *down* the Bishop Creek road, for instance, it is *your* responsibility to watch ahead for cars coming up, and to wait at the nearest turnout until they have passed you. You can always tell a "flatlander," for he roars down the grades expecting others to pull out of his way, never waving or indicating any kind of a "thank you."

Rock and Arrowhead Collections

Besides the large collections in the Eastern California Museum at Independence, many motels and stores have displays of rocks, minerals and arrowheads. Inquire locally for them. Hob-nob a bit with local people. Some have lived in Owens Valley many years, and are happy to share their knowledge.

Rattlesnakes, Ticks, Rabid Squirrels

The eastern Sierra is ideal for camping, for it has much sun, little rain, and few harmful plants or animals. While rattlesnakes are scarce, it is well to know that there are *some,* mostly below 7,000 feet. Fishermen should watch particularly along little-used streams. If you wear boots and watch where you place your feet and hands (do not reach for a ledge you cannot see), there is little to fear. Remember that a snake is afraid of you, and that he will try to get away unless you have him cornered. It is *your* fault if you surprise him. A snake-bite kit is always good insurance.

You are not likely to pick up a tick unless you wander through dense brush. If you find one on your body, the surest way to remove it is to grasp it gently but firmly, with tweezers or tissue. Do not squeeze or jerk; pull slowly and gently. Examine the wound and the tick to make sure you have pulled his head out, then paint the area with antiseptic. If you have broken the tick off or develop a headache and fever, consult a doctor.

Chipmunks and ground squirrels may carry rabies, plague or tularemia. It is fun and harmless to feed them, but dangerous to handle them. Caution children against picking up a "sick one"; very likely he *is* sick, otherwise he would run away.

Lost Children

Small children usually are "lost" fairly near roadside campgrounds. They should be taught to stay in sight, for they can easily lose all sense of direction. Most important, they should be taught that if they are ever lost, they must stop walking immediately and *stay put* until someone comes near.

Inyo National Forest

Most of the mountain country described in this guide lies within the Inyo National Forest, which comprises about two million acres in Inyo and Mono Counties. Help the Forest Service in whatever way you can to keep the trails and campgrounds in good condition, and report vandalism, missing signs or trail damage.

Campgrounds

Our map indicates the public campgrounds, most of them maintained by the Forest Service. You can write the Forest Supervisor at Bishop for a list of the campgrounds, which gives their size, season, and facilities. Inyo County is now building campgrounds adjacent to Highway 6–395, and is planning more.

Camping Tips

An Experienced Camper—

Drinks water only from faucets, or from cold, swift *remote* streams. Lakes and streams near roads are usually polluted. If in doubt, boil it.

Brushes his teeth and throws his wash water away from running streams, thinking of the camper downstream who is using the same stream for his water supply.

Builds his campfire in a designated place, in an area cleared of pine needles and tree roots; *puts it out thoroughly* with water, *testing with his hand* to make sure the ashes are cold.

Leaves picnic sites and campsites cleaner than he found them, burning whatever he can. Places unburnables in a garbage can or takes them along in his car until he finds one.

SOUTHERN APPROACH TO OWENS VALLEY

Redrock Canyon.—A hundred miles north of Los Angeles, 24 miles north of Mojave, the dark hills of the El Paso Mountains break the desert flatness. The Garlock Fault, which for 150 miles separates the Mojave Desert from the mountainous country to the north, bounds the El Pasos on the south. Along it, 40 miles of horizontal movement and thousands of feet of vertical movement have taken place. One branch of the Fault is visible at the mouth of Redrock Canyon, on both sides of the highway. Just before entering the canyon, if you look on the hillside to the right, you can see pale lavender sediments along the fault ending abruptly against hard brown rock.

Highway 6 winds through the El Pasos, following Redrock Canyon. The colorful cliffs consist of alternating thin layers of hard red pebbly sandstone and thick layers of soft gray clay or volcanic ash. Ground waters carried iron oxides into the rocks, staining them rusty red. Water running in rills down the cliffs has worn the soft layers away faster than the hard layers, so that the reddish layers project out from the cliff faces. Deep flutings in the gray layers show the paths of the rills. Some of the sedimentary beds contain animal fossils and fragments of petrified palm wood several millions of years old. Animals that have been identified include horses, camels, a bovid (cow-like animal), and an elephant. West of the highway, beds of volcanic ash are quarried for household cleansers. Holly cleanser is quarried at Holly Camp; ash from Last Chance Canyon formerly was used in Old Dutch Cleanser under the trade name "seismotite."

Indian Wells Valley, N.O.T.S.—The U. S. Naval Ordnance Test Station at China Lake is headquarters for the Navy's largest ordnance research and development organization. Daytime haze often hides this community of over 12,000 people, blending it into the desert gray, but at night a mass of sparkling lights give it size and shape. N.O.T.S. is the birthplace of such

The geologic history of the Redrock Canyon area

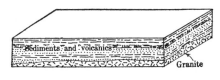

Sand, clay, gravel, volcanic ash, and lava flows were deposited layer upon layer on a nearly flat flood plain and in lakes.

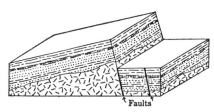

The rocks now exposed along Redrock Canyon were tilted and faulted upward several thousand feet along the south edge of the El Paso Mountains. This tilting and faulting took place a few feet at a time over many thousands of years.

During the tilting and faulting, the uplifted beds were attacked by streams, which continued to erode after the faulting and tilting stopped. In time the region was reduced to a flat gravel-veneered plain except perhaps for a low ridge of granite.

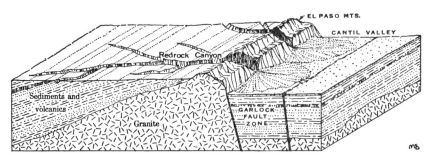

After a period of quiet, faulting was renewed, tilting the beds to the angle they assume today. Streams then attacked the gravel-covered plain, cutting Redrock and other canyons in the El Paso Mountains.

weapons as the guided missile Sidewinder, the air-to-air rocket Mighty Mouse, the anti-submarine Rat, and the high-performance Zuni rocket.

Highway 395, coming over Cajon Pass from San Bernardino, joins Highway 6 near China Lake; the two highways run the length of Owens Valley together. As you continue north, the large steel pipes you see at the mouths of several canyons are siphons of the Los Angeles Aqueduct.

Side trip up Ninemile Canyon to the South Fork of the Kern River.—About 5 miles north of the Highway 6–395 Junction, the Ninemile Canyon road turns off west. Over the summit, 6500 feet, the road winds down to the Kern through a forest of squat gray-green pinyon pine. In early summer you may see cowboys driving herds of cattle to the mountain meadows, a rare sight now that jeeps and stock trucks have largely replaced cow ponies and old-fashioned cattle drives. The meadows provide summer range for about 4500 head of cattle, which winter in the Owens and San Joaquin Valleys.

Near the river, there is a turnoff right (N) to the Kennedy Meadows campground, pack station and Ranger Station. The main road crosses the river and ends now at Troy Meadows. From these two road ends, trails lead into the gentle wilderness of the South Fork, a region known as the Kern Plateau. Since the Forest Service is letting contracts for logging the Jeffrey pine forest, penetrating the Plateau with a network of logging roads, and building new campgrounds, roads and trails will be much changed during the coming years. For the latest information write: District Ranger, Sequoia National Forest, Kernville.

Little Lake.—Little Lake is a commercial resort which offers camping and fishing for a fee. On the lake during spring and fall there are migrating water birds by the hundreds—pintails, ruddy ducks, Canadian honkers and pelicans. Up to a hundred whistling swans often winter on the lake. Early maps called it Little Owens Lake. For a hundred years its springs have been a stopping place for travelers—the prospectors bound for Coso, later the stages and freight teams coming across the Mojave.

Just north of Little Lake, the Southwest Museum excavated house sites, graves, stone slabs used for grinding seeds, obsidian knives, scrapers, and nearly 500 spear points. The first few inches of soil contained tools made by recent Paiute or Shoshoni Indians. The more deeply buried artifacts belonged to an ancient "Pinto" people, who lived here about 5,000 years ago when trees were abundant and water ran in the now-dry streambed.

Near Little Lake, you can see many low black ridges of once-molten lava. Some flowed along the base of the hills; others burst from vents and cascaded down the slopes. In the black lava you may notice some low elliptical mounds (pressure mounds), bucklings of the upper cooled crust caused by movement of still-liquid lava beneath. The black vertical columns just south of Little Lake are lava also. According to a Shoshoni Indian, his people called this long cliff "The Rattlesnake"—its head a high section to the north, the columns representing its belly scales. When a large mass of basaltic lava shrinks in cooling, it sometimes forms such columns. The Devil's Postpile National Monument in Mono County displays this same phenomenon on a more spectacular scale.

North of Little Lake a striking dark red cinder cone, Red Hill, rises above the rubbly lava. It is a small volcano built up of cinders that were thrown into the air in a series of explosions. North of Red Hill, you can see many more basalt flows and cinder cones in the Coso Mountains to the east. Among them are a few smooth-surfaced tan mounds, which from a distance can easily be mistaken for granite. These are rhyolite domes, formed from lava of a different composition. Two mills near the highway crush and screen the abundant cinder and pumice for building material. Some is used for landscaping, roofing, and insulating; most is made into lightweight building blocks.

In April, in favorable years, the area north and east of Little Lake is a colorful garden with some unusual flowers—the gay little reddish Bigelow mimulus, with flowers almost as large as the plants; the tall woolly thistle sage, with flowers as beautiful as miniature orchids; several of the most beautiful desert lupines; and the rare one-inch high pygmy poppy, with shining white petals.

Sideroad to the Fossil Falls.—About two miles north of Little Lake, at a rock daubed with orange paint, turn east onto a wide dirt road. Follow it about ½ mile, turn right onto a less traveled road and drive to its end. A trail, about a mile long, leads to the top of the falls. Along the trail you can distinguish several kinds of volcanic rock. The dark bubbly rock is lava which flowed from a vent to the east. The red is cinder, hurled out from nearby cinder cones. There are also small pieces of pale gray lightweight pumice—solidified molten froth. "It looks like a bad dream," someone said, peering into the 40-foot gorge. Several thousand years ago, when Owens Lake overflowed to the south, its stream carved the dark lava into weird shapes. Feel the slick potholes; perhaps you can find some deep ones that still contain their grinding rocks. Water pouring over the falls swirled these grinders around and around, scouring the holes ever deeper.

Haiwee and the Coso Mountains.—About ten miles north of Red Hill, you can glimpse Haiwee Reservoir. Before the Aqueduct, this area was known as Hayway or Haiwee Meadows, from the Indian word for dove. The thousand-acre meadows at one time supported a ranch of ten thousand goats. In 1864 the McGuire family ran a small way station at Hayway. One of the notorious incidents of the Indian war occurred while McGuire was away. A dozen Indians set the roof on fire, then murdered Mrs. McGuire and six-year-old Johnny. Several days later Lone Pine settlers retaliated by attacking an Indian camp on Owens Lake. Though they were not sure the culprits were there, they massacred some forty Paiute men, women and children, sparing only several youngsters.

The mountains east of Haiwee are part of the Coso Range, bounding

Owens Valley on the southeast, where in 1860 prospectors discovered the first silver ore in Inyo County. "Coso" probably comes from the Indian word for fire. Before the naval base restricted the area, Coso Hot Springs were popular among Indians as well as whites. In 1921 a promotor advertised them as the "Greatest Natural Radio Hot Spring in America," guaranteeing that its 250 springs would benefit stomach diseases, rheumatism and kidney trouble.

Haiwee is known for its flame-colored desert mariposa, which usually blooms early in May. They are plentiful, though not noticeable from the highway. To find them, wander a bit, looking especially in gullies. North of Haiwee, in early April, pepper-grass forms a conspicuous green-gold mat.

OWENS LAKE

Olancha.—The first trees and green fields for many miles mark Olancha. The cottonwoods, some transplanted from Cottonwood Creek over eighty years ago by a pioneer rancher, provide a shady roadside stop. A marker honors Joseph Walker, the famous Mountain Man who discovered Owens Valley and the Walker Pass route across the Sierra. Since there are Central American towns named Olanchita and Cartago, possibly the Mexican prospectors who named Cerro Gordo brought these names with them. For his Olancha mine in the Cosos, M. H. Farley constructed a small mill here about 1861. Later, Olancha was a way station; one of the old adobe buildings still stands. (A "station" or stage stop was seldom more than a tent or one small adobe room —with boxes to sit on, a barrel, a few glasses—where teamsters and travelers could water and feed their stock, buy drinks and meals, and find a bunk or a corner to sleep in.) During the 1870s, Olancha had large corrals for the Cerro Gordo freight teams. It was long a stop for the Owens Valley–Mojave stage.

Just south of Olancha a mill processes Fuller's Earth, a clay used for insecticides and filters, mined from a pit eight miles east. At Olancha a road turns off east and connects with Highway 190 for Death Valley (see Owens Lake Loop Trip below).

Cartago.—In the 1870s Cartago, at the southern tip of Owens Lake, was a bustling "port." Across the blue salty water churned the *Bessie Brady*, loaded with silver-lead bullion from the Cerro Gordo mines. Fourteen-mule teams hauling food, liquor, grain, lumber and machinery from Los Angeles waited for their cargo to be unloaded for her return trip to Swansea.

Near the crest of the Inyos are the mines of Cerro Gordo, whose smelters poured out bullion at such a rate that the teamsters could not keep up with them. Molded into bars or "pigs" shaped like 18-inch loaves of bread, each weighed 85 pounds, worth $20–35. While weary teams plodded across the desert for three weeks to reach Los Angeles, the stacks of pigs at the smelters grew longer and longer. By 1873, 30,000 bars were stacked up like cordwood. Miners piled the big bricks for walls, stretched canvas for a roof, and lived midst silver splendor.

FOURTH OF JULY

CELEBRATION

AND EXCURSION!

THERE WILL BE AN EXCURSION ON OWENS Lake on the approaching Fourth of July, when will be carried out as closely as possible the the following

PROGRAMME:

The Steamer will leave Swansea at 8½ o'clock A. M., to accommodate citizens of Swanson and Cerro Gordo. She will then proceed to Ferguson's landing, at the north end of the Lake, where she will be christened. After this ceremony she will take a trip to the

Southern Extremity of the Lake,

Where there is a delightful spot for a Pic-nic.

The christening and maiden voyage of the Bessie Brady. *Inyo Independent*, June 29, 1872. Acquiring the Cerro Gordo freight contract in 1872, James Brady built the 85-foot *Bessie Brady*. Some say she resembled a barge, others that she looked like a ferry boat. Christened by Brady's daughter, Bessie, the shallow-draught steamboat could carry 700 bullion bars across Owens Lake in three hours, cutting freighting time by three days and expense as well. The *Bessie Brady* moved the accumulated bullion from Swansea to the Cartago landing.

The *Bessie Brady* later burned, and Colonel Stevens' boat, the *Molly Stevens*, named for his daughter, supposedly capsized. In 1962 a Lone Pine pilot spotted something unusual in the dry lake bed; it proved to be a 3-foot, 300-pound propellor, which may have belonged to the sunken *Molly Stevens*.

Desperate, the owners of Cerro Gordo formed the famous Cerro Gordo Freighting Company with teamster Remi Nadeau, who set about establishing a dozen stations between Cartago and Los Angeles, a day's haul apart. Within a few months he had eighty teams, each pulling three huge wagons. Standard cargo for one team was 7½ tons, 170 bars. A third of the teams kept busy just supplying the stations with barley and hay. Within a year the miners had to give up their silver houses as Nadeau succeeded in hauling away the accumulated bullion. When Cerro Gordo shut down in 1879, Cartago's busiest days ceased also. The mound of white material near Cartago remains from the soda plant that operated during World War I and again in the late '20s.

Sideroad to the Cottonwood Charcoal Kilns.—Burning wood slowly with little air, these kilns transformed it into charcoal, essential for the Cerro

Gordo smelters. During the camp's first years, nearby slopes provided enough pinyon pine to fire the steam engines, heat the miners' shacks, and make charcoal. But as the slopes were stripped clean and the pack burros had to plod farther away for their wood loads, and as the teamsters began hauling lumber all the way from Los Angeles, Colonel Sherman Stevens thought of a profitable way to supply the Cerro Gordo wood market. His project included a sawmill up Cottonwood Canyon to the west, where trees were plentiful, and a flume to Owens Lake. He shipped his lumber, mine timbers, fuel wood and charcoal to Swansea on the *Bessie Brady;* later he built the *Molly Stevens.*

Sideroad to Cottonwood Creek.—A paved road follows Cottonwood Creek up its narrow canyon to a pack station and campground. The Cottonwood Power Plant was built to provide power for the aqueduct's construction. The lower part of the stream has little water, for most is diverted to the power plant. Besides many cottonwood trees, there are birch, willow and oak. Trails lead to the old Stevens sawmill, Cottonwood Lakes, and the meadows country of the upper Kern.

Bartlett.—The Pittsburgh Plate Glass Company's chemical plant (capacity, 275 tons per day) at the northern end of Owens Lake crystallizes and refines carbonate compounds from the brine under the lake's crusted surface. The resulting soda products are used in detergents, cleaning compounds, metal processing, and the manufacture of paper and glass. Mining the lake for its salts began in 1885, with the Inyo Development Company soda plant near Keeler. Other companies have produced soda ash, trona, and borax from time to time, locating either near the Carson & Colorado depot at Keeler or along the Southern Pacific tracks near the lake's west shore. Estimated production, 1885–1950, is over a million tons of soda products. Bacteria, and the protozoa and brine shrimp living on them, color the evaporation ponds red.

Owens Lake.—Owens Lake is the natural sump for all the streams flowing into Owens Valley. Before the Los Angeles Aqueduct diverted the river, it was a salty shallow lake, thirty feet at its maximum depth, covering one hundred square miles. By 1921 it had shrunk to half this size, and trona (a sodium carbonate salt) began to crystallize on the lake bottom. North of Bartlett you can see sandy beaches and the shorelines of pre-Aqueduct days clearly. This was only the last chapter in the story of Owens Lake, however, for the lake had been shrinking for several thousand years and was already highly saline. Remnants of ancient beaches, some more than 200 feet higher than the 1913 lake, are preserved at several places around the lake. (See Glaciation, Geology Section.)

Frémont named the lake for Richard Owens, a member of his 1844–45 expedition, although Owens did not go through Owens Valley and never saw the lake named for him. In his *Memoirs* Frémont describes Owens as "Cool, brave, and of good judgment; a good hunter and good shot; experienced in mountain life; . . . valuable throughout the campaign."

Owens Lake supplied the Paiutes with one of their food staples, the salt-marsh fly pupae, which looked like a grain of rice when dried. Oldtimers tell that the salty water had marvelous cleansing properties, though if one left his clothes soaking too long there might be nothing left. Others claimed drinking it cured various ailments. In 1882 some San Francisco promoters planned to ship a carload of water, and began buying all the empty barrels they could find. Commented the *Inyo Independent,* "When railroad connection is made with Bodie there will be no scarcity of empty barrels for this business."

The Alabama Hills—Oldest in the World?—Near the northern tip of Owens Lake, low hills rise west of the highway. While the Civil War was raging, some Confederate sympathizers discovered placer gold in them. They named their mines after the *Alabama,* a famous Confederate cruiser which destroyed northern shipping valued at six million dollars. Eventually the name applied to the entire ridge.

You may hear the Alabama Hills called "the oldest hills in the world." Actually, they are the same age as the Sierra Nevada, and the White and Inyo mountains; all were formed by faulting a few million years ago (see diagram). The granite in both the Alabama Hills and the Sierra is about a hundred million years old. The oldest rocks in the region are in the White Mountains. The weird shapes of the weathered rocks probably inspired the folklore regarding their age. (See Alabama Hills Scenic Route, p. 66.)

The Alabama Hills are the locale for many western TV shows and movies. In favorable years, especially in May, there are outstanding displays of desert wildflowers. For many years there has been talk of somehow preserving the Alabama Hills for public recreation and providing campgrounds and trails. In 1963 real progress began toward establishment of a State Park. Public

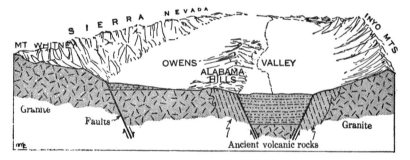

The Alabama Hills are a block of granite and old volcanic rock which slipped down from the Sierra Nevada, but did not sink as much as the bedrock underlying the deepest part of Owens Valley. Several million years ago a long narrow strip of ground that was to become the Valley began to sink along faults. As it sank, the ground on both sides rose to form the Sierra and the Inyo-White Mountains. The Alabama Hills are the eastern edge of the block that slipped to a midway position. Sand and gravel washed from the mountains fill the deepest part of Owens Valley and cover the western part of the Alabama Hills.

support will determine whether this project is given priority among the many State Park proposals.

Junction with Highway 190, Route to Death Valley.—The two million acre desert wonderland of Death Valley National Monument is open all year, although unless you are part lizard, summer is not recommended. Climate is most pleasant between mid-October and mid-April. Favorable years bring flower displays in March or even earlier. There are two excellent museums. The new Visitor Center has displays of geologic features, desert flora and fauna. The Borax Company Museum has a fine collection of old wagons, buggies, an arrastra, and mining machinery. For information write to Death Valley National Monument, Death Valley, California.

Owens Lake Loop Trip to Swansea, Keeler, Dirty Sock.—Starting on Highway 190 you can drive around Owens Lake, looping back to the highway at Olancha. If a high wind is blowing, postpone your trip a day. Sand may damage your car paint, and may cover the road. In mid-summer plan this trip for very early morning or early evening, with perhaps a picnic on the Olancha sand dunes. Heading toward the Inyo Mountains, you will cross the dry bed of the Owens River. Tunnels in the foothills expose white dolomite, a marble. The Mills Building in San Francisco is decorated with slabs of Inyo marble. Limestone for the soda plants was mined here. Dolomite is now being crushed for decorative roofing.

Saline Valley Salt Tram.—The first group of old wooden buildings near the highway was the terminal of the 14-mile Saline Valley electric tramway. Up the hill you can see a few of the towers that have not yet been dismantled. Beginning in 1913, the half-million dollar tram operated intermittently for 17 years, but evidently the salt works were not a financial success. Salt, said to be 99.3% pure, was scraped from the natural salt beds on the floor of Saline Valley east of the Inyos. The tram carried it to the mill, where it was dried, crushed and sacked. Some of the men hired to work in Saline Valley backed out when they learned they had to ride the tram to work, for at one point the buckets swung many hundreds of feet above Daisy Canyon, not much fun in a strong desert wind.

Swansea.—A plaque marks the location of Swansea, one of Cerro Gordo's three silver-lead smelters, named for the famous smelting center in Wales. Shifting sand has covered all except a bit of the smelter's stone foundation. A cloudburst in 1874 buried much of Swansea and filled the smelter with mud. The Owens Lake Silver-Lead Company, involved in a long and costly lawsuit against the Cerro Gordo kings, Belshaw and Beaudry, was in no financial position to rebuild.

Keeler.—Now the bleakest portion of the Valley, Owens Lake was once the busiest. To see the entire lake bed, opposite the Keeler turnoff, drive half a mile up the Cerro Gordo road. The mining, milling, teaming, shipping, wood-cutting and charcoal burning connected with Cerro Gordo kept the shores of the big lake alive with activity. After Cerro Gordo died, it received another boost when the Carson & Colorado railroad built its narrow gauge tracks the length of the Valley, ending at the lake. Captain Julius Keeler—elected to the State Assembly in 1883, and active in milling, the marble works, and a soda plant—realized the financial possibilities of the railroad terminus, and laid out a town of 42 blocks. The railroad yards gave life to Keeler for many years, shipping talc, soda, marble and salt, besides ore from small mines. Here freight and passengers going south transferred from the train to stages and wagons.

At Keeler you can see many old houses, the C & C water tanks and depot. At the end of Malone Street was a fair-sized Chinatown. Perhaps you can find the tunnel and cellar of the busy fan-tan house (opium a sideline), where patrons could hide when the law appeared. The plant now operating is a talc mill. Mines in the mountains to the southeast produce a high quality steatite-grade talc, essential in the manufacture of high-frequency electrical equipment. Along the lake shore there are many evaporating vats, mounds of white limestone and remains of the soda plants. In the hills behind Keeler, you can see tunnels and shacks of small mines which produced gold, silver and lead. North of the highway is the Keeler graveyard, much of it washed away by cloud-bursts. One wonders who placed the elaborate stone with Chinese characters for Mary You.

Dirty Sock.—Five miles past Keeler, the loop trip leaves Highway 190 and follows the south shore of the lake. About 10 miles from this junction, a sandy road leads to Dirty Sock Springs. You will be safer walking, for many a car has been stuck. If you are counting on smoke signals for rescue, there is little to make smoke with, and no one to see it even if you could. The origin of the springs' name is obscure, though obviously they smell like many, very dirty socks. One story is that prospectors—using the springs for their semi-annual bath, laundry and "cure"—hung their clothes on the sagebrush to dry, but forgot to take out their socks before they disintegrated. There is an artesian well, drilled in 1917 by a company exploring for fresh water for a soda plant. At 1200 feet, warm water gushed through the casing; it has been gushing ever since. The concrete pool remains from a resort promotion that fizzled.

Olancha Sand Dunes.—The Olancha sand dunes are a favorite place for winter and spring picnics. Children can have never-ending fun exploring and sliding on them. Movie studios have used them as locations for Egyptian and western movies.

Side trip to Cerro Gordo.—Cerro Gordo (Big or Fat Hill) was a real bonanza, one of the great silver-lead producers in California (see History Section). In its peak year, 1874, its three smelters poured out 5300 tons of bullion worth $2,000,000.

Plan a full day's trip for Cerro Gordo; though only 8 miles from Keeler, there is much to see and the road is slow. Many passenger cars make it up the steep road, though some have trouble. Follow Highway 190 to Keeler as described above, there turn left up a gravel wash. The road winds through a maze of narrow canyons and crazily tilted rock layers—bright red, black, brown, maroon, green—following the general route of the old tollroad. The last mile is the steepest, the infamous Yellow Grade taking its name from the yellowish rocks. How many thousand mule teams clanked up these grades to the roaring camp? The down trip was the more dangerous, wagons heavy with bullion occasionally losing control and careening down the canyons.

Pablo Flores and two other Mexican prospectors discovered silver-lead ore here in 1865. According to those who knew Flores, Indians killed the two but let him go, on his promise never to return. Flores returned later and located several claims.

Among those in San Francisco hearing news of the strike was Mortimer Belshaw, an educated man who had the foresight to spend two years at the Sinaloa mines of Mexico, learning how to work silver ore. At Cerro Gordo, Belshaw found silver quartz so rich that miners were throwing away any ore worth less than $200 a ton. Knowing that lead was essential for smelting silver, he recognized that the galena (lead sulfide) ledges held the key to Cerro Gordo's riches. Realizing that whoever owned the lead and built a smelter would control Cerro Gordo, he wasted no time doing both. For a share in his proposed smelter, he talked himself into a third interest in the largest galena mine, the Union. Raising capital in San Francisco, Belshaw first built a road to the mines, collecting a dollar toll from every wagon. From San Francisco he shipped machinery to San Pedro and sent it across the Mojave by mule teams. Inventing a new smelting technique, by the end of the year Belshaw was producing silver-lead bullion at the unheard-of rate of 4 tons per day. He then joined Victor Beaudry who owned a small smelter, which they enlarged. As dull gray metal flooded from the smelters at ever-increasing rates, Cerro Gordo boomed to a $5 camp (a miner's wage for a 10-hour day) with 2,000 people. With a new pipeline providing plentiful water, the Stevens mill and kilns shipping abundant wood and charcoal from Cottonwood Canyon, and with Nadeau's teams hauling the bullion bars away as fast as the smelters spewed them out, Belshaw and Beaudry again enlarged their smelters. By 1874 their capacity reached 400 bars, 18 tons, per day. You can read details of Cerro Gordo's fascinating story in Remi Nadeau's (great-grandson of the teamster) *City-Makers*. By 1877 the smelters had gobbled up all the known deposits. When the Union works burned Belshaw did not rebuild; Beaudry's smelter ceased production two years later.

Miners worked small deposits off and on until 1911, when Louis Gordon discovered zinc, besides new bodies of silver-lead. The wooden towers you saw coming up the road are remains of the tram built to carry zinc ore to the railroad. One tale of the tram days concerns Chinese miners who would go to Keeler for a fling, then ride the buckets back in a happy stupor. His caution dulled, one might raise up at the wrong instant—and off went his head. Supposedly one could find a few skulls along the tramway. Since the early '40s, Cerro Gordo has been idle.

At Cerro Gordo you can see mine tunnels, dumps, shacks and rock foundations all over the hills. On the slopes you may find traces of the switchback trails where hundreds of pack burros filed up and down, laden with water, wood, charcoal and ore. Among other buildings on the main street is the American Hotel. Some of the buildings date from the 1870s, others from the 1911 operation. Square nails indicate those built before 1900.

Lone Pine Peak 12,944' Mt. Muir 14,015' Mt. Whitney 14,495' Mt. Russell 14,086'

Whitney Portal Road

Mount Whitney and neighboring peaks, Alabama Hills in foreground. Peaks are named for John Muir, naturalist and "father of Yosemite Park"; Josiah Whitney, Director State Geological Survey, 1860–1874; I. C. Russell, geologist, eastern Sierra studies, 1881–1883.

LONE PINE

View of Mount Whitney.—Near the airport, south of Lone Pine, there is an exceptional view of Mount Whitney, the highest peak in the United States B.A. (before Alaska). You are looking at the loftiest portion of one of the earth's great mountain ranges. Some people are disappointed with Mount Whitney. The rounded hump at the end of a toothed ridge is not the Matterhorn-like spire they expect. But the Whitney group is really grander than any one mountain could be. For the Sierra crest culminates not in one isolated peak but in a massive granite wall fifteen miles long, between Mount Langley and Mount Tyndall. Besides Whitney there are six other peaks over 14,000 feet. Whitney is the highest point on this mighty surge of granite that towers two miles above Lone Pine.

Lone Pine.—In 1861 Bart and Alney McGee built the first cabin on Lone Pine Creek, named after a tall Jeffrey pine later washed out by flood. After driving a herd of cattle to Monoville in spring (and seeing not one white person between Walker's Pass and Adobe Meadows in Mono County), the brothers returned to Lone Pine Creek that fall. The mines of Cerro Gordo, Panamint and Darwin brought Lone Pine a floating population of many nationalities, miners constantly drifting in for supplies and pleasures. The many Mexican families, and immigrants from the Welsh and Cornish mines gave Lone Pine more color than the Valley's more sedate farming towns. For many years September 16, the anniversary of Mexico's liberation, was Lone Pine's most celebrated feast day, with guitar music, dancing and cock-fights.

Lone Pine Ranger Station, south end of town.

Mount Whitney Golf Course, 2 miles south of Lone Pine, open to public.

Community Swimming Pool, next to High School, south end of town.

Diaz Lake, 3 miles south. Swimming and water skiing—in wet years.

Lone Pine Park, north end of town. Shaded picnic tables, restrooms, swings, slide.

Lone Pine Cemetery, 1 mile north. There are two small neglected cemeteries, one near Lone Pine Station, the oldest north of the airport.

Grave of 1872 Earthquake Victims, 1 mile north, marked with a plaque.

Sidetrip to the 1872 Earthquake Scarp.—A bank of boulders just west of Lone Pine, miles long though only twenty-three feet high, is one of the most significant features in Owens Valley. If you recognize it for what it is, you can appreciate much of what has happened in this region over thousands of years—why the mountains are so abrupt, why the Valley so deep.

From the center of Lone Pine, drive less than a mile west on the Whitney Portal Road. After crossing the aqueduct, turn north onto an unmarked dirt road. Take the right forks and follow the road about a half-mile to a low ridge of boulders. This is an earthquake "scarp," changed little since the land east of it dropped 20 feet during the 1872 earthquake. The quake centered near Lone Pine; cracks opened as far north as Bishop.

Geophysical studies show that the movement occurred along the major "fault zone" just east of the Alabama Hills—a weak zone in the earth's crust. Since we are prone to think of mountains as immovable and rock unbreakable, it is difficult to realize that tremendous pressures build up within the earth, and that unable to withstand the accumulated stress, great blocks of rock break and move. The weak zone where they finally give under tension is called a fault zone, the break itself a "fault." The abrupt break where the rock has slipped up, down or sideways is a "scarp."

Side trip to Whitney Portal.—Exploring the Sierra in 1864, a State Geological Survey party was astounded to find several peaks higher than Mount Shasta, considered at that time the highest mountain in the west. They named the tallest peak after the Survey's chief, the eminent geologist, Josiah D. Whitney.

For several years there was considerable confusion over which peak was Mount Whitney. Clarence King, one of the survey party, had returned to

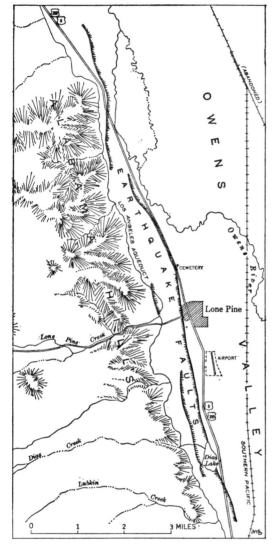

Fault scarps in the Lone Pine area formed during the 1872 earthquake. Cliff-like scarps 5 to 20 feet high, dotted with clumps of green fed by springs, mark the faults. On the map the hachures are on the downdropped sides of the faults. At Lone Pine, two parallel faults half a mile apart bound a sunken strip that extends southward to Diaz Lake. The strip dropped down 10 to 20 feet along the western fault, but less than 10 feet in most places along the eastern fault. At one place along the eastern fault, near Lone Pine, the ground also moved southward 16 feet.

A mile north of Lone Pine, the eastern fault reverses itself, and its east side is downdropped. You can see this scarp readily as you drive along, for it runs parallel and a few hundred feet west of the highway for about two miles.

At the north end of the Alabama Hills the highway crosses the fault scarp that runs along the base of the hills. This scarp continues northward, and at Independence lies three miles east of the highway.

Farther north, between Fish Springs and Big Pine, an 1872 fault scarp runs a few hundred feet west of the highway, across the Crater Mountain lava field and the gravelly slopes west of Big Pine.

Lone Pine in 1871. With summer storm clouds partially obscuring the mountains, he climbed and measured a peak he thought was Whitney. Two years later Mortimer Belshaw and W. A. Goodyear of Cerro Gordo, riding mules to the summit of King's peak (now Mount Langley), realized that the highest peak, the true Mount Whitney, lay several miles north. In a letter to the California Academy of Science, Goodyear publicized King's mistake. Shortly after, local men on a fishing trip—Charles Begole, A. H. Johnson, John Lucas—succeeded in reaching the summit of Mount Whitney for the first time. Two weeks later four other local men climbed it, and in a letter to the newspaper claimed they were first and that the three fishermen "never was on the mountain." In the same issue of the *Inyo Independent*, a letter signed "Fishermen" reasserted their claim for the first ascent, and stated also that they had christened it "Fisherman's Peak."

The dispute over the mountain's name kept on, for Valley people were annoyed with Professor Whitney for not staying long enough to study their earthquake more thoroughly. Fishermen's letter continued, "Whitney's agent . . . finds fault with the people here for their lack of romance in calling it 'Fisherman's Peak.' Ain't it as romantic as 'Whitney'? Wonder who the old earthquake sharp thinks is running this country, anyhow?" Local people even had their legislator introduce a bill legalizing the name Fisherman's Peak. But the governor refused to sign the bill, and Whitney's name has remained.

People from forty-six states and twenty-five foreign countries signed the register at Whitney Portal in 1961. There are two campgrounds, one 7 miles from Lone Pine, the other just below the Portal. In the center of Lone Pine, turn west onto the Whitney Portal road. Take advantage of the turnouts to stop along the way, for there are splendid views of the Inyo Mountains and Owens Valley, from the dry bed of Owens Lake north to Big Pine. Toward the upper end of the road, you can see Mount Whitney towering 6,000 feet above. At the end of the road, circle on around the pond to the parking area. Large white fir and Jeffrey pine shade the picnic area (no overnight camping). Aspen, birch and willow half hide the falls of Lone Pine Creek. Raucous-voiced jays may scold from their perches, or snatch morsels from your lunch table. Sheer granite cliffs loom above, the light gray rock sometimes so glaringly bright it looks snow covered. A large sign marks the trail.

Astronomers instigated the first trails up Mount Whitney. In 1881 a poor trail was built over some of the roughest places, that mules could carry wood and a tent for Professor Langley's party from Pennsylvania's Allegheny Observatory. Twenty years later, knowing that other scientists were planning expeditions, local people raised a small fund to build a pack trail and Gustave Marsh adopted the project as his own. Marsh completed the first trail in July 1904. Dr. Barton Evermann's party from the U. S. Division of Scientific Inquiry camped on the summit a few weeks later during a lightning storm so fierce it knocked down three of the men and killed a packer.

Five years later, when the University of California's Lick Observatory planned observations and the trail needed repair, Lone Pine held a ball to raise money. The Smithsonian Institute provided funds to build a shelter and employed Marsh to supervise construction. Despite scant funds, bitter cold, and helpers deserting him, Marsh completed the stone house on the summit. The trail, however, was far from the graded walkway of today. Dr. Abbot wrote that "even Mr. Marsh said . . . he hardly saw how the mules could go over it, unless they had hooks on their hind feet to hang on by till they found a place for their forefeet. There are places where . . . the mules must step down as far as from a high desk to the floor, landing on jagged rocks . . ." One scientist humorously questioned who was more important, the observers, or "our mute asinine friends" Jack and Lucky, who carried the two delicate mirrors safely to the summit. Sequoia National Park and Inyo National Forest cooperated to build the present trail, completing it in 1930.

Sideroad to Carroll Creek.—If you drive the Carroll Creek road mid-day in August, the summer haze and flat light of the high sun will hide the soft desert colors. But if you will go before breakfast, or in early evening when the shadows have begun to creep down the Sierra slope, you will be rewarded with a magnificent airplane-like view of Owens Valley and its mountains. Follow the Whitney Portal road for about a half mile, then turn left (S) onto the Carroll Creek road. Following Tuttle Creek, the road winds for several miles through the weird, weathered Alabama Hills. After crossing Carroll Creek, it begins the 2,000 foot climb up the shoulder of Wonoga Peak. (There is no place to camp, no wood, no water.) From the road end a trail leads to Cottonwood Lakes. Inyo County has plans well underway to continue this road into the now wild basin of Cottonwood Creek, with a 7-mile extension known as the Horseshoe Meadows road. Campgrounds are planned on upper Cottonwood Creek. If the new road brings greatly increased fishing pressure, some of the golden trout waters may have to be closed to assure enough adult fish for eggs.

Lone Pine and Mount Whitney Stations.—One-half mile north of Lone Pine, a road leads east to Lone Pine Station, the terminal of the Southern Pacific line from Mojave. Two miles farther, trees and foundations mark Mount Whitney Station, once Lone Pine's depot on the C & C narrow gauge. It is well worth driving out this road for the grand view of the Sierra crest north and south of Mount Whitney.

The Alabama Gates.—Four miles north of Lone Pine on the Aqueduct, there is a stone building and spillway, the Alabama Gates. The most publicized incident of the 25-year fight with the City of Los Angeles over Owens River water took place here in 1924 when 60 Valley men "captured" the control station for five days and opened the Gates, cutting off the aqueduct flow and turning the water back into the Owens River. As wives brought picnic lunches the gathering turned into a good-natured 5-day festivity, though the serious purpose of making Los Angeles meet Valley terms was uppermost in everyone's mind. Wilfred Watterson, Valley leader and banker, was in Los Angeles during the incident, pleading with the bankers' Clearing House Association to exert its influence on the City to buy the two remaining irrigation ditches at the Valley's price, $12,000,000. When the Association assured Watterson that they would help obtain a fair settlement, he relayed the word to his friends at the Gates. Thinking they had "won," the farmers turned the water back into the aqueduct, celebrating their "victory" with a final barbecue attended by 1500 people. Newspapers and national magazines headlined the incident and generally condemned Los Angeles. But once the water was flowing down the aqueduct again, the Clearing House Association took no further part in the argument, and the battle over prices continued another three years, Valley men dynamiting the aqueduct sixteen times.

If I am not on the JOB You can find me at the AQUEDUCT

Sign on flagpole, Bishop, November 1924. (Courtesy Charlotte Arcularius.) When the sheriff went through the motions of trying to stop the "capture" of the Alabama Gates, his friends crowded around to make sure he listed *all* their names! Tom Mix and a movie company on location in the Alabama Hills livened the festivities with an orchestra.

Alabama Hills Scenic Route.—See pages 66–67.

The Great Wall of the Sierra Nevada.—As you drive along Highway 6–395 between Lone Pine and Big Pine, you are close to the base of a massive granite wall two miles high—the Sierra's great eastern escarpment (see above, Side Trip to the 1872 Earthquake Scarp, also Geology Section). There are few places in the world where you can see such a gigantic scarp, the product of hundreds of earthquakes and repeated earth movements over thousands of years. Imagine, if you can, a solid mass of rock once extending from the San Joaquin Valley far into the Nevada desert, with no mountains or deep valleys. Then imagine this great mass cracking and moving, as poorly poured cement cracks under tension. On a grand scale, a huge block of granite about 60 miles wide and 400 miles long began to tilt westward, along a break (fault zone) at its eastern edge. A few feet at a time, the mountains were thrust up to their present height, and a narrow strip to its east sank down, forming Owens Valley. Near Fish Springs the mountains have risen more than 3,000 feet.

Manzanar.—North of George Creek two stone entrance markers with Oriental up-swept roofs—which you could easily drive by without noticing—indicate the site of Manzanar. The fertile farmland between George and Shepherd Creek was first known as George's Creek. When Dr. S. G. George was prospecting in 1860, a Paiute leader whose camp was on the creek acted as his guide and took the name Chief George. Later, when farmers planted large apple and pear orchards north of George's Creek, their community with its large packing plant was named Manzanar, presumably from the Spanish word for apple. During the war years, ten thousand Japanese lived here at the Manzanar Relocation Camp. To see the stone monument remaining in the Japanese cemetery, continue north on the highway a short distance, then turn west at the first cattleguard and follow the dirt road.

Loop Trip to Reward Mine, Owenyo, Owens Lake.—About 11 miles north of the town of Lone Pine (4 miles south of Independence) turn east on the Manzanar Reward road. Looking from the railroad bed near the Inyo foothills, you can see the mill of the Reward & Brown Monster Mines at the mouth of a canyon 1½ miles northeast. The Reward has produced small amounts of lead, silver and gold in recent years. The Brown Monster, formerly the Eclipse, was probably the first location made near Owens Valley.

Follow the road paralleling the narrow gauge roadbed, continuing on it south through the sand and sage of the valley's east side. The fine white powder you may notice on the ground is an alkaline deposit, leached from the soil and brought to the surface by ground water. There are glorious views of the Sierra crest, from Mount Langley north to Coyote Flat. Some buildings and a cluster of foundations remain from Owenyo, a busy railroad junction for a time, and before that a Quaker colony. About 1900 the William Penn Colonial Association established the town of Owenyo, center for its 13,000 acres and 42 miles of canal. Inexperienced with irrigating and working desert land, the Quakers had a difficult time. When Los Angeles began buying land in 1905, they were among the first to sell. When the Southern Pacific built its branch from Mojave to Owens Valley in 1910 for hauling Aqueduct construction materials, Owenyo was the junction where the new broad gauge joined the old C & C narrow gauge. From Owenyo continue following the railroad bed south to Highway 190 near Owens Lake. There you can either turn east to visit Swansea and Keeler, or west to join Highway 6–395 near Lone Pine.

Back Roads We Do Not Mention.—Many unsigned ranching and mining roads meander along the valley floor or climb the foothills. Though a few may be too muddy or sandy to travel safely, most are passable, though

Sierra crest west and north of Lone Pine. Peaks are named for Joseph LeConte, geologist, University of California, 1869–1901; George Mallory and Andrew Irvine, British mountaineers who died on Mount Everest, 1924; Alexander McAdie, climatologist, Harvard, 1913–1931, a member of the 1909 scientific party which made observations from the summit of Mount Whitney; Edward Barnard, astronomer, University of California, 1888–1895; Colonel Robert Williamson, Pacific Railroad Surveys, 1853, 1855.

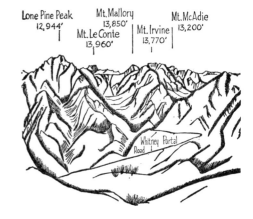

Lone Pine Peak 12,944' Mt. Mallory 13,850' Mt. LeConte 13,960' Mt. Irvine 13,770' Mt. McAdie 13,200'

rough. Try particularly some that head toward the Inyo foothills; from the east side of the valley there are stirring views of the Sierra crest.

Desert wandering is great fun. You need not go far, the open country invites you to go every direction your fancy pleases, landmarks keep you from becoming lost. In April and May desert wildflowers will brighten your way; in fall the rabbitbrush will be in golden bloom. The only equipment you need is sensitivity and curiosity. Wandering, looking, touching, seeing, hearing, imagining, with no particular "goal" except to keep on wandering and wondering. Wondering about the prospectors and cowmen that scraped out the roads; about the creatures and small plants (have you looked near your feet?) that manage to survive the rigorous climate; about the mountains looming above you. And the more you learn, the more you will find to wonder about. Whose tracks made this lacy pattern in the sand? Why are there so many obsidian chips *here?* Which canyon did these brilliant pebbles wash down from? Did water in this dry ditch once turn a water wheel, irrigate a cornpatch? How did these rock layers come to stand on end? Who has nibbled the tips off this shrub?

INDEPENDENCE

Sideroad to Symmes Creek.—The Shepherd Pass trail, leading to the headwaters of the Kern River, starts from the end of the Symmes Creek road. Both Shepherd and Symmes Creek take their names from pioneer families.

Sidetrip to Mazourka Canyon, Badger Flat.—In Mazourka Canyon you can sample the distinctive and subtle attractions of a desert canyon. In favorable years, Mazourka Canyon is a flower garden, a mass of color from late May to July. From a high point near Badger Flat, there is a superb view of Sierra canyons and peaks. Even in mid-summer Badger Flat is high enough (8800) to be cool and pleasant. Why not plan a picnic supper among

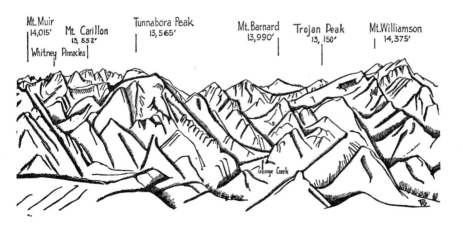

Mt. Muir 14,015' Mt. Carillon 13,552' Tunnabora Peak 13,565' Mt. Barnard 13,990' Trojan Peak 13,150' Mt. Williamson 14,375'
Whitney Pinnacles

George Creek

the scraggly pinyon, and linger into evening, watching the canyons fill with purple-gray shadows as the sun sets over the Sierra?

About three miles east of Independence, after crossing the Aqueduct's open ditch, the road drops down a 15-foot scarp, formed during the 1872 earthquake. Higher up Mazourka Canyon, you can look back and see it clearly, a bank dotted with trees running north and south for several miles. Where you cross the C & C railroad bed, there was a station known as Kearsarge. The sites of San Carlos and Bend City, in 1863 the largest mining camps in the Valley, are near. Both towns were seriously considered for the County Seat. Bend City was near Kearsarge Station. To find San Carlos, drive about three miles north of the Station and wander about the banks of the dry river bed; you may find a few bricks and foundations.

At the foot of the Inyos you turn north into Mazourka Canyon. These slopes comprised the Union and Russ Mining Districts, the first established in Owens Valley. As you drive up Mazourka Canyon, you can see remnants of some old placer gold diggings. At some of the springs there were small mills. Many small mines and prospects are scattered along the canyon, but production has been limited. Besides gold, silver, copper, lead, and zinc, tungsten and talc are most commonly sought. Red, brown, yellow, and gray metamorphic rocks comprise the lower slopes southeast of Kearsarge Station; they extend northward along Mazourka Canyon, where they are sandwiched between two large bodies of granite. Most of the rocks along the canyon are dark shales that were deposited on the sea floor as mud. In early summer purple gilia and Mojave aster, and low bushes of yellow golden heads are abundant. The tall yellow Prince's plume is particularly handsome against the dark rocks. The unusual position of Mazourka Canyon—running not east into the mountains as other canyons do, but north, paralleling the crest for seven miles—is determined by this granite sandwich, the rocks of which eroded more readily than the granite on either side. Unlike the Sierra, the Inyos are composed largely of sediments that were deposited in an ancient ocean. The sedimentary layers have been folded and broken and in many places stand on edge.

About fifteen miles from Highway 6–395, the old Mazourka Canyon road, now washed out, forks right. Stay on the road which forks left (the Al Rose road) for three miles and park by a small corral. Beyond, there are two steep pitches which many cars cannot make. It is about 1½ miles to the viewpoint. In late May and June Al Rose Canyon is colorful with desert mountain flowers. On the viewpoint you can find occasional clumps of the Mojave mound cactus with scarlet flowers, and subalpine plants such as globe buckwheat, mat sandwort, dwarf daisy and a low mountain onion.

From the point you look east across Badger Flat to the Inyo crest. Looking at the Sierra, you can follow the crest from Split Mountain south far beyond Olancha Peak. From sketches in this section, you can identify

Independence Peak by Tom Ross

Have you known Owens Valley

and its mountains only under the summer sun? Then you are still a stranger here, for the seasons bring changes unbelievable.

Poplars near Bishop
William Fettkether

Prospectors bound for Skidoo, 1907

Independence 1873

*Yesterdays
can flavor
your todays*

Burkhardt Bar, Lone Pine, 1895.

From photo collection,
Eastern California Museum.
Reproductions by
David Hamren.

The Slim Princess, 1923.
Dolomite Spur near Keeler

The Sierra wave

is a gigantic updraft which is to gliding enthusiasts what the Himalayas are to mountain climbers. Though the wave is invisible, it produces spectacular telltale lens-shaped clouds.

Most of the world sailplane records have been made above Owens Valley. When westerly winds, pushed by winter storms, speed over the Sierra crest, they set up large waves in the broad river of air whipping over the mountains. Associated with the wave flow is severe turbulence, with strong up- and down-drafts which sailplane pilots have learned to ride to record heights.

The Commander's House and the Hospital are the only buildings remaining today of Camp Independence. They were built in 1872, after the earthquake shattered the camp's adobe structures. Since most of the soldiers were easterners, it is not surprising that their buildings resembled eastern farmhouses. After the camp was abandoned and the buildings auctioned off, many were torn down for their lumber. Photo by Tom Ross

The tule elk is a unique variety of elk native to the Central Valley, smaller than those of Yellowstone Park and other areas. Owens Valley and Colusa County have the only wild herds of tule elk in existence. Photo by George Bruley

Most Valley towns have cemeteries where you may see ornate iron fences typical of the 1890s, as well as many handmade monuments. On many of the markers are the names of near-by canyons and creeks— and many different states and foreign countries. Wind and sand have weathered most of the old wooden markers to silver, and scoured away their lettering. Bishop Pioneer Cemetery by David Hamren

many mountains, including Mount Whitney. From here, you can appreciate what a great bulky wall the Sierra's east slope is. As you look into its canyons, see if you can distinguish the broad basins and U-shaped valleys chewed out by the glaciers from the lower V-shaped canyons cut by streams.

Independence, Inyo County Seat.—Among the first to settle in Owens Valley was Charles Putnam, who in 1861 built the first trading post, on Little Pine Creek. That winter fights with the Paiutes began. On one occasion most of the settlers gathered at Putnam's, whose stone cabin became known as "the fort," and fortified it as best they could with wagons and yokes. As others homesteaded along the creek, the settlement became known as Little Pine. The following summer Colonel Evans established Camp Independence a bit to the north on Oak Creek. Little Pine changed its name to Independence when it became the County Seat in 1866. Later that year Thomas Edwards laid out the townsite of Independence. With the upper story of the Chalfant home serving as press room, P. A. Chalfant and J. E. Parker started the Valley's first newspaper here in 1870, the *Inyo Independent*.

Inyo County Courthouse.—The present courthouse was preceded by three others. The earthquake demolished the first, and fire destroyed its successor. The third, built in 1887, served until the present courthouse was constructed in 1921.

Inyo County Free Library, courthouse basement.

Eastern California Museum, courthouse basement, open daily. Crammed with documents, maps, photographs, exhibits of minerals, Paiute baskets, arrowheads, flowers, guns and other eastern California lore. Some of the Museum's most interesting items show the settlers' ingenuity—handmade furniture, a wheelbarrow put together with whittled pegs and its wheel cut from a section of tree trunk, a hand mill for grinding flour. The Museum Association (address: Independence) conducts monthly exploring trips. For a small fee, you may join, supporting the museum and receiving notices of trips.

Historic Buildings.—Commander's House, corner of Edwards and Main Streets. After Camp Independence was abandoned, the Commander's House was moved to its present location. The Museum Association acquired the building in 1961, and has begun to refurnish it in the fashion of 1872.

Mary Austin Home. Mary Austin, famous author of the classic *Land of Little Rain,* lived here from 1892 to 1903. Many Owens Valley people did not share the literary world's enthusiasm for Mary Austin. Her neighbors criticized her unhappy personal life and found her peculiar and "different." Her bluntness often aroused antagonism rather than friendliness. For an understanding and sympathetic biography, read *Mary Austin: Woman of Genius* by her friend, Dr. Helen Doyle of Bishop.

Camp Independence Hospital Building. Moved to its present location after Camp Independence was abandoned.

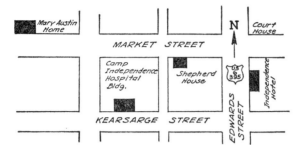

Historic buildings, Independence. The Commander's House and the Hospital Building were built in 1872, replacing the adobe buildings shattered in the earthquake. After the camp was abandoned, the buildings were auctioned off. Some were moved, others torn down for lumber.

The Shepherd House, oldest house in Inyo County. Built about 1865, its front part is adobe covered with boards. Back rooms were added on in the 1880s.

The Independence Hotel, shown above, burned in early 1963.

Dehy Park, roadside rest, north end of town, named for a beloved Superior Court Judge. Shade trees, tables, restrooms, water. The narrow gauge steam locomotive, Number 18, for many years hauled freight and passengers up and down Owens Valley.

Independence Creek Campground, ½ mile west on Onion Valley Road.

Independence Cemetery, Pavilion Street, 2 blocks east of the highway.

Side trip to Onion Valley.—A $1,500,000 road, completed in 1962, climbs the canyon of Independence Creek to Onion Valley (9200), named for the abundant swamp onion. During July and early August when the wildflowers are in their prime, Onion Valley is a jungle of soft colors. Growing four feet high and more in the damp meadows are deep blue monkshood, aptly named corn lily, magenta fireweed, and orange tiger lilies; more modest are white rein orchis and grass of Parnassus. Above the meadow grow clumps of tall-stemmed soda-straw and, close to the ground, mountain hemp with dainty pink flowers.

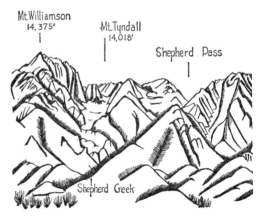

Sierra crest west of Independence. Peaks are named for John Tyndall, British scientist and alpinist, 1820–1893; William Keith, California artist, 1838–1911; Cornelius B. Bradley, professor of rhetoric, University of California, 1894–1911; the University of California itself; Wilson Gould, companion of LeConte when the two climbed the peak in 1896.

The imposing mountain standing apart from the crest, south of the Onion Valley road, is the second highest in the Sierra, Mount Williamson. From the horseshoe bend above Grays Meadow Campground, looking down to the creek, you may be able to make out some rock foundations, the site of the Rex Montis mill. The Rex Montis is one of several gold mines high on Kearsarge Peak, just above you. In 1864, Thomas Hill discovered gold ore in quartz veins. The year before, Southern sympathizers had named their placer finds near Lone Pine the Alabama Mines, after a famous Confederate cruiser. Hill and his friends, Northerners, named their claims after a battleship which had just sunk the *Alabama,* the *U.S.S. Kearsarge.* The ore was promising enough to attract investors who built a $40,000 10-stamp mill. About 10 miles from Independence, if you look carefully in the brush below the road, you can find the foundations of this mill. When Inyo County was established, Kearsarge City, the mining camp below Onion Valley, was the largest settlement in Owens Valley and was seriously considered for the County Seat. By the next year, when elections were held, it was almost deserted. The silver bullion reported to be valued from $3 to $12 an ounce, proved to be worth 12½¢. Near the end of the road is a bunker used for loading gold ore; just below it is the trail leading to the mines. The trail passes some dry-laid stone cabins that probably date from the very early mining days.

The road ends at Onion Valley, where there are two pack stations and a small campground. This is one of the most popular starting points for trips into the high country of Kings Canyon National Park. Almost any summer morning you can see mule trains, families with burros, or hikers with backpacks starting up the trail to Kearsarge Pass. An old Paiute trail led over this pass.

Sideroad to Mount Whitney Fish Hatchery and Oak Creek.—The Mount Whitney Hatchery, operated by the California Department of Fish and

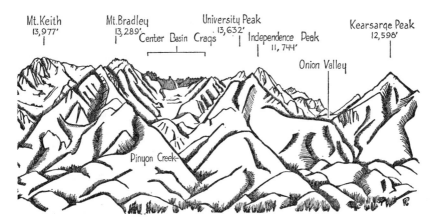

Game, is one of the most important in the State. Under large shade trees, there are pools and picnic tables. The public is welcome to use these facilities and to visit the hatchery from 8 to 5.

First go into the lobby of the large stone building, where pictures and exhibits explain the hatchery's work. Restrooms are to the left. To the right a door leads to a huge room where during winter and spring you may see millions of tiny fish. There are over a hundred long troughs, each holding 25,000 fish or more, where newly-hatched fish are cared for until they are large enough to be planted or trucked to other installations. At the south end of the room is a large incubator which can handle 3,000,000 trout eggs. Eggs are placed in fiberglass trays, and water at a constant temperature is circulated through them. By regulating the water temperature, the rate of egg development may be controlled to produce fish at desired times in order to meet production schedules. The ponds outside contain broodstock. This is the only hatchery which maintains broodstocks of eastern brook and brown trout, and the only hatchery raising goldens in quantity. Kokanee salmon fingerlings are also reared at Mount Whitney Hatchery, but the eggs are obtained from outside sources. Catchable and subcatchable rainbow trout are not produced at Mount Whitney, since they can be reared more economically at installations with warmer water supplies, such as Blackrock Springs. The hatchery's primary work is the production of trout eggs, and fingerling trout for the stocking of back country waters. Each year it produces approximately 10,000,000 spring-spawn rainbow eggs, in addition to large numbers of eggs from the other species. Most of these it ships to other hatcheries throughout the state, which do not have facilities to produce eggs, and occasionally to foreign countries. Recently it shipped 100,000 rainbow eggs, packed in ice, to Brazil by jet.

Below the hatchery on Oak Creek are ruins of the Bell flour mill, which operated from 1866 to 1924. Above the hatchery, the road forks left to a pack station, and right to the North Fork of Oak Creek and a small campground. This is a good road to take if you are looking for a picnic spot. From dozens of places, there are sweeping views of Owens Valley. The Inyo Mountains are particularly beautiful at dusk, as the great shadow of the Sierra climbs their slopes and the last rays of the sun bathe their crest with pink. The Baxter Pass trail begins at the end of the road.

Camp Independence and Soldiers' Cemetery.—North of Independence, at the turnoff to the Fish Hatchery, turn right (E) instead, and drive a half mile. A large sign marks the general location of Camp Independence. When in 1862 Owens Valley settlers appealed for help in fighting the Indians, Colonel George Evans received orders to lead the Owens River Expedition. The troops arrived on July 4, 1862, chose a site on Oak Creek, raised their flag on a 50-foot pole, and named their camp in honor of the day. Some of the men lived in caves in the banks of the ravine (though most are caved in, a few are recognizable) until they had built adobe barracks. The following July the soldiers marched 900 Indian men, women and children off to Fort Tejon. Commanding officer McLaughlin persuaded his superiors that with so many Indians gone, the Valley was safe and there was no further reason to maintain the post. Against the wishes of the settlers the Camp was abandoned for two years. The Camp was reactivated in 1865 and occupied for the next twelve years. When the 1872 earthquake cracked the adobe buildings, it was rebuilt, and was said to be one of the most beautiful posts between St. Louis and San Francisco. Surrounding a parade ground were officers' houses, a hospital, school, store rooms, and a commissary, all buildings painted white. Trees and wide lawns were planted. A memorable ball celebrated its completion.

To see the Soldiers' Cemetery, drive a quarter mile farther and watch for some white monuments west of the road. Relatively few soldiers from the Camp were buried here, for most who died were killed fighting Indians and were buried where they fell. Local people also buried their dead here. After the soldiers left, the Army moved their bodies and headstones to the San Francisco Presidio. A few soldiers are still buried here, those who were mustered out and then remained in the community.

Paiute Monument.—Driving north of Independence, if you will search the crest of the Inyos, you can see an unusual 80-foot finger of granite, long known as Paiute Monument or Winnedumah. There are several Paiute legends about the Monument, one inscribed on a brass plate in the hotel lobby in Independence. Another concerns Tinemaha, a Paiute leader, and his brother Winnedumah, a great medicine man.

Sawmill Creek Campground, on the highway.

Sideroads to Sawmill Pass Trail.—As shown on the map, three roads lead to the beginning of the Sawmill Pass trail. People with stock use the southern

The legend of Winnedumah. When Digger Indians crossed the Sierra to raid the Paiute's hunting grounds, they fought a terrible battle lasting many days. Defeated, the Paiutes fled—some hiding in caves at Blackrock, others escaping into the Inyos. When the exhausted Winnedumah reached the crest, he stopped to wait for his brother. While he prayed to the Great Spirit on behalf of his beaten people, the earth shook and thundered, frightening the Diggers so that they retreated from the Valley; the faithful Winnedumah was turned into a pillar of stone that still watches over his people.

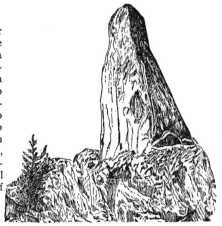

one, which goes to a corral; backpackers use the other two. The pass and creek take their name from the Blackrock Sawmill, built up the Canyon in the 1860s. The Division Creek powerhouse was built by Los Angeles.

Sideroad to Blackrock Springs Rearing Ponds.—At these natural springs, the Department of Fish and Game has built ponds which produce approximately half a million catchable and subcatchable rainbow trout (90,000 pounds) annually. Fingerlings are brought here from Mount Whitney Hatchery for rearing. In addition, rainbow, eastern brook, and brown trout are kept at Blackrock Springs about eighteen months, when they are transferred to Mount Whitney Hatchery for brood stock. The springs' year-round 58° water is conducive to rapid growth.

BIG PINE

Aberdeen.—Aberdeen takes its name from Aberdeen Station, once a stop on the Carson & Colorado railroad several miles east. East of Aberdeen 2½ miles is the intake of the Los Angeles Aqueduct, where Owens River water is diverted to begin its 230-mile flow to San Fernando. Aberdeen is on Goodale Creek, named after pioneer ranchers. Early settlers had some violent arguments over water long before the "civil war" with Los Angeles. There's an old western saying, "steal my horse, carry off my wife, but don't touch my water." On this creek, where the Hines and Goodale irrigation ditches joined, Bill Hines shot one of the Goodales in 1895.

Goodale Creek Campground.—West of highway, just north of Aberdeen.

Big Pine Volcanic Field.—Red cinder cones and dark basaltic lava flows, as fresh as if they had been erupted only a few years ago, lie along the base of the Sierra from Sawmill Creek to Big Pine. (See Geology Section.)

Just south of the Poverty Hills, the highway crosses a flow that broke out from the base of Red Mountain, cinder cone of classic symmetry. Paiute legend says that an old woman who lived at the top of the cone occasionally

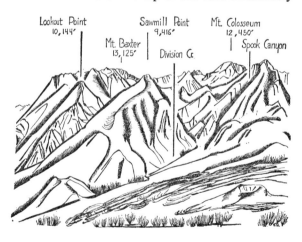

Sierra crest northwest of Independence. Mount Baxter is named for a pioneer rancher.

went on a rampage, building fires and making much smoke. Mothers told their children that if they were not good the old woman would get them. Opposite Red Mountain, a similar flow poured out from a vent along a fault at the base of the Inyo Mountains.

Tinemaha Road.—Begins just north of Aberdeen, rejoining the highway near Fish Springs. Along this back road you can drive slowly enough to get acquainted with some of the volcanic features described above. According to another Paiute legend, the land has a burnt look because in a contest among the sun, the moon, and the animals, the sun lost. The others dumped him into a pit, turning the country red and making the water hot.

Sideroad to Taboose Creek and Taboose Creek Campground.—The Taboose Pass trail, leading to the headwaters of the Kings River's South Fork, starts from the end of the road. Taboose is the Paiute word for a plant growing in the moist soil along many of the lower creeks. With nutlike growths the size of a pea on its roots, it was an important food plant for the Paiutes, who ate it raw and also dried it and ground it into flour. At Blackrock and at Bishop, Indians irrigated the natural plots to make the taboose grow more abundantly. In fall the women dug it up with sticks, or robbed gopher caches, from which they might obtain up to a quart of the sweet-tasting nodules. Down the creek east of the highway a man named Wright had a stage station, eating place, race track and dance pavilion, a popular place for miles around. In an old letter, a soldier from Camp Independence grouses about being sent on a mission, for he will miss a big dance at Wright's.

Charlies Butte.—Three miles north of Aberdeen, east of the highway, is a low lava butte on the river bank known as Charlies Butte. In 1863, members of the McGee and Summers families attempted to go south through the Valley on their way home to Visalia. Helping drive their horses was Negro Charlie Tyler. Traveling the east side of the Valley, they realized their danger when they found the body of a white man and saw Indian signal fires near Fish Springs. Seeing Indians ahead, they attempted to cross the river near the butte. When the horses were unable to pull the wagon up the steep bank, the men cut them loose and mounted them, hoping to make it to Camp Independence. Charlie gave his horse to Mrs. McGee, saying he would catch another and follow. The last they saw of Charlie, he was running toward the butte, Indians after him. Years later a pistol identified as his was found nearby, its empty chambers suggesting a valiant but hopeless fight. The soldiers were annoyed over the incident, for they had warned people not to travel the Valley because of Indian danger. Because the families were known Confederate sympathizers from Texas, some soldiers even said it was too bad the Indians hadn't killed them!

Fish Springs.—The low hills just west of the highway are the Poverty Hills, named by a store keeper who went broke when his prospector customers could not pay their bills. Petroglyphs are evidence of old Indian camps near

Mt. Perkins 12,591'   Mt. Pinchot 13,495'   Goodale Mt. 12,790'

Sierra crest northwest of Aberdeen. Peaks are named for George Perkins, California governor 1880–1883; Gifford Pinchot, first chief, U. S. Forest Service, 1898–1910; the Goodale family, pioneer settlers; Tinemaha, a legendary Paiute chief.

the springs. Near Fish Springs in the 1860s there were some small gold mines, worked by water-powered arrastras. For a time there was a Fish Springs Station. The only activity now is the Fish Springs Hatchery, the second largest producer in the state, which raises approximately 100 tons of trout annually. Visitors are welcome.

Big Pine.—Big Pine lies at the base of the Palisades, the sixteen-mile section of the Sierra crest between Taboose and Bishop passes which is so precipitous that no trail crosses it. Big Pine Creek rises from Palisade Glacier, the largest by far of the Sierra's fifty-odd glaciers. The creek exhibits several qualities distinctive of glacial streams. Silt ground fine by the moving glacier makes the water milky looking, particularly noticeable in late afternoon when the stream is high. Unlike most streams which crest in spring, Big Pine Creek crests twice—first in spring from the snow melt, again beginning in late August as summer heat melts the glacier. Big Pine Creek is one Sierra canyon that hides its glories well. The highway is so close to the base of the front mountains they block your view of the highest peaks be-

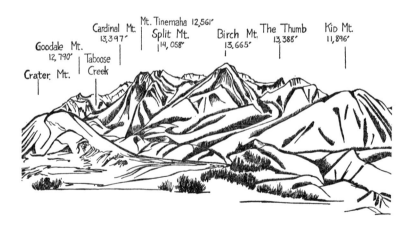

Goodale Mt. 12,790'   Crater Mt.   Taboose Creek   Cardinal Mt. 13,397'   Mt. Tinemaha 12,561'   Split Mt. 14,058'   Birch Mt. 13,665'   The Thumb 13,388'   Kid Mt. 11,896'

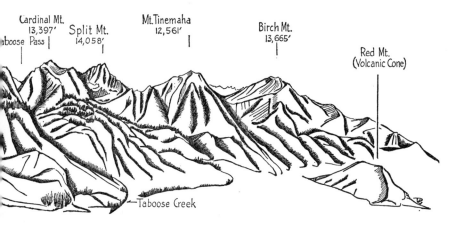

Cardinal Mt.
13,397'
Split Mt.
14,058'
Mt.Tinemaha
12,561'
Birch Mt.
13,665'
Red Mt.
(Volcanic Cone)

aboose Pass

Taboose Creek

hind. To see the glacier and the grand peaks of the Palisades, you must go either by trail to Fourth Lake or the ridge above Grouse Spring, or by road to the east side of Owens Valley, or better yet, part way to Westgard Pass (see below).

Big Pine Park, roadside rest, center of town. Restrooms, water.

Side trip to Big Pine Creek.—The first road up the creek was built for a sawmill, established in 1864 near the first bridge. For a time the hand-made lumber wagons, on solid wooden wheels rimmed with iron, were pulled by 4-yoke teams of oxen. The mill operated for many years, supplying Valley towns and mines as far away as Cerro Gordo.

One-half mile west of Big Pine the road crosses a prominent fault scarp—an abrupt 20-foot bank bordering a sunken place, where the ground slumped during the 1872 earthquake. A mile beyond, just before you cross Big Pine Creek, if you look carefully you will notice that the road drops down a second scarp, the same height but facing in the opposite direction. Thus, the block between the two rose 20 feet above the adjacent ground. These small

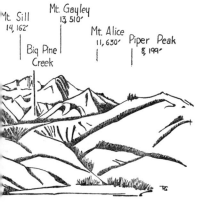

Mt. Sill
14, 162'
Mt. Gayley
13, 510'
Mt. Alice
11,630'
Piper Peak
8, 199'
Big Pine Creek

Sierra crest west of Big Pine. Peaks are named for Edward Sill, poet and literature professor, University of California, 1874–1882; Mrs. Alice Ober of Big Pine.

scarps indicate only the most recent movement along these faults. The fault along the east side of the block is actually the northern end of the "earthquake" fault along the east base of the Alabama Hills. Geophysical studies show that during thousands of years the bedrock here has moved vertically more than 2,000 feet.

Farther on, the road and dump you see on the canyon's south wall belong to the Blue Star talc mine, where talc and marble were last mined in 1946. At the mine, dark volcanic rocks enclose a small body of marble which lies along a contact between two granites, one light-colored, one dark. When the adjoining granite was molten and intruded the rocks, its heat recrystallized the marble, driving out carbon dioxide, which reacted with the volcanic rocks to form talc. In forming talc, iron was expelled from the volcanic rocks and formed veins of iron ore which you can see in the near-by rocks.

There are one large campground and two smaller ones on the creek. Near the end of the road there is a pack station, store and resort. A mountaineering guide has headquarters here also, offering instruction in rock-climbing and guided trips to the peaks and the glacier. The trail to the seven upper lakes and Palisade Glacier begins at the road end. (See Glaciation, Geology Section.) The grand peaks of the Palisades are the special joy of mountain climbers. Almost any weekend you can see climbing parties starting off, their nylon ropes, ice axes, and crampons on their backs.

Side trip to the ancient bristlecone pine.—High on the mountains bordering Owens Valley on the east live the bristlecone pine, the oldest known living things in the world. Do you find it incredible that some were already 2,000 years old when Christ walked the hills of Galilee? "Methuselah," the most ancient of all, pushed rootlets into its gravelly soil a thousand years before the oldest giant redwood sprouted from seed. Do not expect the bristlecone to rival the majesty of the Sequoias, however, for unlike the redwood forests' lush greens and warm browns, the bristlecones' world is bleakly tan and gray and white. It has no streams, almost no underbrush. Most of the trees are less than thirty feet tall—scarred and battered warriors, starving for soil and water, clinging to life in as brutal a climate as you can imagine. It is hard to tell whether some are alive or not. If you search a seemingly dead mass of wind-scoured trunks and twisted limbs, you may find it is living after all, somewhere one valiant branch triumphantly brandishing green needles.

The world of the bristlecone is a remote forbidding land. Unlike the ragged Sierra across the Valley, the crest is a gently rolling plateau. The White Mountains are an unexpected combination of arctic, desert, and forest. You are in a forest, but the trees are so stunted and scattered you seem not to be. You are in a desert, but only twenty miles west rise snow-clad mountains with glaciers. It is something of a surprise, always, to look near your feet and find you are stepping on small plants, so well do their colors blend with the rock. Their springtime, July and early August, is brief and subdued.

Most of the flowers are flat to the ground, their petals so small even the brighter ones are inconspicuous. Windswept gravel mingled with low alpine plants carpets the upper slopes, from a distance looking so drear but on close inspection a mosaic of soft desert colors—lavenders, silvers, pale yellows, gray greens, pinks, tans, dull reds and rusts.

A graded road, possibly the highest you have ever driven (12,000 feet at the locked gate) leads to the bristlecone.

Leave early and plan for a whole day, since the drive alone takes several hours. After crossing the Owens River, the road forks. The right fork goes to Saline Valley, Eureka Valley whose huge sand dune is a scenic winter campsite, and the northern end of Death Valley—all fascinating desert trips during the cool months. Taking the left fork, shift down to a lower gear as you begin the climb. About seven miles from Big Pine, choose a spot to stop for the view of the Palisades. This is one of the few vantage points where you can see all of the sharp peaks towering above their glaciers.

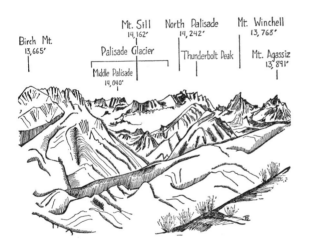

The Palisades, viewed from the Westgard Pass road. Peaks are named for Alexander Winchell, physicist and geologist, University of Michigan, 1853–1872; Louis Agassiz, zoologist, geologist, Harvard, 1847–1873.

The road winds through an impressive narrow canyon that the stream has slashed into the bedrock, exposing its tilted layers. Chartreuse lichen highlights the dark metamorphic rock, older than the Sierra granite by several hundred million years. In the pinyon-juniper forest at Cedar Flat (juniper are often mistaken for cedar) near Westgard Pass, a large sign marks the turnoff to the bristlecone. The pass was named for A. L. Westgaard of the Automobile Association, who in 1913 chose this route for a transcontinental highway. Westgard Pass arbitrarily divides the White and Inyo Mountains, really all one range.

From the turnoff at Westgard as the road curves up to the broad crest, pinyon and juniper are replaced by the timberline trees, limber pine and bristlecone mixed together. Higher yet, the bristlecone alone survive. The

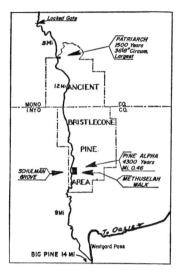

In 1961 Inyo County realigned the Bristlecone Pine Road to a 12% maximum grade; passenger cars in reasonably good condition should have no trouble. Side roads, however, are safe only for 4-wheel drive vehicles. Have a full gas tank and plenty of water. The road is usually snow free from June through October. Check in Big Pine, or with the White Mountain District Ranger, Bishop. Photographers often choose July, when there are more likely to be thunder clouds. There is a dry campground at Schulman Grove; take your own wood and water. The bristlecone are protected; you may remove nothing, nor disturb the area in any way.

From the turnoff at Westgard Pass, the road winds through pinyon country, arid but far from lifeless. Though you may see few, fifty different birds and forty mammals live in these desert mountains. You may see cattle, driven up from Deep Springs Valley for summer grazing.

white rocks and soil near the crest are a limestone called dolomite. Though elsewhere bristlecone grow in other soil, here it is obvious they prefer dolomite. At the sharp contacts between white dolomite and other rocks, notice how few bristlecone straggle over into the dark areas.

Nearing the crest, stop several times and walk a bit west for the superlative view. Of all the viewpoints described in this book, none is better for seeing the Sierra in all its immensity. Stretching north and south as far as you can see is one massive block of granite, the passes barely lower than the peaks. Of the fourteen highest peaks in California, you can see twelve, between the Palisades and Mount Langley.

The Schulman Grove Picnic Area (10,000) honors the memory of Dr. Edmund Schulman, who discovered the trees' great age. For details on the discovery and significance of the bristlecone, read his article in the March 1958 *National Geographic*. Here atop the White Mountains he discovered the oldest tree of all, 4600-year-old Methuselah. A U.S. Forest Service ranger is stationed at the Grove. Two trails lead to the oldest trees. It is a half mile to Pine Alpha, the first 4000-year-old tree which Schulman dated. Methuselah Walk is a two-mile hike among many ancients.

The bristlecone forest is not a dying one, though it may look so because in this dry climate dead trees stand for hundreds of years, their very resinous wood resisting decay. Throughout the forest there are many sturdy young (only several hundred years old!) trees. Timberline trees' growth rate varies greatly. They always grow slowly, but in unfavorable locations they barely grow at all. In dry years they just endure, producing no cones and a microscopic ring. What looks like a sapling with a diameter of only a few inches may be several hundred years old, perhaps adding less than an inch per century. Apparently bristlecones survive not in spite of adversity but because of it. The trees that eke out their existence on the driest slopes, the soil eroded away from their roots and least protected from winter gales, live far beyond the normal life span of more fortunate trees growing in sheltered flats.

These mountains are also the home of the White Mountain Research Station, operated by the University of California, and supported by the Office of Naval Research and the National Science Foundation. Crooked Creek Laboratory (10,500), Barcroft Laboratory (12,470) and the Summit Laboratory (14,246) comprise the mountain sites; at Big Pine there are low altitude facilities. The nature and demands of the work do not allow casual visitors. The Research Station offers the only year-round high altitude research facilities in North America. Barcroft Laboratory is the highest permanently inhabited place in the United States. Problems studied have ranged from cosmic ray measurements to the effects of high altitude on chickens. The main emphasis is on the stress high altitude causes in man, such as the fatigue and nausea caused by oxygen lack. Such research will benefit aviation and space travel.

Beyond Schulman Grove the road continues on to the Patriarch, a whopping youngster of a tree only 1500 years old but with a circumference of 36 feet 8 inches. The Forest Service plans some self-guiding tours here. Particularly unusual are the "pickaback" trees that grow not up but *sideways,* adding inches to their circumference though not to their height. As a tree deteriorates, next to the dying trunk new growth may start, keeping alive the spark of life for another thousand years. As it dies, in turn, again new growth may develop beside it, resulting in a stubby tree with a distorted half-dead trunk.

Three miles beyond, the road ends at a gate, open only to personnel of the research labs. If *your* body is not too oxygen-starved you can walk to the summit of White Mountain Peak, higher than all Sierra peaks except Mount Whitney and Mount Williamson. Carry water and warm clothing.

Cal Tech's Radio Observatory.—North of Big Pine, you may notice two 90-foot saucer-shaped antennae mounted on steel towers. This is not a radar tracking station, but an observatory for radio astronomy, a science only thirty years old. Just as stars and planets give off light waves, something else billions of light years away gives off radio waves. The antennae catch them, as astronomers catch light waves in their telescopes, and focus them into a radio receiver which amplifies them. Other gadgets record them as squiggly lines on graph paper; from them radio astronomers hope to learn much about the universe. With radio waves they can "see" much farther away than the largest optical telescope; in addition they can see through clouds of dust that a telescope may never penetrate. Though a ridge is the best place for a telescope, it would be the poorest location for a radio observatory. The Owens Valley site was chosen because high mountains on both sides screen out interfering waves from radio and TV stations. The big ears are so sensitive that during observations electric razors and fluorescent lights are kept off. For this reason visitors are not welcome, for even an automobile's ignition would be disturbing. The Office of Naval Research supports the installation, hoping that findings will contribute to navigation.

Big Pine to Bishop.—The Sierra Nevada escarpment between Big Pine and Bishop is characterized by long straggling spurs and by slopes much gentler than the sheer scarps to the north and south, for here the summit surface of the Sierra is *bent* down to Owens Valley—it is not *dropped* abruptly along a fault (see Earth Movements, Geology Section).

BISHOP

Keough Hot Springs.—Shaded picnic tables and pool, open May through September. The springs are named for a pioneer family who operated a resort for many years. Without the unpleasant smell many hot springs have, these artesian springs flow over a million gallons a day. The water is 127° when it gushes out and must be cooled before it is piped into the pool.

Bishop.—Though Samuel Bishop stayed in Owens Valley but one season, his name has remained on the creek where he made camp in August, 1861. A man of many financial interests, Bishop ventured into the Valley from Fort Tejon, built two small cabins, and started his San Francis Ranch about three miles west of the present town. His first winter, trouble started between the Paiutes and other newly arrived cattlemen. Evidently Bishop concluded that the hostile Valley was not a likely place for a successful ranch, for he returned to Kern County and became prominent there, being elected one of its first supervisors in 1866. The first structure in the present Bishop was a blacksmith shop, set up in a building hauled from Owensville in late 1864. A small town, called Bishop Creek or Upper Town, grew where Brockman

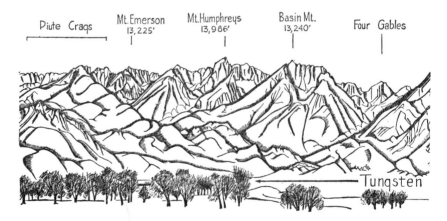

Lane now is. Since much of the land adjoining the creek was swampy, when the Rev. Andrew Clark started the first church east of the Sierra in 1869, jokers nicknamed the town Gospel Swamp.

With abundant water, fertile soil, and square miles of natural grasslands attracting settlers, the northern end of the Valley became a prosperous ranching community with Bishop its center. Today Bishop is the largest as well as the only incorporated city in Inyo and Mono Counties.

Schober Lane Park, just south of town. Picnic tables, restrooms.

Bishop Park, on the highway, north end of town. Heated swimming pool open in summer, wading pond, picnic tables, restrooms, water, barbecues, playground equipment, horseshoe courts.

Bishop Golf Course, on the highway south of town.

Pioneer Cemetery, Cemetery Road, off West Line Street; Bishop Cemetery, East Line Street. The Bishop Cemetery was originally the Oddfellows and Masons cemetery; others used what is now called the Pioneer Cemetery.

Inyo National Forest Supervisor's Office, 207 West South Street. White Mountain District Ranger's Office, 130 Short Street.

Department of Fish and Game, 407 W. Line Street. Anglers' guides and information.

Side trip to Bishop Creek.—With three major canyons cradling the three forks of the creek, each a large stream in itself, Bishop Creek is the largest eastern Sierra basin. There is boating and fishing on the two large reservoirs. There are eleven campgrounds, two pack stations, trailer parks, and several resorts with cabins and boats for rent. Many miles of fishing streams are along the roads; trails lead to many lakes and smaller streams. Rust, red, white and black rocks liven the mountain landscape. Beautiful any time of year, the canyons are breathtaking in late September and early October when the aspen slopes are a mass of orange, scarlet and quivering yellow-gold.

At the center of Bishop turn west on Line Street. Near a black butte a

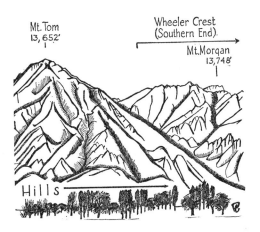

Mt. Tom
13,652'

Wheeler Crest
(Southern End).

Mt. Morgan
13,748'

Hills

Sierra crest west of Bishop. Peaks are named for Ralph Waldo Emerson, philosopher, 1803–1882; General Andrew Humphreys, Chief of Engineers, 1866–1879; Thomas Clark of Owensville, credited with the first ascent in the 1860s; Captain George Wheeler, leader of the Wheeler Survey, 1875–1879; J. H. Morgan, a member of the Wheeler Survey.

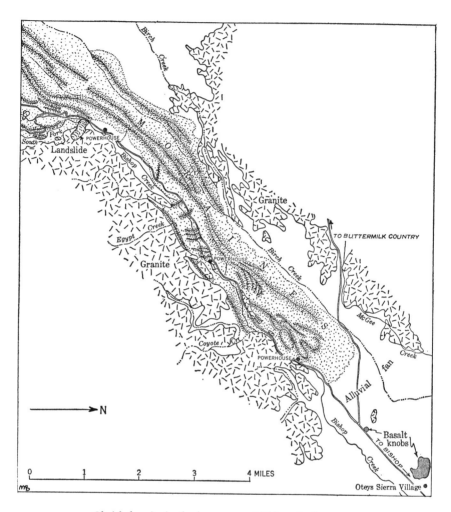

Glacial deposits in the lower part of Bishop Creek canyon

The dotted area shows the glacial deposits; the lines within the dotted area show the crests of moraines. The long lines are the crests of lateral moraines, deposited along the sides of the glacier. Most of these rise 400 feet or more above Bishop Creek. The complexly curved lines in the lower end of the deposits mark crests in the terminal moraine, a great pile of debris deposited at the end of the glacier when it was farthest advanced. The short lines, curved downstream, are the crests of recessional moraines, deposited from the end of the glacier during its last retreat. Though they may appear as low shapeless mounds of debris, when examined carefully they prove to be arc-shaped ridges.

Periods of light winter snowfall or warm summers, when the glacier melted back (retreated) and deposited moraines higher up the canyon, followed periods of heavier snowfall or cool summers, when the ice grew thicker and the glacier advanced. The moraines you see as you drive up the canyon record the advances and retreats.

short way from Bishop is the "Bishop Battlefield," where in 1862 whites and Indians met in their first real battle. A dark knob on the north side of the highway, about five miles from Bishop just below the Buttermilk Road turn-off, is the eroded root of an ancient volcano. Some 20 feet high and 50 feet in diameter, this knob is famous among petrologists (rock scientists), for it shows clearly that molten basalt lava is hot enough to melt solid granite. Microscopic examination shows that where the fluid basalt erupted through the gray granite, the granite adjacent to the dark dikes became glassy and frothy.

Below the mouth of the canyon near Plant 6, Dugan and Blair had a water-powered flour mill in the late 1800s. The power plants, penstocks, and dams on South Lake and Lake Sabrina you will see up-canyon belong to the California Electric Power Company. Two men who came to invest in Nevada silver mines found water more profitable than silver. Recognizing Bishop Creek's potential, they organized a power company backed by Denver financiers. They constructed a 113-mile transmission line (in 1904, the longest in the world) over the White Mountains to Tonopah and Goldfield. Desert heat made the project difficult; when a 4-horse team started on a day's haul, a similar team was needed to haul enough water for the two. The narrow gauge railroad brought the generators and machinery to Laws; long mule teams (42 head, plus 6 pushing behind, for the heaviest loads) hauled them up the canyon. At Plant 4 you can see a set of big wooden wheels from a wagon. The venture was profitable for both the power and mining companies. Electric motors, replacing the gasoline engines powering compressors and hoists, reduced costs from $1.08 per horsepower to 8 cents. Later the company built other plants up the canyon and a power line to San Bernardino and River-side Counties. Bishop Creek falls 5500 feet in 14 miles, enabling the plants in tandem to use the same water five times. The wood-stave flowlines and dam facings are redwood, more hardy and resistant to freezing temperatures than concrete. About fourteen miles from Bishop the road forks, the right fork going to Lake Sabrina and North Lake, the left fork to South Lake.

Bishop Creek Canyon is one of the best places to see evidence of the Ice Age. See how many of the concave shapes typical of glaciated regions— U-shaped canyons, cirques, knife-edged ridges—you can recognize. (See Glaciation, Geology Section.) Glaciers hundreds of feet thick moved slowly down-canyon, plucking out rocks along their routes and transporting all loose material in their way. Along the edges of the glaciers the rock eventually melted out of the ice, forming heaps of gravel and boulders called moraines, such as the one you can see near the mouth of the canyon. It marks the end of the glacier that lay in this canyon. The shapes of the canyons are further evidence of the glaciers' work. For about three miles above the canyon mouth the road follows the narrow canyon cut by Bishop Creek; abruptly the canyon widens into the broad U-shaped valley sculptured by the Bishop Creek glacier. Moraines occur along the valley floor between the lower end of the U-shaped valley and the junction of the South Fork at intervals of a few hundred feet or more. The landscape has been little modified by erosion since the end of the Ice Age. The narrow slot in the floor of the Valley, which contains Bishop Creek, is the only significant modification that could have occurred since the ice disappeared.

South Fork of Bishop Creek.—The road branching left follows the South Fork up its broad glacial canyon. Where it crosses the first ridge into the basin, if you will walk a few hundred yards west of the highway to the top of the ridge, you will have an exceptional view of a fossil Ice Age landscape. As you look northwest you can see three parallel ridges, moraines the glacier deposited along its edges at different times. The lowest was deposited during the glacier's last advance, the other two during earlier advances. The greater age of the highest is indicated by its more rounded shape and less bouldery surface, evidence of a much longer period of weathering and erosion. Opposite Habegger's Ranch (formerly Andrew's Camp) the long gently sloping ridge scarred by a mine road is another moraine, deposited by the South Fork glacier. The road leads to a tungsten mine which during World War II produced ore worth $370,000. The South Fork road ends at a large parking area a quarter mile past the dam. South Lake is the largest of the reservoirs, its 75-foot dam impounding 13,700 acre feet of water. From the road end, trails lead to dozens of lakes and to Bishop Pass.

Middle Fork of Bishop Creek.—The road branching right follows the Middle Fork, beneath the steep east canyon wall. Across the creek you can see the large dump of the Cardinal Gold Mine, its buildings now used as a resort. From the resort you can walk the mine road to the ruins of the mill and cyanide plant. Gaylord Wilshire of New York, who was endeavoring to outdo William Randolph Hearst in gold mining, had high hopes for his Cardinal Mine. In a 1906 issue of his *Wilshire's Magazine,* he wrote: "It is indeed the 'World's Greatest Gold Mine.' . . . With our unlimited ore body and prac-

Thompson Ridge

Mt. Haeckel
13,435'

tically unlimited power, there is no reason why we should not install five mills of 1000 stamp capacity and mill 20,000 tons a day. This sounds large, but it must be remembered that we have absolutely the largest ore body in the world—and every facility for working it cheaply. . . . if we get only $3 per ton in values that will give us $2 a ton net profit, and if we mill 10,000 tons per day that would be over seven million dollars a year profit . . . However, this is a very modest estimate, because there is hardly any doubt that the ore will run very much over $3 a ton." According to a subsequent State Mining Bureau report, the mine produced 5,000 tons of ore worth $11 a ton. Despite Wilshire's dreams, operations were not profitable enough, the "ifs" won out, and in 1915 the 10-stamp mill shut down. From 1933 through 1937 the mine produced gold worth $1,600,000, but closed the following year when no new ore was discovered; it has not operated since.

As you drive along the boulder slope, do you notice that the rocks change color from light gray to rust to darker gray? In the late afternoon sun, you can have a fine view of the cliff above and the relations of these rocks to each other from the North Lake road, see below. Lake Sabrina is named for the wife of a power company superintendent. From the roadend trails lead to the many lakes and open country of the Middle Fork canyons.

North Fork of Bishop Creek.—Below Lake Sabrina, a steep road turns off to North Lake. Just before reaching the lake, you have an outstanding view back across the Middle Fork. Rarely are the relations between granite and the much older rocks it intruded so easily seen and so wonderfully exposed. At the top of the grade, look for a tractor trail to the right and walk a short way along it.

Layers and layers of mud, silt and sand had accumulated on the floor of the ocean that once covered most of the western states. (See Older Rocks, Geology Section.) These layers, compacted and hardened into rock, were further changed (metamorphosed) when great earth movements squeezed,

Sierra crest south of Lake Sabrina. Still an array of wild peaks, many without names.

tilted, and folded them. Much later, masses of molten granite welled up into them, intruding cracks and weak zones.

Streams eroded the cap of overlying metamorphic rock and part of the granite, filling the San Joaquin and Owens Valleys with their sand and gravel. Almost all of the old metamorphics are gone, but there are occasional remnants such as the rust-colored mass you see across the canyon. It is this ancient metamorphic rock which provides the colors in Bishop Creek and Pine Creek canyons. It extends eastward to form the rusty ridge above North Lake, and westward to form the red, black, and white rocks of the South Fork canyon and Coyote Ridge.

Beyond North Lake, the road passes a prominent steep-faced pile of iron-stained rubble, looking somewhat like a mine dump. Perhaps this is a rock slide, or it may have been a rock glacier, an ice-lubricated mass of rock fragments. Rock glaciers live in many of the larger basins above 11,000 feet. One of the largest is on the north side of Mount Powell, south of Lake Sabrina. From the Bishop Pass trail you can see two smaller ones, one half a mile northwest of Saddlerock Lake, the other east of Bishop Lake. If you walk across a live rock glacier, huge boulders will often move underfoot, showing that they are not at rest, and suggesting that the mass is in motion. Rock glaciers feed on rock debris; all are at the base of long boulder slopes. Unlike true glaciers, they do not require a snow pack at their heads, but they do require a climate cold enough to keep the ground perennially frozen (permafrost conditions).

In the lodgepole forest at the roadend there are scattered meadows with a marvelous variety of mountain flowers—orange tiger lily, blue iris, lavender lupine, shooting stars, daisies, and wild onion, red columbine, orange-red paintbrush, yellow cinquefoil and monkey flowers, small white rein orchis and tall woolly parsnip, dark blue monkshood. You likely will see hummingbirds darting among the flowers, many black-capped juncos and white-crowned sparrows hopping about hunting for seeds, and you may hear the flute-like song of the hermit thrush. The Piute Pass trail begins at the roadend.

Side trip to Pine Creek Canyon.—In this canyon is the Union Carbide Nuclear Company's Pine Creek Mine, one of the world's largest tungsten producers. (See *Bishop Tungsten District,* Selected Reading, Geology Section.) Tungsten is a metal used in exceptionally hard heat-resistant steel alloys, for cutting tools and engine parts. The mill recovers molybdenite, a little copper and gold, and most important, scheelite (calcium tungstate). When the federal government suspended tungsten stockpiling in 1956, price declined drastically; by 1958 every other tungsten mine in the United States had closed. The Pine Creek operation continues because the mill can recover molybdenite, a profitable co-product of the tungsten ore, and because in 1960 the company developed a pioneer commercial process to produce high-purity ammonium paratungstate. APT is a tungsten compound in great demand for lamp filaments, tool tips and high temperature parts for the aero-space program.

Some frightening disasters have occurred in the steep-sided canyon. In the summer of 1946 when heavy rains raised Gable Creek to flood stage, a mass of boulders and gravel were washed down Gable Creek canyon into the mining village near its mouth, burying it to depths up to 8 feet and destroying seventeen of the houses. In 1952 avalanches destroyed part of the mill and several houses. A baby was lost for two hours; rescuers found him with the family's two dogs protected by his overturned playpen, buried under six feet of snow.

Pine Creek Canyon has magnificent displays of rock structure and glacial features. As you start up the Pine Creek road in Round Valley, you can see two low ridges extending more than two miles from the canyon mouth to the company town of Rovana. These are long moraines, rock debris the Pine Creek glacier deposited along its sides. The road goes between the moraines to enter the canyon, a splendid example of a U-shaped glacial valley. In miniature, it resembles Yosemite Valley, and was formed in much the same way. The position of the steep-walled canyon head is no accident; here, glaciers from Gable Creek, Morgan Creek, and upper Pine Creek combined to form one huge powerful glacier which gouged deeply into its bed.

The precipitous canyon walls are chiefly granites, which can be dis-tinguished by their different shades of gray. In the lower part of the canyon dark bands or "dikes" cut through the granite, molten material forced up-ward under pressure, that invaded the granite wherever there were cracks or weak zones. At the head of the canyon, the light-colored bands which look like layers are also dikes, offshoots of a granite body that cut through a variety of rocks. The rusty-colored rocks are part of the "Pine Creek pendant," a remnant of the ancient metamorphic rock which antedates the granite by several hundred million years. (See Older Rocks and Structures, Geology Section.) The public road ends at the bridge and pack station below the mill; a trail leads to Pine Lakes and Pine Creek Pass.

The Volcanic Tableland.—An enormous volcanic flow, which forms the pink cliffs beyond Bishop, blocks Owens Valley on the north. You can see into the heart of the flow in the Owens River Gorge, and from the top of the Tableland you can see how large broken blocks of the volcanic rock have been tilted and moved. (See Volcanism and Earth Movements, Geology Sec-tion, for details and trips.)

Chalk Bluff Road.—Chalk Bluff, the prominent white exposure in the cliffs of the Tableland north of Bishop, is not chalk at all, but cross-bedded white pumice which was deposited there by streams before the flows of molten material that compose the upper layers of the Tableland rolled down to cover it. Above the pumice is a 220-foot layer of soft pinkish tuff, and capping that a 50-foot layer of hard orange-brown tuff. Below the pumice layer you can see older gravel beds, deposited by an ancient and much larger Owens River. The Chalk Bluff Road runs along the base of the cliffs, a short drive that in addition to its geologic interest provides scenic views of the meandering Owens River and the Sierra crest. This portion of the river provides popular year-round fishing. If you take pictures, plan a morning trip when the sun is shining into the Sierra canyons. For even better views, scramble up to the top of the Tableland.

From Bishop drive north on Highway 6 a little over a mile. Where the highway makes a right-angle turn east, proceed straight ahead for another two miles to the point where the road forks three ways. The Chalk Bluff Road is the left of the three; it joins Highway 395 near Round Valley.

Side trip to Owensville, and the Carson & Colorado Depot at Laws.—From Bishop drive north on Highway 6 about four miles. Where the highway bends north after crossing the Owens River, go a few hundred yards on the Silver Canyon Road which forks right, and park by the depot.

Owensville.—In 1863 prospectors established the mining camp of Owensville, the first settlement in the northern part of Owens Valley, near the present junction of the Silver Canyon Road and Highway 6. During its short boom, corner lots sold for $1,000. In 1864 its July 4th celebration attracted a gay crowd of 150. But Owensville "lasted soon." When their claims in the White Mountains proved disappointing, the prospectors wandered elsewhere. By the end of the year most of the cabins were torn down for their lumber or moved away. There are few traces of the camp. Hollows that do not seem natural may indicate fireplaces or cellars. If you wander in the grass near the river, you may find some worn building blocks of pink tuff, quarried from the cliffs of the Tableland. A two-foot-high ring of earth and rock was a corral.

Laws.—For thirty years the narrow-gauge train affectionately called the Slim Princess was the connecting link between isolated Owens Valley and the outside world, hauling Valley cattle, farm produce, and passengers north (see History Section). Without air-conditioning, reclining chairs, or a coffee shop, still the three-day train trip to San Francisco was luxury compared to the

White Mountain Peak
14,246'

The White Mountains east of Bishop may have been named for the snow that lies on them into late spring or for the white limestone on the crest. Perhaps the name was first applied to the granite mountain to the north (now Montgomery Peak) and later transferred.

twelve-day stage to Los Angeles or the rough wagon roads over Walker and Sonora Passes. In summer the trip was hot. In winter, if you sat in the red plush seats near the stove you roasted; at the other end of the car you froze. Fortified with ample picnic baskets, Owens Valley settlers boarded the little train in the morning, stayed overnight at Sodaville, Nevada, transferred to the Virginia & Truckee near Carson City, reached Reno the next evening, and there waited for the transcontinental train to San Francisco. Wood-burning engines chugged along the eastern side of Owens Valley, several miles from the towns. Each town had its station to the east—some of them oases with trees, hedges and flowers, most of them sad dull-red buildings with a few scraggly trees. Freight wagons and stages made the trips from stations to towns, often through hub-deep sand or mud.

Laws, named for an assistant superintendent, served Bishop. The ties and rails have gone for salvage, and there is little to see of the C & C except at Laws. During its busy days Laws had three hotels, a school and several stores. Today you can see the depot, and walk down the roadbed to the water tower and hand-pushed turntable. The S.P. has donated these installations, steam engine Number 9, and several cars to Bishop and Inyo County, which plan a railroad museum or park.

Petroglyph Loop Trip.—Within half an hour's drive of Bishop, there are acres of rock alive with fascinating designs—spirals, circles, wavy lines, footprints, men, deer, and mountain sheep. Ancient peoples throughout the world have painted such pictures (pictographs), or chipped them in rock (petroglyphs). This 50-mile signed loop trip takes you to four of Owens Valley's most accessible sites. (See Petroglyph Makers, History Section.) Photographers need early morning sun for the first two. If you time your trip to include a late picnic supper, you will be rewarded with a glorious sunset panorama of the Sierra and White Mountain crests.

The 5-foot circle designs among the Chalfant group are among the largest known in the west. To reach them, walk north along the base of the bluff. For at least a quarter mile north and south of the parking area, you can find more petroglyphs pecked into the soft rock (Bishop tuff). The route turns west and takes you on top of the Tableland to the Red Canyon petroglyphs, so extensive you could spend a day rambling along the ridge and still not find them all. West and north of the sign, perhaps you can discover pictures of men, deer, and bighorn sheep, and on the ridges, hand and footprints.

Panorama Stop is reason enough to drive the loop, particularly when the mountains are snow covered. Here is an extraordinary full-circle panorama, with over a dozen 13,000-foot peaks cutting a jagged skyline.

At Chidago (Shi-dáy-go) Canyon, children can have a grand time scrambling up the jumbled rocks and hunting for petroglyphs hidden around corners. The boulder that is crowded with designs is nicknamed the Newspaper Rock. Could this really have been its function, a place where nomadic In-

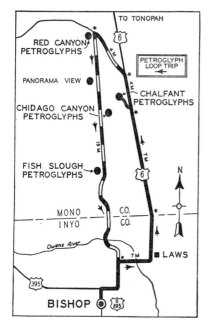

From Bishop, follow Highway 6 through Chalfant Valley, named for Inyo editor and author W. A. Chalfant. A short detour will take you to the old depot on the C & C narrow gauge. Watch for the 80-year-old roadbed in the brush near the highway; when you turn off west to the Chalfant petroglyphs, you will cross it. Near Laws, there is a plant for processing nonmetallic ore such as talc and kaolin.

South of Fish Slough the road loops back to Highway 6. If you prefer a longer way home, at the mouth of Fish Slough turn east on the Chalk Bluff Road which joins Highway 395 in Round Valley.

Local sponsors who have placed signs on the petroglyph sites hope that visitors will prize them and help prevent any vandalism. Marring the designs in any way will make them useless for scientific study and research.

Adapted from map by Automobile Club of Southern California, Copyright 1961

dians "wrote" about their travelings and "read" about those who had camped there before? Professor Robert Heizer, University of California, has recently advanced a new explanation of the petroglyphs. After studying six hundred California and Nevada sites, and finding that all are on game trails, Heizer has concluded that they are magic symbols to foster good hunting.

Though at Fish Slough petroglyphs are scarce, there is abundant evidence of Indian camps—obsidian chips, bits of pottery, mussel shells, and house rings, circles of stones which may mark the outlines of shelters. Near the sign is a large rock with dozens of holes and shallow depressions in its flat top, where Indian women ground pinyon nuts and wild seeds. Near the springs at the upper end of Fish Slough, there was a stage station, on the wagon road between Bishop and Benton. The stream was first called Sand Springs Creek, for the sandy-bottomed springs where you can see water bubbling up.

Winter Trips to the Desert.—Though beyond the scope of this book, we mention briefly a few of the many possible trips to the desert and ghost towns east of the White Mountains. Books listed at the end of this chapter and the history section will give you further information.

Candelaria.—Take Highway 6 over Montgomery Pass, turn left at Basalt on Nevada State Highway 10, drive 17 miles to a wooden sign, turn right on the dirt road to Candelaria.

Loop Trip to Tonopah and Goldfield.—Take Highway 6 to Tonopah (possibly staying overnight there), go south on Highway 95 to Goldfield, west on Highway 3 to Lida and Oasis, southwest to Deep Springs Valley and Westgard Pass, and rejoin Highway 6–395 at Big Pine.

Loop Trip to Fish Lake Valley.—For a scenic drive along the eastern base of the White Mountains, take Highway 6 over Montgomery Pass, turn south on Nevada State Route 3A through Fish Lake Valley to Oasis, southwest through Deep Springs Valley and Westgard Pass, and back to Big Pine.

Back Roads.—There are many square miles to explore, and miles of unsigned roads. The following will get you started:

Ed Powers Road.—About 3 miles west on the Bishop Creek Road, where the highway bends south, continue straight ahead and turn north onto the Ed Powers Road. From it you can turn west and drive to the Tungsten Hills; or turn west onto Sawmill Road, and go on back roads to Round Valley.

Buttermilk Road.—About 5 miles west on the Bishop Creek Road, turn right onto the Buttermilk Road which leads to the grazing lands of the Buttermilk Country, named for the dairy where teamsters stopped for buttermilk during the 1870s.

Old Sherwin Hill Road.—Take Highway 395 to Round Valley. Where the highway swings right up Sherwin Grade, take the left fork which rejoins 395 near Sherwin Summit. Near the base of the grade, you can see the first silo built in Inyo County.

Poleta Laws Road.—Drive out East Line Street to the Poleta Laws Road. If you turn north you will reach Laws and Highway 6. The large irrigation ditches you will follow are part of the McNally Canal, which figured prominently in the water war of the 1920s.

Highway 395, Bishop to Sherwin Summit.—At Bishop Highways 6 and 395 separate, the former climbing over Montgomery Pass into Nevada, 395 following the eastern base of the Sierra to Reno. Driving the dry gray land between Bishop and the base of Sherwin Hill, it takes some imagination to picture it as prosperous ranch country, with a network of irrigation ditches, thousands of cattle, orchards and vineyards on the foothill slopes. Old-timers are nostalgic as they recall "how green was their valley," before they sold their precious water to the Los Angeles Aqueduct.

Three miles west of Bishop near Brockman Lane, the large trees north of the highway are said to be the place where a posse hanged the convicts of Convict Lake fame (see *Mammoth Lakes Sierra*). One and one-half miles farther the road climbs a 75-foot bluff to a boulder strewn terrace. The low rounded mounds are inactive sand dunes that have been stabilized by vegetation; road cuts through the dunes expose clean sand. Desolate and seemingly uninteresting, the terrace has a story to tell—of a much larger and more powerful river, and of earth movements which tilted the land (see Earth Movements, Geology Section).

The low hills to the southwest are the Tungsten Hills, where three partners who were mining placer gold found a heavy white mineral which proved to be scheelite, a tungsten mineral. The high price of tungsten in World War I stimulated considerable mining and the camp of Tungsten City. When the price of tungsten dropped at the war's end, the mines closed; a few have been worked intermittently since. The pink cliffs of the Volcanic Tableland rise on the opposite side of the highway. As the road bends north you can see the remains of a quarry, where the soft volcanic rock was mined for building stone and decorative purposes.

As you approach Round Valley, its large green fields may give you an inkling of how parts of Owens Valley looked during ranching days. These ranches are among the very few whose owners did not sell to Los Angeles. In the horse and buggy days, when Bishop was half a day away, Round Valley had its own small community. In the foothills, the Jones brothers built the first grist mill during the 1860s. Bits of its handmade wooden machinery can be seen at the Eastern California Museum. The steep slopes of Basin Mountain, Mount Tom, and Wheeler Crest make up the spectacular Sierra scarp rising behind Round Valley. Like the escarpment south of Big Pine, it was formed by faulting. Round Valley is a large depressed block; its bedrock, now covered several hundred feet deep with sand and gravel, was once continuous with the main block of the Sierra.

South of Round Valley, between the Tungsten Hills and the Sierra itself, lie the high meadows and brushland of the Buttermilk Country. Cattle graze it in summer; in winter it is an important deer range.

Beyond Round Valley, the highway swings up the Volcanic Tableland. Road cuts expose sparkling pink below the weathered tan surface of the volcanic rock (Bishop tuff). Mounds fifty feet high, readily visible from the road, mark places where escaping gases hardened and bleached the tuff, making it more resistant to erosion. The road cuts across the edge of one of these mounds, where you can see that the white was pink before bleaching.

Sherwin Summit, 3,000 feet above Owens Valley, was named for James Sherwin, who had a ranch at the base of the hill and who later built the Sherwin Tollroad up the grade during the rush to the Mammoth Mines. Be sure to stop at some of the turnouts along the grade for the view south into the heart of the Bishop Creek drainage. For roads and trails north of Sherwin Summit, see our companion book, *The Mammoth Lakes Sierra*. You can make an interesting loop trip back to Owens Valley by driving north to Mono Lake, east on highway 120 to Benton, then south on Highway 6 to Bishop.

Alabama Hills Scenic Route.—A graded road completed in 1962 takes you on an unusually scenic 18-mile loop trip into the strange world of the Alabama Hills. There are marvelous possibilities for family picnics (take your own wood and water), with no end of caves and rocks for children to climb. It is said that the Paiutes cached pine nuts in some of the hollows, covering the openings with adobe. Water, seeping into the

SOURCES OF ADDITIONAL INFORMATION

Inyo National Forest.—Information, maps, campfire permits.
Forest Supervisor, Bishop.
Lone Pine District Ranger, Lone Pine.
White Mountain District Ranger, Bishop.

For Accommodations and Resort Information, Write.—
Southern Inyo Chamber of Commerce, P O Box 552, Lone Pine
Bishop Chamber of Commerce, 125 East Line St., Bishop
Eastern Sierra Motel & Hotel Association, 1025 N. Main St., Bishop

Selected Readings

AUSTIN, MARY. *The Land of Little Rain.* Boston: Houghton Mifflin, 1950. 132 pp. This edition of the 1903 classic is illustrated with 48 full-page photographs by Ansel Adams. Sensitive to the people and the land east of the Sierra. Out of print. A 1961 edition by Doubleday is available as a 95¢ paper-bound Anchor Book.

Indian Wells Valley Handbook. Box 73, China Lake: The China Lake Branch, American Association of University Women, 1960. 87 pp. Trips, history and natural history of the desert country south of Owens Valley.

MILNE, LOUIS J. and MARGERY. *The Mountains.* New York: Time Inc., 1962. 192 pp. The fundamental, fascinating relationships between mountains and their plant and animal inhabitants. Extraordinary illustrations.

PUTNAM, GEORGE PALMER. *Up In Our Country.* New York: Duell, Sloan and Pierce, 1950. 224 pp. The peace and endless delights the famous publisher found during his retired years in a Sierra cabin below Mount Whitney.

REED, ADELE. *Old Bottles and Ghost Towns.* Bishop: published by the author, 1961. 55 pp. Nearby ghost towns; lavishly illustrated. Available locally or send $2.00 to the author, Route 1, Box 96, Bishop.

SCHUMACHER, GENNY, ed. *The Mammoth Lakes Sierra.* San Francisco: Sierra Club, 1961. 160 pp. Companion book to *Deepest Valley*, dealing in the same fashion with the eastern Sierra country between Bishop and Mono Lake.

WOLFE, LINNIE MARSH. *Son of the Wilderness: The Life of John Muir.* New York: Knopf, 1945. 364 pp. A biography of the great conservationist, John Muir, telling of his inspiring fight to preserve wilderness beauty.

---

parallel cracks (joints, characteristic of many granites) and decaying the rock, and wind have weathered the granite into grotesque shapes. The worn, rounded Alabamas are noticeably unlike the splintered peaks of the Sierra crest, although both are granite and both are the product of weathering. Desert climate has fashioned the former, while alpine climate with its continual freezing and thawing has produced the latter.

Six miles north of Lone Pine, turn west off Highway 395 and follow the signed "Alabama Hills Scenic Route." A rocky outcrop on the left, 2½ miles from the highway, is believed to be the location of one of the first fights between settlers and Paiutes. The Indians fled to the rocks and drove the whites back with showers of arrows. A grove of cottonwoods farther on indicates the old Moffett homestead. Many side roads invite you to wander and explore. If, at the junction with the Whitney Portal Road, you are not yet ready to leave the Alabamas, turn right, cross the bridge, turn left onto the Tuttle Creek Road, and drive on through the southern portion of the Hills.

Trails

THE HIGH SIERRA ABOUNDS WITH GOOD trails. During August the most popular trails abound with people. Some complain that the Sierra is overpopulated. Don't be fooled. If you hike only the best known canyons and camp right beside the trail, then you may have good reason to think the Sierra crowded.

But have you never pitched your tent a quarter mile off the trail, on the *far* side of the stream? Never wandered cross-country along an unnamed stream to an unnamed lake? The Sierra Nevada is over four hundred miles long, over fifty miles wide. No quietness and solitude left here? Once you are familiar with the country, have followed the trails described in this guide and learned the landmarks, then the real fun begins—exploring the trail-less wilderness, discovering the countless meadows, streams, and ridges we do *not* mention. A lifetime of summers would not be enough to know them all.

On the following pages we describe all the well-defined trails into the the eastern Sierra from Owens Valley. Unless otherwise noted, all are suitable for stock. Most trails are well signed and easily followed. Where they are indistinct, look for blazes or ducks (cairns). Mileages are from the most recent measurements (made with a bicycle wheel) available from the Forest Service, and from Starr's *Guide to the John Muir Trail*. For those trails that have not been measured, we qualify the mileage with the word "about." For details on the roads leading to the trails, consult the end-paper maps and use the index to look up particular roads.

Army, Trail Crest, Shepherd, Baxter, Sawmill, Taboose, Kearsarge, and Bishop passes lead into Sequoia and Kings Canyon National Parks. Park rules differ in one important respect from National Forest rules. *Firearms, dogs (even on leash), and cats are prohibited on all Park trails. Motor scooters and other mechanized vehicles are prohibited on all Park trails, in all Wilderness Areas, and on many Forest trails.* Check with local rangers.

Tree blazes are conspicuous markings at eye level, where bark has been removed. The rock piles are called *ducks*.

Plan for Strenuous Trips

The earth forces that fashioned the Sierra have made its eastern slope above Owens Valley a massive rock wall two miles high, its passes but a little lower than its peaks. There is a striking difference between Sierra trails north of Pine Creek Canyon, and those south. In our companion book, *The Mammoth Lakes Sierra*, which covers the country north, we classified trails as easy, intermediate, and strenuous. Of all the trails south of Pine Creek, which this book covers, there is only *one* easy trail and few are intermediate. Not only are most trails out of Owens Valley strenuous; we had to add an additional class, "very strenuous." We grade trails chiefly on the basis of elevation gains, for in the mountains this determines how long and how rough the trip will be, far more than do miles traveled. In this section we classify trails generally as follows:

easy hike	less than 500 foot gain
moderate hike	600–1500 " "
strenuous hike	1600–3,000 " "
very strenuous hike	over 3,000 " "

The three least strenuous passes are Kearsarge, Bishop, and Piute passes. The others are tough, even for hardy backpackers who are used to high altitude and are in top physical condition. There are several ways to make a trip into this rugged country less of a grind and more of a joy. One is to rent a horse for yourself and a mule for your load. The cost for packing in, if split among several people, is nominal. Or, walk in, but let a mule carry your gear. If you do not wish to use animals, then take two or even three days to cross the passes.

Most important for backpackers, on the trails that begin low—plan your time of day. Hiking miles up shadeless brush slopes under a searing late-morning sun is no fun; avoid it by starting an hour before sunup or in the late afternoon. Colors are more intense. The canyon walls so monotonously gray in the noonday glare may be green, rust, red, and blue-gray in the kinder sidelight early and late. Flowers are brighter, oaks and pinyon deeper green, the copper bark of the birch more glowing. Dawn in the foothills is exhilarating, breezes are cool. Broad blue shadows still deepen the canyons of the Inyos behind you, while Sierra ridgecrests are gold in the sunrise. Or if you prefer, start late in the afternoon, when the mountains have begun to cast their shadows. Though you can make only a few miles before dark, they will be pleasant miles in the cool of evening.

Maps

The map inside the front and back covers has been drawn especially for this guidebook. For larger scale, more detailed maps, best by far are the topographic maps which show elevation and relief, invaluable information when traveling a new region or exploring cross-country. Find someone to show you how to read a topo map; it takes only a little study and practice. The new "15-minute series" is large scale, one inch equaling approximately one mile. Each map, known as a quadrangle, covers 15 minutes of latitude and longitude. Topo maps can be purchased in many stationery and engineers' supplies stores, or order them from the Geological Survey, Federal Center, Denver 25, Colorado (30 cents each). Write also for the free sheet of Topographic Map Symbols, and the latest Index to Topographic Mapping in California, which shows all maps available. Besides asking for the quadrangle by name, be sure to specify you want the 15-minute series.

The Forest Service supplies reliable maps. The Outing Maps of the Sierra, published by the large auto clubs for their members, are good maps. The Sierra Club publishes a small-scale map of the entire High Sierra.

The John Muir Trail

The famous John Muir Trail winds among the highest peaks and passes of the Sierra crest, from Yosemite Valley south to Mount Whitney. Named in honor of the man who did so much to ensure that some of the Sierra's wild beauty remain wild and beautiful, the Muir Trail is the longest mountain wilderness trail in the country, touching no towns nor paved roads along its two hundred miles. Yet for all its wildness, the Muir Trail is readily accessible, trails intersecting it from dozens of roadends. Most of the trails out of Owens Valley connect with it.

Emergencies

Though there are few emergencies and few lost people in the back country, knowing how to help rescuers locate you could save precious time. A series of three—shouts, whistle blasts, or smoke signals—means distress. (A whistle is cheap insurance.) If help is needed for serious illness or accident, send someone to notify the Sheriff's office or the nearest Ranger. The Sheriff's posse and the Civil Air Patrol, volunteers who risk their lives to save others, assist mountain rescue operations. Most lost people can find their own way eventually if they do not panic. If lost, never travel in the dark. Keep warm and save precious energy for daylight hours. If you are truly lost, in an open area make signals that can be seen from the air, such as a smoky fire, a flag, or light-colored clothing spread in a meadow.

Altitude Sickness

Physically fit people are often surprised and puzzled when in the mountains they have nosebleeds, headaches, and nausea. Age has little to do with it; athletic teenagers are sometimes the most distressed. Driving to a roadend 9,000 feet high is so easy and quick that one tends to forget that the human body needs several days to adjust to the tremendous change in elevation from sea level where most of us live. Dr. Andrew J. Smatko of Santa Monica, a mountaineer who has climbed over one hundred and fifty Sierra peaks, has contributed the following discussion on altitude sickness.

The disagreeable sensations one may experience at high altitudes, commonly called "altitude sickness," are the body's reactions to the lack of oxygen. Most of these symptoms would disappear quickly if oxygen could be administered or if the individual were promptly returned to a much lower altitude. As one ascends from sea level, the amount and pressure of oxygen in the air constantly decreases, causing symptoms such as headache, lack of appetite, nausea, vomiting, irritability, shortness of breath, rapid pulse, and insomnia. Whether or not one experiences these symptoms depends on many factors, among them general good health, physical (muscular) fitness, a capable heart, good lung capacity, and elastic arteries in all the vital organs, especially the brain. Headache and slight nausea occur most often above 8,000 feet, after exertion, frequently because of inadequate intake of carbohydrates.

One should walk *slowly* and *steadily,* resting briefly, eating small amounts of carbohydrate-rich foods, particularly quick-energy sugars, frequently. In addition, drink as often as you are thirsty. The dry air of the eastern Sierra increases the body's demand for water.

However, there is a limit to the body's ability to adjust. The only safe way to acclimatize is to give your body the rest and time it needs to adjust to the lack of oxygen. An hour or two of rest may take care of acute discomfort; but one must not conclude that he is cured or that the symptoms will not recur if exertion is continued. Further traveling may need to be postponed until the next day. The severity of the symptoms is the best guide. Those individuals who do not acclimatize readily (categorized by the vague but true designation "not in shape"), may need to remain camped at the same altitude for several days, or better still, descend a thousand feet. There are various medications which lessen nausea, others that ameliorate headache, and stimulants to combat fatigue, but the treatment par excellence is *oxygen.* Oxygen is richer at lower altitudes, and is free.

The Experienced Mountaineer . . .

. . . *has these essentials in his knapsack,* even on short hikes: sunburn preventative, mosquito repellent, first-aid supplies, small flashlight, matches, extra food, map, and dark glasses (or an exceptionally good squint).

Doesn't succumb too often to local legends that "it never rains at night" and "it never rains in August." No matter how clear the sky when he sets out, he is always prepared with tent or tarp, poncho or rain jacket, for those unexpected days and nights when it pours and even hails.

Wears comfortable, broken-in shoes or boots. Boots need not be heavy, but they need thick enough soles for rocky trails. Leather soled shoes are poor, for they provide no traction. The best for all around wear is the lug sole, available at all large mountaineering equipment stores. It can be attached to almost any boot; it is suitable for snow, talus, scree, mud, rock, as well as woodland trails. Get the best, which is made of hard black rubber (Vibram, Dufour). Though expensive, it will outlast any other sole several times, and is safety insurance as well. Some hikers are well satisfied with thick-soled, arch-supported basketball shoes, for they are light and inexpensive. However, such rubber-soled shoes are taboo on ice or hard snow.

Travels with a companion (he enjoys solitude more if he can talk to some-one about it) and always tells someone where he is going and when he expects to return.

Never underestimates the hazard of snow slopes, stream crossings, steep mountainsides, and high exposed places in storms.

Stays on the trail, whenever cutting across switchbacks could conceivably start gullies (which in one season can wash out an expensive trail) or other-wise break down the trail's upper or lower edges. Does whatever else he can to improve or preserve trails, such as clearing away loose rocks, reporting broken or misplaced signs to a ranger.

Gives stock the right of way—moves several yards off the trail, on the *up* side or beyond the end of a switchback when possible, then stands still until the animals have passed. He stands out in the open and talks quietly so that the animals will see and hear him and not be spooked. He does *not* crouch behind a tree, wave arms, or shout, or start a movie camera whirring. He parks his gear and pitches his tent well off of any stock trail. Mules have been known to kick packs to pieces, perhaps because they didn't like the shiny frame or just because they don't like backpackers' competition.

Allows at least 150 yards from streams or lakes if there are no toilet facilities; digs and covers.

Leaves his campsite cleaner than he found it, burning what he can. Since disturbing meadow sod to bury debris can in time destroy a meadow, he *carries out* his unburnables. He knows that if both ends of tin cans are removed, the cans then burned and smashed flat, they take up almost no space and weigh little—much less than when he carried them in, and by now he is in better shape to carry them anyway.

Leaves no evidence that he passed; he finds it wild, treads softly, keeps it wild.

Most important, he does all these things without being odiously virtuous about it—like a reformed smoker, for instance. He simply sets a quiet, un-ostentatious example. He is almost a paragon, but there are more and more of him; this is a good thing, because there are a lot of people visiting the Sierra wilderness, and his kind take up less room. His sensitivity to the beauty of wildness—carried even to the extreme of not breaking off and burning the sculptured artifacts of old dead albicaulis at timberline—will help wildness last longer.

Bristlecone Pine, White Mountains   William Fettkether

Trail country

"You get the best of what this country
has to offer only if you do it yourself."

Pack Train,
Bishop Pass Trail
Philip Hyde

William Fettkether

Tom Ross

Bullfrog Lake, west of Kearsarge Pass   Tom Ross

The animals silhouetted against the snow in the picture below are bighorn sheep. Extremely wary, and frequenting the most inaccessible areas, bighorn sheep are rarely seen. There are about four hundred in the Sierra in five herds, scattered between Convict Creek and Cottonwood Creek. The largest herds are near Mount Baxter and Mount Williamson. Photo by Fred L. Jones

There is an Assyrian tablet of 2000 B.C. which says:

THE GODS DO NOT SUBTRACT FROM THE ALLOTTED SPAN OF MEN'S LIVES THE HOURS SPENT IN FISHING

Dorothy Petersen photos

Bishop Creek
Stephen Lucacik

"Fishing reduces the ego of . . . even presidents . . . for all men are equal before fishes. It brings meekness and inspiration from the glory and wonder of nature, and charity towards tacklemakers. It brings mockery of profits, the quieting of hate, and the lift of the spirit. And it brings rejoicing that you do not have to decide a darned thing until next week."—Herbert Hoover

The Assyrian tablet quotation is reprinted from *Ford Times.*

THE KERN PLATEAU

South of Mount Whitney the elevation and spectacular quality of the Sierra Nevada dwindle abruptly. The meandering South Fork of the Kern River drains this region, half a million acres known among past generations of cattlemen as the "meadows country." This unglaciated part of the Sierra differs markedly from the rugged High Sierra to the north. It is the Gentle Wilderness—low, forested ridges (the higher peaks under 10,000 feet), many small streams, few lakes, and dozens of mile-long meadows (a few up to five miles long). Though the Plateau has other fish also, it is known particularly for its golden trout. The South Fork is planted with catchables, but the back country has only native fish. Since elevations are lower, the season is longer, the days warmer. When the high passes to the north are still snowbound in June, the Plateau is usually open and just right for the early family vacation. Many of the old trails have not been maintained, some are poorly signed, and some have been partly obliterated by the trampling of cattle. Landmarks are harder to distinguish than in the higher mountains. Careful use of a map is essential to keep yourself located. From Highway 395 on the east, you can reach the Kern Plateau by air (landing strips at Monache and Tunnel Meadows), by the Ninemile Canyon Road, and by trail over Haiwee, Olancha, and Cottonwood passes. Few people travel Haiwee and Olancha passes other than cattlemen and hunters. Both trails can be unpleasantly hot when the summer sun is high, for they start low and are shadeless.

Topographic maps: Kern Peak, Monache Mountain, Hockett Peak, Olancha, Mount Whitney, Triple Divide Peak quadrangles.

Haiwee Creek (5000) to Haiwee Pass (8200)

Strenuous hike, 4½ miles.

Starting Point: North of Little Lake, take the Haiwee Canyon Road, which leads southwest from Highway 395 to the mouth of Haiwee Creek canyon.

The trail stays in the bottom of the canyon for over a mile, and then continues up its right (N) fork. Leaving the stream, the trail climbs steeply the remaining two thousand feet to the summit, through a desert forest of oak and pinyon pine. From the summit, it is about 1½ miles down to the South Fork of the Kern.

Sage Flat (5750) to Olancha Pass (9200)

Very strenuous hike, 6 miles.

Starting Point: South of Olancha take the Loco Ranch Road, which turns off west from Highway 395 and ends at Sage Flat, where short spur roads lead to several corrals. The trail begins behind the Forest Service Maintenance Station.

There is no water from Sage Flat to the pass; over the pass, the small stream draining Summit Meadows may also be dry. Over the broad sagebrush-covered saddle that Olancha Pass is, the trail swings right into Summit Meadows, a series of long meadows rimmed with lodgepole pine, then drops down to the South Fork of the Kern River.

COTTONWOOD LAKES BASIN

Though the Cottonwood Lakes are often called the "Home of the Golden Trout," strictly speaking, tributaries of the upper Kern River are the golden's true home. In 1891 goldens were first transplanted to the Cottonwood Lakes. They thrived there, and the lakes became the primary source for golden trout eggs (see Fish Section). Cottonwood Creek Canyon is interesting also for its ninety-year-old sawmill, now a skeleton of huge notched timbers held together by wooden pegs and square nails. This is one of the few eastern Sierra canyons where there are beaver (imported). Many current maps of this basin are incorrect, showing the Army Pass trail circling behind Lake 4. Because snowbanks often blocked that route even in midsummer, the trail was relocated in 1951.

Topographic maps: Olancha and Lone Pine quadrangles.

Cottonwood Creek (5300) to Cottonwood Lakes

Sawmill (9300), very strenuous hike, 5½ miles.

Golden Trout Camp (10,150), very strenuous hike, 8½ miles.

Cottonwood Lakes (11,000), very strenuous hike, 10½ miles.

Starting Point: The end of the Cottonwood Creek road, beyond and to the left of the pack station.

The trail follows the creek, at the bottom of its narrow canyon. Delicate pink blossoms of wild rose brighten the tangle of willow, cottonwood, oak, and pinyon pine. Peach-colored granite walls rise three and four thousand feet on either side. Along the way perhaps you can find ruins of the old flume, boards now splintered and weathered gray, which carried timbers from the Stevens' sawmill down the canyon. According to the *Inyo Independent*, September 1873, "As the work progresses the material is sent down the flume from the sawmill. . . . Sections 12 feet long are put in at the mill and often ridden down by the men." Much of the trail is sandy with granite grit, a coarse sand formed as granite weathers and disintegrates. About four miles up the trail there is a steel bridge for crossing during high water. In early summer Cottonwood Creek can be belly-deep on a horse. The trail climbs steadily, finally topping out at the sawmill.

You could spend hours poking about the remains of the mill. There is also an old wagon, its solid wooden wheels still encased in their metal bands. Take pictures while you can, for every year winter snows damage these relics more. Thousands of stumps, for several miles upstream, will help you appreciate Cerro Gordo's tremendous appetite for wood and charcoal. (See Cottonwood Charcoal Kilns, Roadside Section.)

The trail follows the creek through willow thickets, lodgepole pine, and small meadows with white and lavender daisies, white Queen Anne's lace, scarlet paintbrush, dainty yellow cinquefoil, and in late summer, small blue gentian. Watch along the stream for beaver ponds, dammed with lodgepole and willow. Perhaps you can find some pointed stumps with fresh toothmarks. The Department of Fish and Game introduced beaver into selected areas of the Sierra in the 1940s. Their purpose was threefold: to provide a fur resource, to improve fish habitat, and most important, to stabilize the water flow. While often fulfilling all three purposes, in some areas beaver have gone further, attempting to restore wilderness by flooding roads and trails. On Cottonwood Creek the beaver have thrived, have improved the stream fishing, and have interfered with no one. Since beaver are wary creatures, you are not likely to see any unless you hide and watch for them at dusk or dawn. Should you camp near the ponds, during the night you may hear water splashing and trees falling.

Golden Trout Camp is a private commercial resort reached only by trail. Above and below the camp there are several gates across the trail. Always close any gate that you open. From the camp, the massive gray mountain you see to the northwest is Mount Langley (14,042), the southernmost of the Whitney group of 14,000-foot peaks. This is the mountain that Clarence King climbed in 1871 and mistook for Mount Whitney, causing much confusion over who climbed what first. Mount Langley's gently sloping back is quite unlike its abrupt eastern face. Somewhere in this guide you may find some clues to explain the marked contrast between its east and west slopes. To reach the Cottonwood Lakes, continue on the trail above Golden Trout Camp. Where it forks, take the right (N) fork which leads over a low ridge. The first two lakes lie in a grassy meadow; the third is a short distance above them. As you enter the meadow, you will find a short trail turning off right to Muir Lake. To reach Lakes 4 and 5, timberline lakes walled in by almost vertical granite cliffs, follow the trail at the inlet of Lake 3.

Cottonwood Creek (5300) to South Fork Lakes and Army Pass

South Fork Lakes (10,900), very strenuous hike, 11½ miles.

Army Pass (12,300), very strenuous hike, 14½ miles.

Proceed as described above to Golden Trout Camp, and continue on the trail about one mile to a trail fork. Take the left fork. As you top a boulder slope, the first of the Cottonwood Lakes lies on your right. The trail bears left, along the south shores of Lakes 1 and 2, then skirts the upper end of "the rockpile," an extensive mass of huge granite boulders. Beyond is the basin of the South Fork of Cottonwood Creek, dominated by rusty-colored Cirque Peak (12,900). Two lower lakes lie below, off the trail. Above High

Lake, long switchbacks climb to Army Pass. For the best view, walk out on
the slope left of the pass. The dark jagged mountains west of the great canyon
of the Kern River are the Kaweah Peaks. North is broad-backed Mount
Langley. From the pass the trail follows Rock Creek down to a junction with
the Siberian Pass trail.

Cottonwood Creek (5300) to Mulkey Pass, Cottonwood Pass

Horseshoe Meadow (9900), very strenuous hike, 8 miles.
Mulkey Pass (10,500), very strenuous hike, 10 miles.
Cottonwood Pass (11,200), very strenuous hike, 11½ miles.
Proceed as described above to the sawmill, and continue on the main trail
for about a mile. Take the trail which turns off left (S), crosses the creek,
climbs a low ridge, and then forks again.

To reach Mulkey Pass (named for Cyrus Mulkey, Sheriff 1871–1874),
take the left (S) fork which crosses the lower end of Horseshoe Meadow.
You might become confused here, for signs indicate two different directions
for Mulkey Pass. This is no problem, for there are two Mulkey Passes. (Both
lead to Mulkey Meadows.) "Old" Mulkey Pass, farther east, is used for
driving cattle to summer pasture. The better trail goes over "new" Mulkey
Pass. (The Olancha quadrangle spoils the confusion by calling the new pass
Trail Pass.) The trail may be lost in the sand or obliterated by cattle tracks.
Follow the edge of the meadow, past the turnoff to Mulkey Stock Drive.
Blazes on some large lodgepoles indicate where the trail starts up to the pass.

To reach Cottonwood Pass take the right (W) fork, which skirts the north
edge of two-mile long Horseshoe Meadow. The log cabin at its upper end
was built over seventy-five years ago for a cow camp. The trail zigzags up
a thousand-foot rocky slope, forested with foxtail pine, to Cottonwood Pass;
beyond, it drops to Whitney Meadows and the headwaters of Golden Trout
Creek.

Carroll Creek Road (7300) to Cottonwood Lakes

Golden Trout Camp (10,150), very strenuous hike, 8½ miles.
Cottonwood Lakes (11,000), very strenuous hike, 10½ miles.
Starting Point: The end of the Carroll Creek Road.
Trails lead to Cottonwood Lakes from two roadends, from the Cotton-
wood Creek Road described above and from the Carroll Creek Road. Though
the distance is the same either way, the Carroll Creek trail starts much
higher (it also climbs higher, to 10,700) and the trails are quite different.
In contrast to the former trail which follows the shaded creek, the Carroll
Creek trail works its way high onto the sunny brush slope of Wonoga Peak.
Backpackers might try a loop trip, going up Cottonwood Creek and returning to the Carroll Creek Road.

The trail starts a few hundred yards below the end of the road, and switchbacks up a long sagebrush slope. At its highest point, just before the drop down to Little Cottonwood Creek, there is a sweeping view into the deep gorges of the creeks. At Little Cottonwood Creek a trail branching left connects with the Cottonwood Creek trail at the sawmill. The trail follows Little Cottonwood Creek for about two miles. Leaving the stream, it climbs through a parklike stand of foxtail pine, the forest floor carpeted with clean white granite pebbles and sand. From the top of a ridge, the trail drops down 500 feet to Golden Trout Camp, joining the trail already described to Cottonwood Lakes.

MOUNT WHITNEY

Mount Whitney is an immense good-natured mountain; its summit is not reserved for the daring. Though not easily come by, all who will plod and persevere on their own good two feet (possibly with the aid of a mountain horse's four) may reach it. There are no tricky stream crossings, the trail is wide, and gradual enough, someone said, "to push a baby buggy up it." The climb is really just a long walk—but a *very* long walk at high altitude, with a 6,000-foot elevation gain.

Any physically fit person who prepares himself should be able to reach the summit. Reread Altitude Sickness in the introduction to this section. Make several breaking-in trips first or climb it at the end of a high-mountain vacation. Or ride a horse. The more time you take, the easier and more enjoyable your trip will be. Only experienced hikers in top physical condition are likely to make it in a day. (The 1961 winner of the annual Mount Whitney Marathon covered the 21-mile roundtrip in 3 hours 55 minutes, so there is no further point in trying to make a record.) Plan a two-day trip; three is better. Backpack to either Outpost Camp or Mirror Lake. Though the lake is more popular, Outpost Camp has more wood and sheltered campsites. Start early or late enough to avoid the midday heat. The second day, start at dawn for the top. Take a canteen, very warm clothing, and a wind jacket, for icy winds often whip over the crest. The summit is within Sequoia National Park; firearms and dogs are not permitted. For a detailed map of the Mount Whitney trail, write the District Ranger, Lone Pine.

Topographic maps: Lone Pine and Mount Whitney quadrangles.

Lone Pine Creek (8367) to Mount Whitney

Lone Pine Lake (9900), 2½ miles, moderate hike.

Outpost Camp (10,365), 3½ miles, strenuous hike.

Mount Whitney (14,496), 10½ miles, very strenuous hike.

Starting Point: End of the Whitney Portal Road.

The trail starts with a long switchback up a brush slope of silver-gray sage, chinquapin with its spiny brown burrs, and black-barked mountain mahogany. In the shaded moist places you can find many mountain flowers —wild rose, blue lupine, pinkish Indian paintbrush. Among those several feet tall will be deep blue monkshood, woolly parsnip, and big-leaved corn lily. Most of the trees are lodgepole pine; as you climb higher you will find a few limber and many foxtail pine. (Limber pine has cones the scales of which look like the ears of a cony, which should make identification easy.) To reach Lone Pine Lake and its sandy beach, take the short trail that turns off left. The trail climbs relentlessly, leveling off only at the meadow below Outpost Camp (Bighorn Park on the topo map). After passing Mirror Lake, which lies below impressive granite cliffs, it continues to follow the creek, crossing and recrossing it several times. Behind boulders you may see some low rock walls; campers have built them for shelter from the cold winds.

Trail Camp (12,000, no wood) is the last dependable place for water. Then begins the long grind to Trail Crest, 1500 feet above. It would spoil the fun to tell how many switchbacks there are; what's *your* count? In the boulder slope to the north, perhaps you can make out traces of a steeper trail, abandoned when the present trail was relocated in 1948. Lichens of many colors—chartreuse, gray-green, yellow ochre, black, rust—brighten the gray granite. You may be surprised at the number of plants growing among the rocks in this high land of bitter weather. Most are small with very short stems—tiny white or yellow cresses, red buckwheat, pale lavender daisies and cushion phlox. But two are nearly a foot tall, the robust yellow alpine gold and the refreshing blue sky pilot (polemonium). These amazingly sturdy flowers seldom grow below 12,000 feet. You will find them on many of the highest passes and peaks. At the end of the last switchback, suddenly you top the crest. In all directions, Sierra ridges and canyons sweep away, as far as you can see. The trail drops over the sharp crest, and heads north for the summit. Scientific parties in 1910 and 1913 used the stone shelter while studying the solar system. Since then it has not been maintained.

Pray for a clear day; so vast a view you will never forget. East of the Inyo-White Mountains, you can see range after desert range. The twin peaks just north are Mount Russell. Over its shoulder you can see part of Tulainyo Lake (12,802), the highest Sierra lake. The distant ridge circling west and south is the Kings-Kern Divide, which divides the drainage basins of these two large rivers. Farther in the distance, perhaps you can make out Mount Goddard and the Palisades, at the head of the Middle Fork of the Kings. To the west, beyond Mount Hitchcock in the foreground, Kern Canyon lies 6500 feet below. The dark jagged mountains across the canyon and a little south are the Kaweah Peaks, on the Great Western Divide.

Mount Whitney's "peak" is a surprise to many, for it is large and flat enough to accommodate a football field. Though perhaps less glamorous than the pyramid-shaped peaks nearby, its summit expanse of frost-split rocks is a far older and more significant feature. The renowned geologist, François Matthes, was moved to write, ". . . the more fully I comprehend its story . . . the more venerable, the more precious seems that bit of flat land on its lofty summit. Upon it I have never set foot without a certain sense of reverence." It is a remnant of the ancient landscape that existed several million years ago. Could you have been here then, instead of mountains and canyons you would have seen only a vast plain stretching to the horizons. As the Sierra block was uplifted and tilted, streams cut a network of canyons into the old plain, transforming it into the steep ridges and narrow valleys that is the Sierra landscape of today. A few small remnants of that ancient plain have survived the attacks of water and ice. Mount Whitney's broad back is one. During the Ice Age, on the shaded sides of the mountain, glaciers gouged out amphitheater-shaped basins and chewed away at their headwalls, forming the sheer cliffs of the north and east faces. There are a few other Sierra peaks, with distinctive flat tops and abrupt east faces, which also have retained remnants of the ancient plain. Lie back against one of the contour-shaped summit rocks and look for other fragments of the ancestral landscape. Really lie back and narrow your eyes as you look. If you are quiet, you may hear the old voice of the earth.

Lone Pine Creek (8000) to Little Meysan Lake (10,100)

Strenuous hike, about 2 miles.
Starting Point: Near the end of the road leading to the summer homes tract, about 1 mile below Whitney Portal.

The trail follows the north side of the stream to Little Meysan Lake, named for a pioneer French family. It may be difficult to follow in places, owing to rerouting some years back, but any route up the canyon will do. Colonies of blue-balls grow on the sandy slopes. There are good campsites near the lake. It is a climb of about 1300 feet more to the large Upper Lake, which lies in a barren cirque under Mount Irvine and Mount Mallory.

SHEPHERD, BAXTER, SAWMILL, TABOOSE PASSES

West and north of Lone Pine, the Sierra crest reaches its greatest height. Dozens of peaks are over 13,000 feet, so many that most are not even named. Over this most rugged portion of the crest, there is only one easy pass, Kearsarge Pass. All the others are eight to twelve miles from roadends, and involve climbs of more than 6,000 feet. The passes themselves, 11,000 to 12,000 feet, are as high as many Sierra peaks. The trails to these four passes start low in the shadeless foothills, below 5700 feet. These trails demand much, and they give much—vast scenic canyons, soaring mountains, solitude, quiet. If you find the Sierra too crowded, head off over these passes. Choose a campsite even a short way off the main trail and chances are you will see no one.

Topographic maps: Mount Whitney and Mount Pinchot quadrangles.

Symmes Creek (5700) to Shepherd Pass

Anvil Camp (10,000), very strenuous hike, about 7½ miles.

Shepherd Pass (12,000), very strenuous hike, about 9½ miles.

Starting Point: ½ mile south of Independence, take the dirt road heading southwest. Park just beyond the corrals. The trail starts on the right (N) side of Symmes Creek.

The trail to Shepherd Pass begins in a foothill brushland of grays and greens—gray granite boulders, pale gray-green sage, darker gray-green pinyon pine, yellow-green leafless ephedra (Mormon or squaw tea), deep green bitterbrush, gray-tan soil. It follows Symmes Creek into its narrow canyon, then zigzags up the south slope through pinyon and red-barked manzanita. On the saddle, the high shrubs with small dark green leaves are especially large mountain mahogany, a favorite deer browse. The great peak you see directly south is Mount Williamson, second highest Sierra peak. Splotches of reddish and greenish rock liven the gray granite of Shepherd Creek canyon. From the saddle, the trail drops into the canyon, and follows Shepherd Creek most of the way to the pass. Mahogany Flat (locally called Manzanita Flat) is the first good campsite. Anvil Camp, a mile farther, is another. Parkinson Meadows, about a quarter-mile up the old Junction Pass trail, is the choicest of all. (See topo map for these locations.)

Beyond the timberline meadows, the trail crosses a great jumble of huge boulders. You will wonder where the trail could possibly be; every cliff looks impassable. It switchbacks steeply up the last 500 feet, finally reaching the broad western slope of Shepherd Pass. Flat-topped Diamond Mesa looms to the right. The striking monument-shaped mountain to the west, across

Kern Canyon, is Milestone Peak. Just left of the pass is pyramid-shaped Mount Tyndall, the northernmost of the Whitney group of 14,000 foot peaks. From the pass you can join the Muir Trail several miles downstream, or go into the headwaters of the Kern, a little-traveled, wild portion of Sequoia National Park.

North Fork Oak Creek (5500) to Baxter Pass (12,300)

Very strenuous hike, about 8½ miles.
Starting Point: End of road, North Fork Oak Creek.

The canyon of Oak Creek is stunning, from the roadend with its large oak trees, through its flowered slopes, to the colorful rocks and sheer cliffs at its end. Unlike the trails to the other three passes, the Baxter Pass trail does not have a long shadeless stretch at its beginning. Among the brush, flowers grow abundantly—buckwheat with its rounded heads of pink, white, yellow and bronze, mountain mint, lupine, and scarlet Indian paintbrush. From a vent on the north side of the canyon at about 8400 feet, lava burst out and flowed down the canyon. You can see small remnants of this dark fine-grained rock between the beginning of the trail and the vent area. About five miles up the trail, before it starts to climb steeply, there are some good campsites.

The upper part of the canyon cuts through a two-mile wide mass of pregranitic, metamorphosed rocks, rust-colored and greenish tinged, streaked with black. The bright red mineral forming small seams and pockets is piedmontite, a manganese-bearing silicate. Red heather, lavender shooting stars and penstemon, and white Laborador tea brighten the trail. Near an upper meadow there are some dwarf lodgepole pine about two feet high, creeping along the ground. There are also some unusually small whitebark pine, not much higher than your head. The last mile is steep and rocky. From the pass the trail swings down to Baxter Lakes and the South Fork of Woods Creek.

Sawmill Creek or Division Creek (both 4650) to Sawmill Pass

Sawmill Meadow (8400), strenuous hike, about 6 miles.
Sawmill Lake (10,000), very strenuous hike, about 8½ miles.
Sawmill Pass (11,347), very strenuous hike, about 10 miles.
Starting Points: 9 miles north of Independence, after passing the Sawmill Creek Campground, take the first dirt road west. From the end of the road at the mouth of Sawmill Canyon, the trail climbs steeply up the cinder cone. Or drive 10 miles north of Independence and take the paved road to the Division Creek Powerhouse. Half a mile beyond it a sign marks the trail. It heads south toward the red cinder cone, circles behind it, and joins the trail from Sawmill Creek.

The trail from Sawmill Creek is shorter, though steeper. The more gradual trail from Division Creek gives you a closeup look at the cinder cone.

At its northern base is a smaller crater. The mileages above are from Division Creek; subtract a mile if you start from Sawmill Creek.

For three miles, the trail zigzags up a steep shadeless slope, dry brown in midsummer, but in early summer alive with flowering shrubs and blossoms of bright blue woolly gilia and yellow and white buckwheat. You may hear the warning notes of quail, and dove cooing. There are good views of the Big Pine Volcanic Field, with cinder cones and lava flows that erupted from both Inyo and Sierra slopes. Rounding Sawmill Point, the trail drops into Sawmill Creek's steep-sided canyon. Watch ahead, on the hogback rising in the center of the canyon, for the well preserved flume of the Blackrock sawmill, built in the late 1860s. Perhaps you can discover other traces of the mill along the creek. As far as Sawmill Meadow you can find scattered stumps, felled trees, and logs used as gliders.

On the trail at about 7600 feet, you can find volcanic "bombs" a foot or two long, formed when molten lava was hurled into the air and solidified in falling. From a vent nearby black lava flowed down the canyon to its mouth, filling it about 150 feet deep. The stream has since eroded away most of the flow, leaving only remnants here and there. Perhaps you can locate some along the trail. If you look into the canyon from the corral near the canyon mouth, you can easily see some of them.

Sawmill Meadow has good campsites. If its stream is dry, there is usually water at a small spring which crosses the trail just above it. Above the meadow, the trail climbs steeply among large Jeffrey pines, their long needles glinting in the sun, and red fir. Below Sawmill Lake, the tumbled rocks at the north end of Mule Lake are one of the best places to see conies (rock rabbits or pikas), gray animals about the size and shape of guinea pigs. Listen for their sharp nasal call. Sawmill Lake, sheltered by foxtail pine, is the last good camping place below the pass. From Sawmill Pass, the boundary of Kings Canyon National Park, the trail winds down into the basin of Woods Creek and joins the Muir Trail.

Taboose Creek (5500) to Taboose Pass (11,400)

Very strenuous hike, about 7 miles.
Starting Point: North of Aberdeen, just after crossing Taboose Creek, turn left onto a graded dirt road. Stay on what looks like the most traveled road; turnoffs to the left deadend at the creek. Go through the cattle gate, closing it behind you, and drive to the end of the road, past the corrals.

The Taboose Pass trail, formerly one of the roughest routes in the Sierra, was rebuilt in 1962 and is now a good stock trail. In early summer the brush slopes are spangled with bronze and yellow sulfur flowers, white morning glory, lively blue woolly gilia, and yellow-centered thistle poppy. Taboose Creek is one of the wildest of mountain streams. It rises in the wide snowbanks and melt ponds of a high rock basin, then dashes over granite cliffs and tumbles down 4500 feet in four miles. Though the trail follows Taboose Creek all the way, you seldom see it for the jungle of copper birch, willow, and wild rose that hides it. Other than the streamside trees and a few scattered pine, this is a canyon with no forest at all. Gray and rusty-colored granite spires rise sheer on both sides of the narrow canyon.

The trail heads straight up the canyon to the base of the red-orange cliffs you see from the bottom. It then turns right and zigzags along a high waterfall. The only good campsite this side of the pass is at the third stream crossing. Above, the trail becomes extremely rough and rocky. At the fourth crossing, there is a gem of an alpine garden, perhaps more precious because the canyon is so austere. Short-stemmed alpine flowers of many varieties are scattered throughout a carpet of inch-high alpine willow. From the pass, you look down into the great canyon of the Kings River's South Fork. The large lake to the southwest is Bench Lake; the black and red peak directly north, Cardinal Mountain.

ONION VALLEY, KEARSARGE PASS

Kearsarge Pass is the shortest, lowest, easiest pass over the Sierra Crest from Owens Valley, and therefore one of the most traveled. The canyons above Onion Valley abound with foxtail, a timberline pine with distinctive cinnamon-colored bark that is restricted to the southern end of the range. It could also be called the "bottlebrush pine," for its stiff short needles are clustered at the tips of the twigs. Photographers particularly will delight in the older trees, their stubby limbs twisted by wind and storm, their bark grooved and cracked. Some of the dead trees are more striking than the living. Stripped of bark, the wood grain raised high by years of natural sandblasting, their trunks are radiant in the early and late sun. Though the canyon's rocks range from white to very dark gray, they are all granites, of different age and chemical composition.

Topographic map: Mount Pinchot.

Onion Valley (9200) to Kearsarge Pass

Gilbert Lake (10,400), moderate hike, 2½ miles.
Kearsarge Pass (11,823), strenuous hike, 4½ miles.
Starting Point: End of the Onion Valley Road. Just before the road crosses the creek to the campground, a large sign marks the Kearsarge Pass trail.

The trail ascends gradually with many long switchbacks. After climbing a dry hillside it enters the forest, predominantly lodgepole and foxtail pine, with scattered red fir at the lower elevations, wind-stunted whitebark pine at the higher. The first lake along the trail is Gilbert Lake, named for an Independence pioneer who tried to obtain its water rights for an irrigation project. Shallow Flower Lake, with many good campsites, lies just above it. A fisherman's trail turns off left to Matlack Lake, named for the man who first planted fish in it. (See topo map for other lakes nearby which can be reached easily through the open forest.) On the slope going down to Matlack Lake, there is a stand of unusually large old foxtail pine, their bark richly colored and deeply furrowed. Near timberline there is a good chance to compare the foxtail with the more common timberline pine, the whitebark. Not only are their barks different colors; the squat purple cones of the whitebark grow close to husky upright branches, while foxtail cones droop down.

From Kearsarge Pass you look down on Kearsarge Lakes, lying below the Kearsarge Pinnacles. On the skyline to the southwest is the Great Western Divide. Over the pass the trail drops down to Bullfrog Lake, considered by many among the most beautiful Sierra Lakes, and joins the Muir Trail.

Onion Valley (9200) to Robinson Lake (10,450)

Moderate hike, about 2 miles.
Starting Point: East end of the Onion Valley Campground. Though you may have to hunt for it, eventually you will find a trail that crosses the stream coming down the steep slope from Robinson Lake.

Though the trail is fairly well defined, if it seems to disappear in the rocks, look for ducks. It stays left of the stream; toward the top it follows the lower edge of a boulder slope. Robinson Lake lies in a small basin below granite crags. In late summer, you are likely to find noisy gray nutcrackers whacking open whitebark cones with their strong black beaks. The lake may be named for the pioneer family which packed snow out on muleback, to sell to Independence townspeople. There is a good view north of Kearsarge Peak. Looking through binoculars, you can see workings of the Kearsarge Mine and remains of cabins on its slope about 11,500 feet.

Onion Valley (9200) to Golden Trout Lakes (11,300)

Strenuous hike, about 3 miles.
Starting Point: Behind the upper pack station, follow the dirt road to its end. Then walk straight ahead into the brush, keeping left of the willows. Just keep looking; the trail is there, though overgrown with brush.

The trail to Golden Trout Lakes has not been maintained and is partly washed out. But if you would try your skill at following a faint trail and exploring a side canyon, here is your chance. The trail zigzags up, to the right of the waterfall. Among the shrubs toward the top of the bench, in fall California fuchsia make a splash of scarlet color. In a small meadow, streams from two higher basins intersect. In summer the meadow is dotted with flowers, including both sierra blue and alpine gentian; in fall it is tawny gold. On its west slope there was a fine stand of whitebark pine until a careless camper let a fire get away. To reach the higher basins, follow the streams.

Faint trails and ducks are there but take some looking for. Golden Trout
Lakes lie up the right fork.

Pinyon Creek Canyon

Starting Point: From the Onion Valley Road, just below Grays Meadow
turn off to the southwest on a dirt road which leads to the mouth of Pinyon
Creek Canyon.

This is one of the many Sierra canyons without signed roads or well-
defined trails. Most we do not mention, but leave them for you to discover
and explore for yourself. A fisherman's trail follows the stream about a mile
to the base of a waterfall. To reach the choicest spot, however, from the end
of the road climb the sandy slope to the north, and continue up the slope of
Pinyon Mesa. Eventually you may pick up a trail which crosses a ravine or
two as it enters an area of scattered pinyon trees. There is a rocky outcrop
in the center of the canyon over which the stream falls. Go around the outcrop's north side, drop down to the stream, and follow it to the top of the
fall, where an exquisite mountain flower garden thrives in the spray. You
may see an eagle watching from the tall trees.

BIG PINE LAKES, THE PALISADES

Though fishermen, hikers, and artists prize them for their lakes and dramatic
mountain scenery, the Palisades are the special paradise of the rock-climbing
mountaineer. Many consider the Palisades the finest collection of alpine
peaks in the Sierra. Though Mount Whitney is higher, the Palisades "look as
mountains should"—bold, jagged, knife-edged, a rock climber's joy and
challenge. All are difficult climbs; there are no easy routes. The best known
feature is Palisade Glacier; horses can take you within one-half mile of it.
Hiking to the glacier and back in a day is very strenuous. Make it a two- or
three-day trip, camping somewhere between First and Fifth lakes. Mileages
are from the end of the road. If you start at the pack station, add about two
miles.

Topographic maps: Big Pine and Mount Goddard quadrangles.

Big Pine Creek (8400) to Big Pine Lakes and Palisade Glacier

First Lake (9950), moderate hike, 3 miles.
Fourth Lake (10,700), strenuous hike, 5 miles.
Summit Lake (10,900), strenuous hike, about 6 miles.
Palisade Glacier (12,200), very strenuous hike, about 7½ miles.
Starting Point: End of Big Pine Creek Road.

The trail zigzags to the top of Second Falls, then follows Big Pine Creek
up the canyon to its headwaters. In early summer this is a canyon of
lavender shooting stars. Later many other wildflowers—such as tiger lily,
red-orange paintbrush, exotic white rein orchis, and red columbine—are

abundant along the streams and in the many small meadows. There are dozens of good campsites on the creek and on all but the two highest lakes. Cienega Mirth is the level area along the creek above Second Falls; the origin of its name is obscure. "Cienega" is Spanish and "Mirth" is Scotch for a swampy place. According to an old-timer, a party camped there had such a good time they named it Camp Mirth. The large stone house left of the trail was built by movie actor Lon Chaney about 1925.

Near First Lake the trail forks, the main trail going left. If you plan to visit the upper lakes, you can make an interesting loop trip by taking the right fork which goes to Black Lake, described below, and returning on the main trail. In the lodgepole pine forest, listen for the clear flutelike song of the hermit thrush, two phrases repeated over and over. Big Pine farmers dammed Second Lake about 1895 for irrigation purposes. The City of Los Angeles enlarged the dam in 1923, and now uses the stored water to operate its power plant downstream. The imposing dark mountain, tinged greenish with lichen, behind the two lakes is Temple Crag (12,999). To its left is white, rounded Mount Alice (11,630). Both are granites, but of different ages and mineral composition. Between them you can see a striking geologic contact, the place where two different rocks meet.

Notice the milky quality of the water. The glaciers above, grinding over the rock, produce a silt so fine it is known as glacier flour. Water from the melting glacier carries it downstream; too fine to settle out, it colors all the waters below. First, Second, and Third Lakes all have the distinctive milky turquoise (sometimes greenish) color of glacial lakes. Third Lake is fed directly by Palisade Glacier. At its inlet you can see a dramatic change from morning to evening. Toward evening—when the stream, high from the hot sun's melting the glacier ice all day, carries much flour—you can see a milky streak at the inlet. In the morning, when the stream is low, it carries little flour, making a clear streak into the milky lake. In contrast, Fourth Lake is clear, for it is not fed by a glacial stream.

Fifth Lake, one of the most beautiful of the Big Pine Lakes, is ½ mile beyond Fourth Lake. About 100 yards below Fourth Lake, a trail forks left and follows the creek to the outlet of Fifth Lake. Sixth and Seventh Lakes (11,100) are about a mile beyond. To reach Summit Lake, above Fourth Lake, follow an unsigned trail leading ½ mile east. This trail deserves more use, for from it there are magnificent views of Palisade Glacier and its peaks.

To reach Palisade Glacier, just below Fourth Lake turn left onto a less well defined trail; if willows and grass hide it, look for ducks. The trail zigzags up among sparkling granite boulders to Sam Mack Meadow, where it forks. The trail straight ahead leads to Sam Mack Lake. The trail to the glacier crosses the stream and climbs to the top of a ridge. Whitebark pine is the only tree able to survive the inhospitable climate, but there are several alpine flowers, marvelously adapted to this windswept, seemingly soil-less high country. The delicate long-stemmed alpine columbine—white, or pastel yellow, pink, or blue—looks more like a hothouse flower than one that must withstand icy winds and eight-month winters. White heather, with its small bell-shaped blossoms, grows in dense mats a few inches high. The sturdy blue sky-pilot is restricted to the highest ridges.

The last half-mile to the glacier requires much boulder hopping. If you have pictured glaciers as being glaringly blue or white, you may wonder at its dirty gray color. The later the season, the grayer it is from dust and falling rocks. The blue ice beneath reveals itself only where the glacier cracks open. It is safe to wander about the lower part of the glacier where the slope is gentle. But to see the cracks (crevasses), you must go to its steep upper part—with a guide experienced on ice if you are not. Glaciers can be dangerous, even this one. Unstable snow bridges often hide deep crevasses. At the lower end of the glacier, see if you can recognize a series of arc-shaped ridges. These are moraines, rubble deposited by the glacier at its margin when it was much larger.

Big Pine Creek (8400) to Black Lake (10,640)

Strenuous hike, about 3½ miles.
This high, view trail enables you to look down on Big Pine Creek and the lower lakes, as well as across the canyon to the crags of the Palisades. Take the main trail as described above for about 2½ miles, then take the fork branching off to the right (N) and climbing steeply up a brush slope. As the trail levels off and cuts west across the slope, there are splendid views up and down the canyon. Black Lake is clear and quiet. About ½ mile beyond it, take the trail going around the left (S) side of a swampy puddle; shortly it joins the main trail near Fourth Lake.

Big Pine Creek (8400) to Ridge above Grouse Spring (10,270)

Strenuous hike, about 3 miles.
Starting Point: End of Big Pine Creek Road.
Of all trails in the area, this one provides the most spectacular view of Palisade Crest. You are far enough away to see the canyons of both forks of Big Pine Creek and all the high peaks rising above their glaciers. The panorama is most impressive in early summer, before the snow has melted. At the second long switchback on the Big Pine Lakes trail, two trails head east across the brush slope; take the upper one. Over the ridge, the trail winds through a stand of widely spaced Jeffrey pine. Logging in this flat began in the 1880s. Two-yoke teams of oxen skidded the logs down to a wagon road in the bottom of the canyon. You may notice that all the stumps are small. The largest trees were left uncut, for they were too difficult to handle. The trail passes Grouse Spring and climbs to the highest point on a gentle ridge

Opposite you (S) across the canyon is Middle Palisade Glacier, with Middle Palisade and Disappointment Peak towering above. To the right (N), the largest white mass is Palisade Glacier. (To identify peaks, see the sketch in Roadsides Section.) To the north are the high rolling meadows of Baker Creek and Coyote Flat, a remnant of the ancient plain that existed before warping and faulting formed the mountains (see Geology Section). Several generations of Owens Valley ranchers have brought their cattle here for summer pasture. The trail on to Baker Creek is seldom used now, for the creek and Coyote Flat can be reached by jeep road from Bishop.

Big Pine Creek (8400) to Brainard Lake (10,240)

Strenuous hike, 4½ miles.

Starting Point: Near the end of the Big Pine Creek Road, where it makes a hairpin turn up the hill, the trail takes off to the left (S).

This little-used trail follows the South Fork of Big Pine Creek to the small lake basin lying below Middle Palisade Glacier. The trail starts on the west side of the creek, then crosses it and proceeds through the brush on its east side, heading for the bottom of a large cliff. Near its base, the trail forks. Follow the left (E) fork, watching for ducks if brush has overgrown the trail, and zigzag up the cliff. The twisted trees clinging to the steep slope are limber pine. All at once, as you top the cliff, you see the southern portion of Palisade Crest, half a dozen small glaciers scattered along its base. After dropping down a bit, the trail forks; a fisherman's trail leads to Willow Lake. The main trail goes left, down to a meadow. If it seems lost, look for ducks to follow. A short pull brings you to Brainard Lake, lying in a steep-sided rock basin.

BISHOP CREEK

Bishop Creek's canyons have abundant water, trees, and wildflowers. There are dozens of streams, some meandering quietly near small meadows, others cascading over waterfalls and spraying mossy grottoes. Fed by small glaciers, most of them are lively even in late summer. There are more than a hundred lakes this side of the crest; just over the mountains there are many more. On almost all the lakes below 11,000 feet, sheltered campsites are plentiful. Bishop and Piute passes are relatively easy entrances to the wilderness back country, and connect with the John Muir Trail. They require only a 2000-foot gain in elevation, far less than any of the passes south except Kearsarge. Yet despite its popularity, in this big open country you can find all the isolation you desire if you will seek out the countless unnamed, seldom visited small streams and lakes.

Topographic map: Mount Goddard quadrangle.

South Lake (9750) to Bishop Pass

Long Lake (10,700), moderate hike, 2½ miles.

Bishop Pass (11,972), strenuous hike, 5½ miles.

Starting Point: End of the road, ¼ mile beyond South Lake dam.

This is one of the busiest trails in the eastern Sierra. The roadend is the highest out of Owens Valley, the trail gradual, the canyon colorful. The trail follows the chain of lakes along the South Fork of Bishop Creek. A dozen more lakes lie within ½ mile of the main trail. Signed trails lead to some of them; others can be reached easily cross-country with the help of a topo map. Marie Louise Lake is named after Mrs. W. C. Parcher, who with her husband established Parcher's Camp in 1922. The Parchers also named Treasure Lakes, inasmuch as their son had backpacked golden trout and had planted them there. At the upper end of South Lake, left of the trail where it makes its first sharp bend, some large timbers and rusted metal mark the site of a sawmill belonging to the power company. It produced lumber for both South Lake and Sabrina dams. The high ridge to the right is Thompson Ridge; to the left is the precipitous face of the Inconsolable Range; the light gray mountain at the head of South Lake is Hurd Peak (12,219), named for an engineer who climbed it in 1906. The far side of Long Lake, its intricate shoreline having many small coves shaded by lodgepole and whitebark pine, is a particularly lovely place for picnics. Wildflowers, changing with the season, grow here and there—lavender shooting stars and mountain mint (crush the leaves and you will *know* it belongs to the mint family), Indian paintbrush, tall magenta fireweed, low-growing red heather. Along the trail perhaps you can find glacial striations, parallel scratches a great glacier scoured into the bedrock.

The higher lakes have clumps of scrubby whitebark pine scattered around them. Saddlerock Lake (11,100) is named for the odd-shaped rock on its far shore. Beyond Bishop Lake, you may see some orange and black signs, which

Snow course markers are guides for men who ski or fly in during winter to measure the snow pack.

are snow course markers. As you zigzag through boulders to the pass, the high mountain just to the left (E) is Mount Agassiz (13,891). Bishop Pass is the boundary of Kings Canyon National Park. Over the pass, the trail drops into Dusy Basin and follows the creek down to the Muir Trail and the Middle Fork of the Kings River.

South Lake (9750) to Chocolate Lakes, Ruwau Lake

Chocolate Lakes (11,000), moderate hike, about 3 miles.

Ruwau Lake (11,000), moderate hike, about 3 miles.

Though these lakes lie less than a mile off the main trail, they seem quite isolated. The red rocks of Chocolate Peak make their setting particularly colorful. Bull Lake (10,750) and the lower Chocolate Lake have unusually scenic campsites. To reach them, proceed on the Bishop Pass trail as described above for about 2 miles. A good trail branches off left to Bull Lake, and follows the stream up to the Chocolate Lakes.

To reach Ruwau Lake, continue on the Bishop Pass trail to Long Lake. About three-quarters of the way to the inlet, look for a trail (there may be no sign) branching off to the left and climbing steeply up the hill. The lake's odd name comes from a combination of the names of two power company engineers, Rhudy and Waugh. Going cross-country from Ruwau Lake, over the ridge to the north, you can loop around to the Chocolate Lakes and meet the main trail below Bull Lake.

South Lake (9750) to Treasure Lakes (10,646–11,200)

Moderate hike, 3 miles.

Treasure Lakes lie at the head of South Lake, in a small basin circled by high ridges. Proceed on the Bishop Pass trail as described above for about ½ mile, the trail to Treasure Lakes branches off right. The first part of the trail is gentle and shaded, crossing small streams lush with wildflowers. Among them will be lavender lupine, daisies, and wild onion (smell them?), blue forget-me-nots, Labrador tea with its white azalea-like blossoms, tall woolly parsnip with their marble-shaped clusters of tiny blossoms. The trail then climbs up a broad open canyon, over slabs of granite bedrock. From the lower lakes a poorer trail (not suitable for stock) follows the cascading creek to the upper lakes, 600 feet higher. Clumps of large yellow mimulus brighten the gray slope. At the top of the cascades, cross the stream and walk over the low hump on the left (E) to the three rockbound upper lakes.

South Lake (9750) to Green Lake

Brown Lake (10,800), moderate hike, 2 miles.

Green Lake (11,100), moderate hike, 2½ miles.

Starting Point: Drive to the end of the road beyond South Lake dam. From the upper end of the parking area, walk up a dirt road a few hundred yards until you see a pipeline.

The horse trail to these lakes branches off from the Bishop Pass trail below South Lake. Hikers can save almost 500 feet of climbing by starting at South Lake and following the pipeline that intersects the stock trail. Add ½ mile to the above mileages if you start at the pack station. Leave the pipeline and follow the trail up a granite slope. Higher, the country opens up into a large meadow, bordered by colorful ridges of red, rust, brown, white, and black rock. Beyond Brown Lake the trail heads left, crossing a swampy meadow and then climbing a boulder slope. To reach Green Lake, when the trail forks, go left.

The right fork climbs to the broad saddle (11,800) of Coyote Ridge. With jeep roads to Coyote Flat, this trail is little used. But a trip to the saddle is interesting for it takes you to a gently sloping, treeless country that is quite different from most of the High Sierra. It is a remnant of the ancient plain described in the Geology Section.

South Fork of Bishop Creek (9,000) to Tyee Lakes

Lake 1 (10,300), moderate hike, 1½ miles.
Lake 4 (10,900), strenuous hike, 3 miles.
Starting Point: About 5 miles beyond Bishop Creek Lodge and Habeggers Ranch, on the west side of the road, a sign and small parking area mark the beginning of the Tyee Lakes trail.

A steep rocky trail zigzags to the six Tyee Lakes, one stepped above the other, each on a small bench all its own. Lakes 3 and 6 lie about ¼ mile off the trail, but can be reached with no difficulty.

Lake Sabrina (9132) to Dingleberry Lake

Blue Lake (10,398), moderate hike, 1½ miles
Dingleberry Lake (10,500), strenuous hike, 3½ miles.
Starting Point: End of the road, east edge of Lake Sabrina dam.

The Middle Fork of Bishop Creek, draining three broad canyons, is the special heaven for cross-country hikers; there is only one maintained trail. The canyon floors slope gently and the forest is open. There are a dozen large lakes and many more small ones. Small meadows are gay with varied alpine flowers. The trail follows the south shore of Lake Sabrina, then switchbacks up through a forest of lodgepole pine into a broad granite basin. The trail follows the north shore of Blue Lake a short way to a fork in the trail. Take the right fork, which climbs to the top of a low rise. From it you can see into the upper basin of the Middle Fork, a high country of space and sky, lakes and peaks.

The maintained trail ends at Dingleberry Lake, a favorite campsite, but you can easily follow the streams and wander to the upper lakes, which lie below the Evolution group of peaks, Mounts Darwin, Mendel, Wallace, Haeckel, and Powell. Many of the lakes have dramatic settings, at the base of sheer cliffs. Some, fed by glaciers, have the peculiar milky turquoise color that distinguishes glacial lakes. Packer Art Schober named many of the lakes in the 1930s: Midnight for a large black horse, Donkey for a burro, Baboon after some CCC boys who were badly sunburned, Hungry Packer for a packer who had to spend a night without blankets or food, Drunken Sailor after a camper, and Topsy Turvy for the huge boulders scattered every which way.

Lake Sabrina (9132) to George Lake (10,750)

Strenuous hike, about 4 miles.

Proceed on the trail around Lake Sabrina as described above. At the upper end of the lake a post (no sign) marks the turn off to George Lake. The trail climbs 800 feet up the slope above the lake. Among the sage and prickly fruited chinquapin there are scattered limber pine, and in early summer dry-hillside flowers such as tall white soda straw, red-orange paintbrush, lavender mountain mint and lupine, and low white cushion phlox. The trail tops out in a small valley. Though it is well blazed much of the way, in the tall grass of the meadow it may be difficult to follow. Watch for bent grass as the trail wanders from one side of the meadow to the other. George Lake lies in a narrow basin between Thompson Ridge and Table Mountain.

For an exceptional view, climb another 800 feet to the table of Table Mountain, east of George Lake. The trail is poorly defined but marked with ducks all the way. The summit is almost barren, a few wind-whipped white-bark pine managing to survive among the weathered granite boulders. The coarse sand formed from the disintegrating rocks. From the summit you can see the canyons of all three forks of Bishop Creek and most of the high peaks. The flat expanse of Table Mountain invites you to wander about, offering additional views northwest to Mount Tom (the large mountain above Round Valley standing well in front of the crest), and east to Coyote Ridge. You can make a loop trip down to Tyee Lakes (see above), by following the ducks as they lead over the summit and down a tiny stream. From Tyee Lakes on, the trail is well defined.

North Fork Bishop Creek (9350) to Piute Pass

Loch Leven (10,700), moderate hike, 2½ miles.
Piute Lake (10,950), moderate hike, 3½ miles.
Piute Pass (11,423), strenuous hike, 5 miles.

Starting Point: End of road, about ½ mile beyond North Lake.

The trail to Piute Pass eases up through a dense forest of lodgepole and white-barked aspen, then follows the North Fork of Bishop Creek. Along the mossy-banked stream wildflowers are abundant—pink spiraea, orange tiger lilies, red columbine, dark blue monkshood, crimson paintbrush. As you climb higher, under the rusty-colored cliffs of Mount Emerson, the forest thins out and you enter the open slopes of the high country. The broad glaciated valley is floored with smooth granite, and decorated with clumps of white-bark pine, snow patches, short grass, and alpine meadows. In the meadows you may see Belding ground squirrels sitting stiffly erect, hence their nickname "picket pins." You may also see fat marmots sunning themselves on their boulder lookouts, or hear their sharp whistle. Over the pass, the trail leads to Humphreys Basin with its many high lakes. A popular several-days' loop trip is to cross Piute Pass, travel the Muir Trail south through Evolution Valley and over Muir Pass, and return via Dusy Creek and Bishop Pass (or vice versa). Since the roadends to the two passes are close, car shuttling can usually be arranged.

North Fork Bishop Creek (9350) to Lamarck Lakes

Grass Lake (9900), easy hike, 1 mile.
Lower Lamarck Lake (10,700), moderate hike, about 4 miles.
Starting Point: Just before you reach the end of the road beyond North Lake, the trail to Lamarck Lakes branches off left (S).

The trail crosses the creek (look upstream from the horse crossing for logs or rocks to cross on), and climbs through a grove of large aspen. Where the trail forks, a short spur goes left to Grass Lake, lying in a swampy meadow. The right fork climbs 800 feet to the lower lake. From the upper portion of the trail, there is a fine view north of the rusty ridge of Mount Emerson. This is rugged rocky country, with sheer cliffs of massive granite and rough boulder slopes. Lower Lamarck Lake lies in a small granite basin. Cross the stream at its outlet and follow the flowered trail on to the upper lake, which lies 200 feet higher.

HORTON LAKES

A mining road leads all the way to Horton Lake. A locked gate closes it to cars, for Horton Lakes lie within the High Sierra Primitive Area. To retain the wild character of small portions of national forest lands, logging, motor vehicles, and commercial development are prohibited. Miners with legitimate claims are allowed to build access roads; hence the road up Horton Creek is closed to all but the mine operators.

Topographic map: Mount Tom quadrangle.

Buttermilk Road (7750) to Horton Lake (10,000)

Strenuous hike, about 4½ miles.
Starting Point: About 5 miles from Bishop, on the Bishop Creek Road, turn right onto the Buttermilk Road and follow it for about 8 miles. Turn off right (W) onto a dirt road that heads for the mouth of Horton Creek canyon (you can see the road switchbacking up the sagebrush slope to the right). Park by the locked gate where you will not block the road.

At the top of the sagebrush slope there is a large meadow, grazed in summer by sheep. After crossing the creek take the lower road to Horton Lake. The buildings near the lake are not for public use, but belong to the Hanging Valley tungsten mine, which is beyond the high ridge north of the lake. The colorful peak to the north is Mount Tom. The creek and lakes were named for a Round Valley rancher. The creek is surprisingly large for such a small drainage basin; melting ice from two small glaciers keeps it high even in late summer. There is a sort-of trail to the Upper Lakes, though it is hard to find and even harder to follow, since it is overgrown with aspen and willow. If you prowl about the inlet of Horton Lake, eventually you will find a trail that follows the right side of the creek to a shallow lake. The easiest way to reach the large lake 600 feet above is to follow the stream up its boulder strewn cut. It takes some scrambling over huge boulders, but it looks worse than it really is.

PINE CREEK CANYON

The canyons of Pine Creek are tremendously impressive, great deep gashes in dark red and black rock. The trails are steep; the scenery is magnificent.
Topographic map: Mount Tom quadrangle.

Pine Creek (7500) to Pine Creek Pass

Pine Lake (9942), strenuous hike, 4 miles.
Pine Creek Pass (11,100), very strenuous hike, 7 miles.
Starting Point: Follow the Pine Creek Road for about 10 miles. Just before it crosses a bridge, turn off left and park among the trees. The trail starts at the pack station.

The trail joins a mining road coming from the Brownstone tungsten mine, which operated 1932–53. Looking back down the canyon, you have a bird's-eye view of the mill and the road going to the Pine Creek Mine. You pass some large stubby juniper trees and the remains of the Brownstone workings and tramway. A rocky trail continues up the canyon. Along the trail perhaps you can discover glacier polish and striations (parallel scratches). As you run your fingers over the marvelous smoothness of the granite bedrock, you may begin to understand the power of the glacier that ground and scoured, as it inched down the canyon. From Pine Lake on, the trail is gentler, following a stream to the pass.

Pine Lake lies below a stunning (unnamed) dark mountain, shot through with dikes of light colored granite. As the trail rounds the north shore, you can see fresh boulders of this unusual rock, black laced with sparkling pink and white. At the inlet of Upper Pine Lake the trail forks. The right fork leads to Honeymoon Lake—ringed with rounded rock cliffs, a waterfall at its inlet—which has some especially scenic campsites. Continuing on the left fork to the pass, look in the meadows for the small magenta meadow paintbrush, related to the common red-orange variety but restricted to very high meadows. Watch also for fat waddling marmots, and listen for the sharp nasal notes of conies. From the pass you look into a high basin with many very large lakes, headwaters of French Canyon. The towering peak to the southeast is Mount Humphreys. The trail continues down French Canyon to meet the John Muir Trail.

Gable Creek (7350) to Gable Lakes (10,400–10,800)

Strenuous hike, about 3 miles.

Starting Point: Park as described above, and follow the dirt road to the three-story mill building. Straight ahead, just behind two large Jeffrey pines, is the trail, which zigzags steeply up the slope to the right of the mill and tramway.

This very steep, little-traveled mine trail climbs the west slope of Gable Creek's deep narrow canyon to the Lakeview tungsten mine. Mules packed out the ore while it operated from 1940–43 and again in the 1950s. The trail goes no farther than the mine cabins at the outlet of the first lake. A second lake lies just above it in an open basin surrounded by high peaks. Another chain of lakes lies to the left (S). The 2½-mile tramway that you see on the way brought ore from the Tungstar Mine, high on the slope of Mount Tom, to the mill where you started. This tungsten mine operated 1939–46. Fire burned the upper buildings; in 1951 snowslides destroyed the lower buildings.

SOURCES OF ADDITIONAL INFORMATION

For a list of eastern Sierra pack stations write: Eastern Sierra Packers Association, Box 147, Bishop.

For information on commercial back country camps (meals, cabins, or tents) write: Dutch Flats, Deer Mountain, and Casa Vieja Camps, Box 3, Coso Junction (Inyo County); Golden Trout Camp, Lone Pine; Jordan Hot Springs Guest Ranch, Olancha; Lake Lodge, Box 267, Big Pine; Monache Meadows Lodge, Box 76, Olancha; Tunnel Air Camp, Lone Pine.

For information on back country air strips and air pack service write: District Ranger, Lone Pine; Bob White's Flying Service, Box 98, Lone Pine.

For information on mountain-climbing guide service and instruction write: Mountaineering Guide Service, Box 658, Big Pine.

Selected Reading

BROWER, DAVID R., ed. *Going Light—With Backpack or Burro.* San Francisco: Sierra Club, 1961. 152 pp. Equipment and techniques for light-weight traveling.

STARR, WALTER A., JR. *Guide to the John Muir Trail.* San Francisco: Sierra Club, 1962. 130 pp. The bible of Sierra trails. Separate folded map.

VOGE, HERVEY, ed. *A Climber's Guide to the High Sierra.* San Francisco: Sierra Club, 1962. 301 pp. Describes climbs any good hiker can make, as well as routes for experienced climbers only.

WHEELOCK, WALT and TOM CONDON. *Climbing Mount Whitney.* Glendale: La Siesta Press, Box 406, 1960. 36 pp. $1.00. Detailed description of the trail, also routes for climbers.

Geology

AT FEW OTHER PLACES IN THE world are geologic features as well exposed or as diversified as in the Owens Valley region; nowhere else is the operation of geologic processes more evident. The story of the magnificent Owens Valley landscape is, first of all, one of earth movements. Tremendous movements have bent and broken the earth's crust, lifted the mountains thousands of feet, and dropped the valley so low that its bedrock surface lies below sea level. In more stable parts of the world, mountains stand high because they are composed of especially hard rocks that resist erosion. Here the mountains are high because they are uplifted, the valley low because it is downdropped between them.

EARTH MOVEMENTS AND STRUCTURES

Because earth movements are very slow, we tend to think of the great geologic events as all having taken place at some remote time. This is not true—geologic events are taking place now, probably as rapidly as in the past. Movement of a few feet per century has been measured. The northwestern part of the Baldwin Hills near Inglewood, for example, is rising at the rate of about three feet per century. The Cajon Pass area was uplifted 8 inches during 35 years—a rate of 20 inches per century. An accurate survey across Tioga Pass shows that the Sierra Nevada east of Yosemite is tilting westward, carrying the crest upward. A station at Tioga Pass is 2½ inches higher above a station at White Wolf than it was 17 years ago—a rate of 23 inches per century, or 19,000 feet per million years.

Some movements involve *bending* of rocks; some involve *breaking*. Breaks in the earth's crust are called faults; the ground on one side has slipped up, down, or sideways (laterally) relative to the ground on the other side. (Cracks whose sides merely move apart are not faults.)

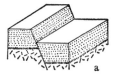 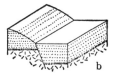 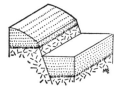

a. Most Owens Valley faults are steeply inclined and form cliff-like scarps where they intersect the surface. b. As the fault scarp grows older, it is eroded back and slopes more gently. c. If faulting is renewed before the scarp is entirely destroyed, a fresh scarp will be formed at the base of the old one. Some low scarps were produced by only one movement, but the great scarps of the Sierra Nevada and Inyo-White Mountains were produced by many movements.

Most geologists believe that many miles of lateral movement have taken place along the San Andreas and Garlock faults, California's two best known faults. The principal movement along the faults in Owens Valley has been up and down.

Fundamentally, Owens Valley is a long narrow block of the earth's crust which is dropped down in the crest of a broad arch that extends from the San Joaquin Valley eastward to Death Valley, and perhaps beyond.

During a period of exceptional movement 1½ to 2 million years ago, Owens Valley was downdropped many thousands of feet to very nearly its present position. Since then movements have continued at a reduced rate, most probably of about the same magnitude as those of the 1872 earthquake, from a few inches to more than twenty feet.

A few million years ago the Sierra Nevada was part of a gently rolling plain.

Then the earth's crust began to bend upward and form a great arch. The arching caused the crust to stretch and the crest and east flank to break along faults.

Sinking of a strip of ground along the crest of the arch formed Owens Valley. The west flank of the arch became the Sierra Nevada; perhaps because it was composed of granite it retained its unity as a single enormous westward-tilted block. The east flank broke into a series of eastward-tilted blocks, which became the ranges east of Owens Valley.

Structures along the East Side of Owens Valley.—The summit surface of the Inyo and White mountains is three miles higher than the same surface beneath the east side of Owens Valley, where in some places it is 4000 feet below sea level. A single very great fault lies along the base of the range. Part of the movement was distributed in a broad zone of faulted and tilted blocks that lies east of this master fault. This zone can be examined by driving east of Bishop on Line Street to the base of the White Mountains, then south about a mile, and then east on a branch road leading into Poleta and Redding canyons. After the turn south, the road is near the base of an eroded west-

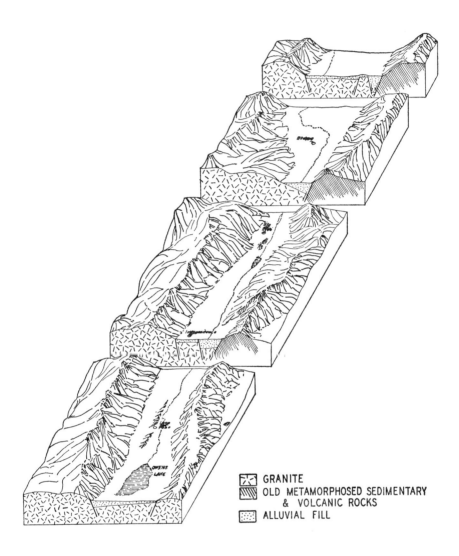

GRANITE
OLD METAMORPHOSED SEDIMENTARY
   & VOLCANIC ROCKS
ALLUVIAL FILL

facing scarp composed of old gravel deposits. This 300-foot scarp marks the master fault, and gives a rough measure of the movement since the gravel washed down from the mountains.

About half a mile above the road fork, old gravel deposits appear along both sides of the road. Layers in them dip toward the valley at about 15 degrees, much steeper than is usual in undisturbed layers, showing that this block of ground has been tilted westward.

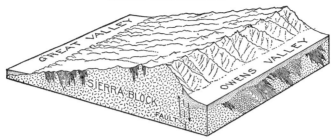

This diagram drawn by the late François E. Matthes illustrates the structure of the Sierra Nevada escarpment south of Crater Mountain (near Big Pine) and west of Round Valley. Debris eroded from the upfaulted mountains was deposited on the downfaulted floor of Owens Valley to depths of thousands of feet. The arrows show the relative motion of the mountain block and the valley block during faulting.

Structures along the West Side of Owens Valley.—Though the Sierra crest is higher than the Inyo-White crest, since bedrock is buried deepest along the east side of the Valley, the difference in altitude between both mountain summits and their adjacent bedrock surfaces below the valley is about the same. West of Independence, along the road to Onion Valley, the bedrock is so shallow it sticks up through the alluvium in low hills. Most of the Sierra escarpment along Owens Valley is a deeply furrowed, precipitous wall of simple structure, which was produced by the erosion of a steep fault scarp.

Although the escarpment seems to tower upward in sheer walls, measurements show that rarely does the average slope from top to bottom exceed 30 degrees. Along the base of the scarp, fault surfaces dip toward the valley at 60–70 degrees, requiring that a great downward-tapering wedge of rock has been eroded away.

At one place along Wheeler Crest is the scarp of a fault where a mountainside slipped down, dammed a stream, and formed a small lake, now almost filled with debris.

In some places, rather than a single fault, there are two or more parallel faults. Opposite the Poverty Hills, peculiar nearly horizontal furrows run along the lower slopes of the escarpment on both sides of Red Mountain Creek. They result from faults along which the mountainside rather than the valley side has slipped down. Similar furrows are present on the east side of Mount Tom, and one also runs high along Wheeler Crest.

The escarpment between Big Pine and Bishop (Crater Mountain to the Tungsten Hills) has a different appearance and origin, and was formed by *bending* rather than faulting. This 20-mile span is characterized by long straggling spurs and gentle slopes that rarely average more than 10 degrees. Along this span the summit surface of the Sierra is *bent* down to the valley, rather than dropped down along a fault. Because warping takes more space than faulting, the warped span bulges into Owens Valley and constricts it to half the width that exists farther south.

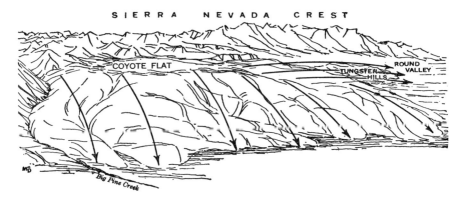

The warped span of the Sierra Nevada escarpment.

The warp is shown by remnants of an old plain that existed before the Sierra Nevada was uplifted and Owens Valley downdropped. The warp is two-sided: from Crater Mountain to the jutting bend in the range front three miles south of Bishop, the old surface bends down to the east; from there to Round Valley it bends down to the north. The gently sloping spur between Big Pine Creek and Shannon Canyon, and the broad ridge north of Rawson Creek are remnants of the old plain in the east flank. The smoothly sloping surface south of Bishop Creek and the rolling surface of the Tungsten Hills are remnants in the north flank. The shape of the warp can be seen best from an airplane or from the crest of the White Mountains.

The surface cracked as it bent and the cracks became faults. In several places, pairs of parallel faults bound narrow sunken strips. Faults that formed in connection with the warping account for the many ridges parallel with the range front west of Big Pine.

The most recent chapters in the story of this great warp are told by the three gently sloping, boulder-strewn river terraces between Bishop and Round Valley. These terraces are former flood plains of the Owens River and its tributaries, which at one time included Horton Creek and Pine Creek. In flood these streams swept back and forth, grinding the underlying rocks to smooth surfaces veneered with boulder gravel. The gravel-veneered surfaces became terraces when they were uplifted and the streams that formed them cut down to new levels. North of Bishop $4\frac{1}{2}$ miles, Highway 395 climbs a 75-foot bluff to the highest and oldest terrace; 2 miles farther on it descends about 50 feet to the middle terrace; $\frac{3}{4}$ of a mile farther it drops to the lowest and youngest terrace. Since the lowest terrace was formed the streams have cut down to their present flood plain. The terraces were cut by streams larger and more powerful than the streams of today, suggesting that they were formed during the Ice Age.

But what caused the terraces to be uplifted and the river to cut down three times? The best explanation is that the whole block of ground between Round Valley and the base of the White Mountains was tilted eastward three times. At the far edge, the terraces end abruptly against the lush fields of Round Valley in a remarkably straight line, marking a fault. The most recent movements along this fault are recorded in a scarp, in places more than a hundred feet high. Sinking of Round Valley west of this fault finally caused Pine and Horton Creeks to change their courses and join Rock Creek in Round Valley, as Pine Creek still does. Doubtless, extensive ponds or even a broad lake formed in Round Valley and collected sand and silt, making possible the soils there today. Each tilting forced the Owens River to flow east, directly down the tilted slope, and so to cut the cliff along the south edge of the Tableland.

Structures Buried beneath the Valley Floor.—The bedrock beneath Owens Valley undoubtedly is broken along many faults, but the evidence is buried. Bedrock is deepest along the east side of the valley. South of Big Pine and north of Bishop, deep downfaulted troughs lie between the base of the Inyo and White mountains and concealed fault scarps parallel with but far removed from the Sierra escarpment. The concealed bedrock scarp south of Big Pine, which records the total movement along the fault, rivals the Sierra Nevada escarpment in height, but the only exposed part is the east side of the Alabama Hills (see diagram Alabama Hills, Roadsides Section).

Between Bishop and Big Pine the east flank of the great downwarped span of the Sierra escarpment continues to slope eastward beneath the valley floor to the base of the White Mountains. Geophysical studies show that it is covered there with more than 7000 feet of alluvial fill. The north flank of the warp slopes northward to the edge of the Volcanic Tableland where, at a depth of about 4000 feet, it bends upward again.

Structures of the Volcanic Tableland.—The Tableland has been bent out of shape and broken along faults, the scarps of which are nearly as fresh as when they were formed. Originally the Tableland sloped smoothly and gently

View northeast into Fish Slough from road to Chidago Flat.

The cliff in the middle distance is a fault scarp. The layer beneath you is 50 feet thick; the cap rock of the distant scarp is the same layer of rock, uplifted more than 400 feet. The two southward tilted blocks in front of the scarp are capped by the same layer. Their tilt suggests that the country east of the fault has risen and moved slightly south.

southeast into Owens Valley. Now it has the general shape of a broad arch with one flank sloping into Owens Valley and the other into Round Valley. Superimposed on this arch are numerous faults and minor folds.

To view some of the fault scarps, drive north from Bishop on Highway 6 about 2 miles. Where the highway bends east, continue straight ahead. At the entrance to Fish Slough, take the middle of three forks, which leads onto the Volcanic Tableland. Half a mile beyond the road fork, stop and look across Fish Slough at one of the largest fault scarps. For the next several miles there are fault scarps after fault scarps, most of them a mile or two long and 50–100 feet high, lying along the flanks of broad northwest-trending wrinkles in the surface of the Tableland.

THE WORK OF WATER

Wind, ice, and especially water battle incessantly to reduce the landscape to a flat and featureless plain, in contrast to earth movements, which increase differences in altitude. One of the paradoxes of the work of water is that the initial step in attacking a newly uplifted block is to dissect it with a network of canyons, converting it from an elevated plateau to a rugged mountain range. A mountain range is a transitory creation; in time the areas between the canyons will also be attacked, and the region will be worn down to low hills, finally to a plain. Earth movements predominate in the Owens Valley region, but if they stop or even slow down very much, the mountains will gradually be worn away.

Water is by far the most effective agent in weathering and erosion. It works into rock along cracks and permeable zones and combines chemically with minerals, causing them to decay and the rock to disintegrate. Flowing streams carry away loose rock, using it to grind down their stream beds. A slight change in the rate of flow greatly alters a stream's carrying power and its ability to cut down its bed. During the summer months, when Sierra streams are clear, they are transporting little rock debris. In spring flood they are muddy with suspended material, and gravel, and even boulders slide and bounce along their bottoms. Carrying power of a stream is greatest when cloudbursts in the mountains cause flash floods. Then it carries enormous amounts of material downstream, forming a field of huge boulders, such as you find near the mouths of many canyons.

Many of the larger Sierra canyons have been enlarged by glaciers, but they were already deep stream-cut canyons when glaciers began to form. Stream-cut canyons are V-shaped, as are, for example, the Sierra Nevada canyons south of Lone Pine, and all the canyons cut into the Inyo-White mountains. Streams have washed rock debris through ever-deepening canyons into Owens Valley, where it has collected three and four thousand feet deep (see diagram Alabama Hills, Roadsides Section). A buried ridge just south of Owens Lake has trapped most of the detritus within the valley.

Streams rushing from the mountains drop their loads when they meet the gentler slopes of the valley. Heavy boulders and cobbles drop out close to the mountain front; gravel, sand, and silt are deposited farther down the slope; only clay and the finest silt are carried to the center of the valley. Debris piles up highest at the canyon mouth and slopes off in a crude half circle, forming an alluvial fan. As the stream changes course, flowing down one side, then the other, it keeps the fan symmetrical. As fans grow larger they coalesce; in this way the sage-covered slopes that flank the base of the mountains were formed.

Alluvial fans east of Bishop along the base of the White Mountains. The large fan with the form of a half circle is at the mouth of Silver Canyon. Laws is at its lower edge.

GLACIATION

Much of the scenic interest of the High Sierra results from sculpturing by ice. Glaciers have widened and deepened great valleys, sharpened the ridges, and scooped out basins for lakes.

The Ice Age generally is thought of as a time much colder than now, when the polar ice caps extended into temperate regions. This is only partly true. The Ice Age was a time when the climatic pendulum was swinging wildly—periods of arctic cold alternated with times much warmer than now. The climatic changes required to bring a new wave of glaciation to the Sierra Nevada may be quite small—perhaps only a few feet more snow each winter or a few degrees lower temperature each summer. Following heavy winters, snowbanks in the High Sierra linger through the following summer. Many consecutive years of heavy snowfall would cause them to grow, especially if during the same period the summers were cloudy and cool enough to inhibit melting. Carried on long enough these slight changes could cause the small Sierra glaciers to advance and new ones to form.

Ice fields and glaciers form from snow. When it accumulates to great thickness, the deeper snow is compacted and recrystallized to ice, the weight from above causing it to flow. Variation in the thickness of ice at the head of a glacier causes the glacier feeding from it to advance or retreat. The critical factor is whether the pack supplies more or less ice than the glacier loses by melting and evaporation. If more is supplied, the glacier advances; if less, it retreats. Glaciers do not release a great rush of water as they retreat; they waste away because of lack of nourishment from their icefields. Thus, the levels of glacial lakes were highest when the glaciers were largest, not when they were retreating.

The Ice Age began more than a million years ago; the last glacial advance in the Sierra Nevada culminated 15,000 to 20,000 years ago. Glaciers disappeared from the main canyons about 10,000 years ago. A brief glaciation 2,000 to 4,000 years ago, called the little ice age, is not generally considered part of the Ice Age.

The Sierra Nevada is glaciated as far south as Cottonwood Pass, ten miles south of Mount Whitney. Along Big Pine, Bishop, and Pine creeks, glaciers extended as low as 5000 feet. The White and Inyo mountains are almost as high, but only the northern part of the White Mountains is glaciated. The glaciers still present in the Sierra are clustered along segments of the crest shielded from the hot noonday sun by north- and northeast-facing cliffs. The largest is Palisade Glacier, with an area of about three-fourths of a square mile. Though it is often referred to as the most southerly glacier in the United States, smaller glaciers are scattered along the Sierra crest for ten miles farther south. These are relics of the little ice age, not of the Ice Age glaciers, which entirely melted away. Although they have been shrinking in recent

The almost flat slope on the left skyline is the summit of Mount Whitney. The Mount Whitney trail is in the middle ground. Photo by Cedric Wright

The story of the magnificent
Owens Valley landscape

is, first of all, one of earth movements. Tremendous forces have bent and broken the earth's crust, lifted the mountains thousands of feet, and dropped the valley so low that some of its bedrock surface lies below sea level.

Basalt columns,
Little Lake
Gerhard Schumacher

*The work of the land-shaping
forces—earthquakes, volcanoes,
wind, water, ice—*

Red Hill, cinder
cone near Little Lake
Gerhard Schumacher

Olancha Dunes by Edward Jacobs

Weathered Rocks, Alabama Hills by Tom F

Palisade Glacier   David Hamren

—is on dramatic display

Bergschrund, Palisade Glacier   Tom Ross

A feature of Palisade glacier is its bergschrund (highest crevasse), where the ice pulls away from the mountain as the glacier moves. A bergschrund usually indicates a true glacier, rather than a permanent snowfield.

This 23-foot cliff is one of the keys

to understanding the Owens Valley landscape. If you recognize this fault scarp for what it is, you can appreciate much of what has happened in this region over thousands of years, why the mountains are so abrupt, why the Valley so deep. It is an earthquake scarp near Lone Pine formed when the land east of it dropped twenty-three feet during the 1872 earthquake. Scarps may be only a few feet high; or, where there has been repeated movement, as along the Sierra Nevada's great eastern escarpment between Lone Pine and Big Pine, they may be thousands of feet high. Directions in the Roadsides Section explain how to find the scarp and the boulder in the foreground, looking exactly as they did when this photograph was taken in 1909 by Willard Johnson of the U. S. Geological Survey.

Temple Crag, Big Pine Creek Canyon   William Fettkether

S·I E R R A   N E V A D A   W H I T E   M O U N T A I N S

Contrast the serrated crest of the High Sierra with the rounded unglaciated summit areas of the White Mountains. The left view is northward across Pine Creek Canyon; the right view is of the White Mountains just north of Black Canyon. Since the White Mountains are in the Sierra rain shadow, too little snow fell to form glaciers.

years, they have shrunk and swelled before, and there is no reason to suppose that they are on their way to extinction. Some glaciologists hold that we still live in the Ice Age, and that eventually the climate will turn colder and ice will once again sweep down Sierra canyons.

Features Formed by Glacial Erosion.—Mountain landscapes that have been shaped by glacial erosion are at once more forbidding and more hospitable than unglaciated mountain landscapes—more forbidding because of steep walls and pinnacles, and more hospitable because of broad flat valley bottoms and benches, many dotted with lakes or covered with flower-decked meadows. Characteristic of glaciated mountains are the conspicuously concave shapes which so enhance the beauty and interest of the Sierra landscape. The concave

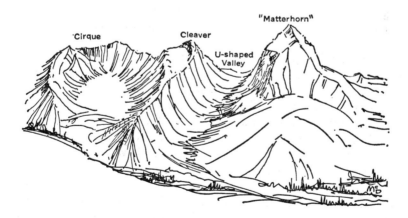

Concave forms resulting from glacial erosion. Sketch looking southward along Bishop Creek's North Fork. The U-shaped valley is the valley of the North Fork; the cirque is the basin that holds the Wonder Lakes; the "matterhorn" is Mount Emerson.

forms resulting from glacial erosion include steepsided U-shaped canyons, lake-filled basins (cirques), knife-edged ridges between basins, and many-sided matterhorns.

In glacially eroded regions there are also grooved and polished rock surfaces, and glacial staircases. Sierra glacial valleys rise in a series of steps. The canyons of Big Pine, Bishop, and Pine creeks are typical glacial valleys. The trunk canyon for half a dozen miles or so above its mouth is smoothly graded; higher up, the canyon rises in a series of long flat treads and short steep risers. Along Big Pine Creek the first riser is at First Falls, at the junction of the North and South forks; the next riser is at Second Falls, beyond the road-end. Higher along the North Fork, each of the lakes occupies a depression in the tread of a step.

Typical profile of stream-cut valley

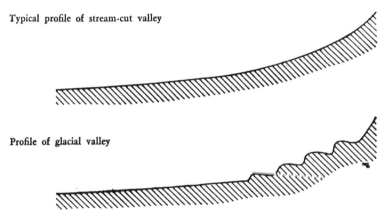

Profile of glacial valley

Stream-cut valleys generally rise gradually headward, whereas Sierra glacial valleys rise in a series of steps—the so-called glacial or Cyclopean staircases.

How the steplike profile formed is something of a puzzle. Some steps, including the very largest ones, occur where two glaciers joined. The first steps along Big Pine, Bishop, and Pine creeks are at major forks in the canyon. Where glacial streams join, the glacier must flow faster and cut deeper to accommodate the ice from both glaciers and still maintain grade. The spectacular heads of Yosemite-like canyons are formed in this way; Pine Creek canyon is a splendid example. The headwall, just above the end of the public road, was formed where glaciers along Morgan and Gable creeks and an unnamed stream joined the glacier from upper Pine Creek. A contributing factor is a belt of marble (a rock peculiarly resistant to glacial erosion) which forms part of the headwall. Another explanation for glacial staircases is that steps form where the rock is least fractured. Cracks speed glacial erosion by permitting water to enter and pry the rock apart by freezing and thawing. The loosened block can then be easily plucked and carried away by glacial ice.

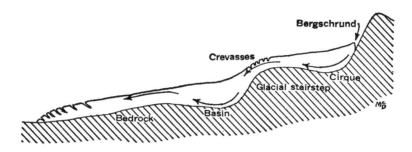

The bottom part of a glacier moves faster after it plunges over a glacial staircase in an icefall. This causes the glacier to scour out a basin on the step below. The arrows show the trace of the most rapid movement in a glacier as it moves down a glacial staircase. (After F. E. Matthes.)

The steepness of cirque headwalls is caused by a glacier sapping the base, along a great crack called the bergschrund. The bergschrund permits air circulation, and freezing and thawing. Water percolating along cracks freezes, dislocating blocks of rock which are carried away in the glacier. Removal of rock at the base of the headwall keeps the upper part of the headwall steep; rocks loosened by frost action fall onto the glacier and are carried away by it.

Glacial Deposits.—The chronology and climatic conditions during the Ice Age are written chiefly in glacial deposits. Deposits which are so recent that every original feature is preserved may be seen to cut across or overlie weathered, older deposits. Most of the bouldery material deposited by Sierra glaciers is in forms called moraines. A terminal or end moraine is a pile of rock debris deposited at the end of a glacier at its farthest advance. Lateral moraines are narrow-crested, steep-sided ridges deposited along the sides of a glacier. As a glacier retreats it may do so in a series of still stands. At each still stand an arcuate moraine, convex on its down canyon side, is deposited from the end of the glacier. Glacial deposits are present along most Sierra canyons from Independence Creek north; the most complete and best preserved display is along Bishop Creek (see Bishop Creek, Roadsides Section).

The Story of Owens Lake.—During the little ice age, and also during the Ice Age, when precipitation was much greater than now, Owens Lake was filled to overflowing with fresh water. Water poured out the south end of the lake into Indian Wells Valley. The 100-foot-deep lake formed there quickly spilled over into the much deeper Searles Lake basin. When the water level in the Searles basin rose to the height of the Indian Wells lake, the two coalesced to form one large 380-square-mile lake, about twice the size of Lake Tahoe. At times water also flowed into Panamint Valley, forming a lake 60 miles long; it in turn may have spilled over into Death Valley.

During much of the last 50,000 years, Searles Lake was the lowest lake in the chain. Only with the close of the little ice age did Owens Lake become the terminal sump of the Owens River system. As the lake dried up, the accumulated salts concentrated to a brine, and then crystallized to form a crust nine feet thick (see also Bartlett and Owens Lake, Roadsides Section).

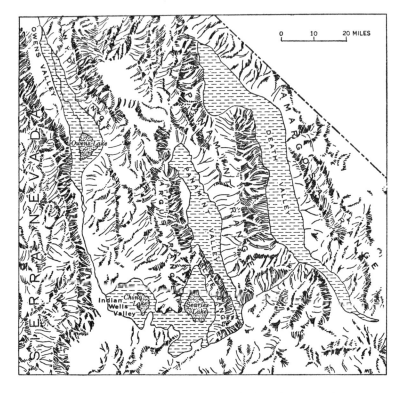

During the Ice Age, Owens Lake was the highest of a chain of lakes

VOLCANISM

As Owens Valley slowly sank between the mountains, volcanoes periodically erupted, hurling ash and cinders high in the air and pouring out flows of lava and glowing ash. The volcanic material originated deep within the earth and broke to the surface along some of the faults.

Basalt.—The most common volcanic deposit is basalt, which forms flows of dark gray lava. Most vents for basaltic eruptions are marked by cones of reddish gray cinders; lava has broken out through the base of many of them. The cinders and lava are the same composition, despite their color difference. Basalt contains an abundance of iron which in cinders has been oxidized by escaping gases to form reddish iron oxide.

Molten basalt generally is thin enough to flow freely and form extensive sheets. The surface of most basalt flows is rough because of cavities formed by expanding and escaping gases, and because liquid lava tends to flow away from cooler congealing lava. Rows of parallel ridges were caused by buckling of the cooled crust, in turn caused by movement of still-liquid lava beneath. The rough vesicular part of a basalt flow generally is confined to the upper few feet. Where streams cut through lava flows, the lower part appears massive and contains few voids. Where basalt lavas have been buried, ground waters commonly deposit minerals in the cavities. In Redrock Canyon, gas cavities in the basalt contain such minerals as chalcedony, opal, analcite, natrolite, and other minerals prized by collectors.

Big Pine Volcanic Field.—One of the most extensive fields of basaltic cones and flows lies along the base of the Sierra between Sawmill Creek and Big Pine. The Poverty Hills, near the center of the field, is not volcanic, but is an upfaulted block of granite and marble. South of the Poverty Hills, several flows have moved down the slope across the position of the highway. Most of these flows have their source in a group of cinder cones that lie along two faults. Crater Mountain, rising 2,000 feet above the valley floor, is mantled with lava, but borings for water show that its interior consists of alternating layers of black lava and reddish cinders. Although it is one of the largest volcanoes in the region, it is not as large as it seems because it is built on top of an upfaulted block of granite. Crater and Red mountains (south of the Poverty Hills) lie along a fault that is marked by a low scarp, which can be seen by taking the Tinemaha road. A branch road to a quarrying operation

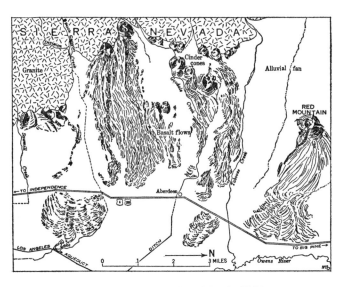

South half of Big Pine Volcanic Field

west of the Hills crosses the scarp just below the quarry; it is marked by springs, lush vegetation, and an abandoned orchard.

Rhyolite.—Less common than basalt but of greater aggregate volume because it forms the varicolored rocks of the Volcanic Tableland, is rhyolite. Rhyolite contains very little iron; much of it is white or buff, although it may be red, orange, purple, brown, or gray. Molten rhyolite usually is much more viscous than basalt, rising above its vents in blobs that move downslope in short stubby flows. Solidified blobs are called domes and are composed chiefly of volcanic glass, varying from black obsidian, which contains few crystals and almost no bubbles, to white frothy pumice. The most spectacular rhyolite domes in the eastern Sierra are the Mono Craters, north of Owens Valley. You can see small buff-colored domes in the Coso Range from the highway and a single dome is present just west of the Poverty Hills. This dome has an unusually high content of water, which causes the rock to expand explosively when heated. It is quarried and trucked to Los Angeles, where it is expanded and sold as perlite. Rhyolite also forms light-colored ash and pumice layers in Redrock Canyon and along the base of the White Mountains northeast of Big Pine.

The Volcanic Tableland.—The outstanding rhyolite deposits are the ash flows of the Tableland. A million years ago burning clouds of incandescent volcanic ash and pumice swept from vents, probably in Long Valley or beneath Mono Lake, into Owens Valley. Unlike viscous rhyolite lava, gas-fluxed rhyolite ash moves freely and forms extensive sheets, some covering hundreds of square miles.

In some places the ash flows followed one another so closely that the later ones overran the earlier ones before they had cooled, as you can see in Owens River and Rock Creek Gorges. To examine them, turn east from Highway 395 onto a paved road about two miles north of the Pine Creek road. About $4\frac{1}{2}$ miles after leaving the highway, turn right (northeast) on a dirt road for about $\frac{1}{4}$ mile. Park at the locked gate; then walk the road to the bottom of the Gorge, a distance of half a mile and a drop of 400 feet.

Across the gorge are layers of various colors and thicknesses. The surface layer is light orange brown, and the layers successively below it are white, pinkish purple, pink, and pale grayish purple. Huge 4-, 5-, and 6-sided columns standing at various positions can be inspected along the road. Like basalt columns, they formed as a result of shrinkage during cooling. The 50-foot orange-brown tuff layer at the top is denser than the underlying white layer, and contains fresh and unaltered pumice fragments, showing that it erupted after the layers beneath had cooled and been drained of gases. The tuff layers beneath cooled together. The pumice fragments in these layers have been altered by gases that escaped from the layers beneath and weather out of the rock readily. With depth, the pumice fragments in the tuff are progressively flatter, and the enclosing rock is denser. The lower third of the canyon is composed of rock almost twice as dense as the rock in the white layer; no pumice fragments are visible, not because none were ever there, but because they were welded with their ashy matrix into homogenous rock during cooling and compaction.

The base of the ash flows is exposed in the cliff along the south margin of the Volcanic Tableland (see Chalk Bluff Road, Roadsides Section), and in quarry faces along its east side, which can be reached from Highway 6 north of Laws. At the quarries you can see the soft pinkish tuff and an underlying white pumice layer, though the top orange-brown layer is missing, having been eroded away.

OLDER ROCKS AND STRUCTURES

The modern landscape is built on the ruins of structures much older than any described thus far. The granites of the Sierra Nevada are a hundred million years old; the rocks in the White and Inyo mountains are much older. The history of the region is increasingly hazy as we go back in time, but the broad story can be deciphered for the last half billion years. (See diagrams on pages 120, 121.)

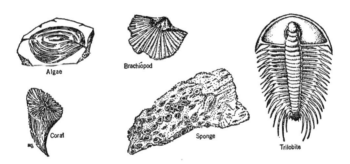

Some representative fossils that can be found in the strata of the White and Inyo mountains. Trilobites are hard to find but are in shales along the Westgard Pass road. Sponges, corals, algae, and brachiopods are in layered rocks near Mazourka Canyon.

The oldest rocks, the ones that were deposited from 200–600 million years ago, are exposed in the White and Inyo mountains. In the Sierra, only scattered remnants are left. Trips into Mazourka Canyon and to Westgard Pass give excellent opportunities to examine these rocks. In most places the layers are inclined, and in some places they stand on edge. Fossils can be found of the organisms that lived in the ancient seas in which they were deposited.

Remnants of these strata in the Sierra Nevada are recrystallized and contain pyrite, which weathers to the iron oxides which stain most of the remnants rusty and brownish colors, making them easy to identify. Two of the largest remnants are the north part of the Pine Creek pendant, from the summit of Mount Tom northward across Pine Creek, and the Bishop Creek pendant, which crosses both the South and Middle forks of Bishop Creek. As the name suggests, a pendant is a downward projection of the deformed strata that overlies the granite. Smaller remnants are found in many other places— such as in the Tungsten Hills, poking through the moraines between Big Pine and Baker Creek and along the crest between Cardinal Mountain and Red Mountain Creek.

The younger rocks that were deposited in the narrow trough 130–200 million years ago are found only in scattered remnants, mostly in the Sierra

Diagrammatic summary of the older history of the
Sierra Nevada and Owens Valley region

About 600 million years ago, most of the western United States was submerged beneath the ocean. Although the sea floor was flexed periodically and lifted above sea level at least once, it lay below sea level most of the time until about 200 million years ago. During this span of 400 million years, sediments eroded from land areas collected layer by layer on the ocean floor to thicknesses of many thousands of feet. In the Owens Valley region these sediments were ordinary mud, silt, sand, gravel, limy sand, and marl (limy mud) such as are accumulating along the edges of the continents today.

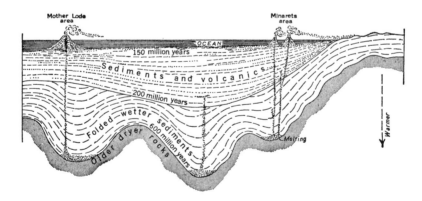

About 200 million years ago the sedimentary layers that had piled up on the ocean floor were folded, broken along faults, and lifted above sea level, where their upturned edges were eroded. Then a long narrow trough began to bow down and to collect debris. The sinking of the trough was accompanied by volcanic outbursts, and vast quantities of lava and volcanic ash were spewed forth. Some of this material flowed or fell directly into the trough, which was near or below sea level most of the time, but large volumes were deposited on land. Much of this material was then eroded into the sinking trough.

Nevada. The rocks in these remnants generally are gray to black, but some are white; they are rarely iron-stained as are the older rocks. One remnant makes up the east side of the Alabama Hills. An especially large remnant lies west of Independence, extending from Independence Creek northwestward over the crest. A long narrow belt in the Inyo Mountains runs southeast from Owenyo; the Cerro Gordo road crosses it.

The various granite bodies differ in appearance. Some have many dark minerals, others few; some are coarse grained, some fine; some have large crystals.

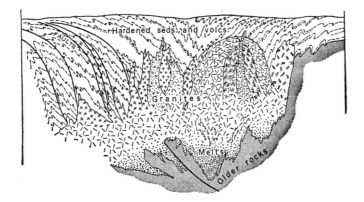

About 150 million years ago, when volcanic and sedimentary deposits had collected to a depth of at least 50,000 feet, the strata that had piled up on the sea floor and in the trough were tightly folded and broken along faults. The squeezing altered the strata; mud became slate, and the other rocks were recrystallized and hardened. The sinking of the trough and subsequent squeezing pushed the strata in the bottom of the trough deep in the earth where temperatures and pressures are very high—so high that the sedimentary and volcanic strata with the lowest melting points were melted. The older rocks did not melt, chiefly because they were very dry, and dry rocks melt at much higher temperatures than wet sedimentary and volcanic deposits. The melts worked upward into the overlying strongly deformed rocks, where they solidified to granite. Because different bodies of molten granite traveled upward by different paths and at different times, we find not just one body of granite, but many. Other explanations for the origin of granite have been proposed, but the one shown here is strongly supported by field studies and by experimental work with granite melts.

After the granite was solidified, the trough began to rise. The uplift was so great that when the uplifted rocks had been eroded away the granites were exposed. After uplift ceased, erosion continued until the land was reduced to a broad rolling plain—the same plain that later was bent upward into an arch and broken into the fault blocks that form the Sierra Nevada, Owens Valley, the White and Inyo mountains, and the desert ranges farther east (see sketch page 101).

They can be distinguished by their different shades of gray, if the light is right. Different granites can be inspected in any of the Sierra canyons. In some places swarms of thin dikes of granite extend outward from a granite body into cracks in its walls. A splendid example of such a dike swarm is on upper Pine Creek near Pine Lake.

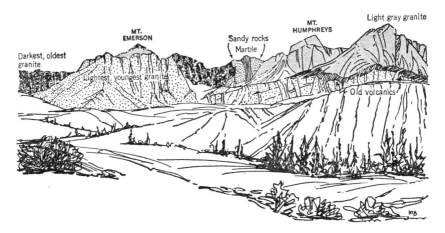

Sketch of the Sierra escarpment west of Bishop showing different bodies of granite that can be distinguished under the morning sun. Afternoon shadows obscure the distinction.

Selected Reading

BATEMAN, PAUL C. *Economic Geology of the Bishop Tungsten District.* California Division of Mines, Special Report 47, 1956. 87 pp. A technical report; many illustrations, 13 separate maps.

BROWN, VINSON and DAVID ALLAN. *Rocks and Minerals of California.* Healdsburg: Naturegraph Co., 1955. 120 pp. Keys for identifying rocks and minerals, maps showing locations. The same authors and publisher have also a 35-cent pocketsize *Illustrated Guide to Common Rocks.*

CASANOVA, RICHARD. *Illustrated Guide to Fossil Collecting.* Healdsburg: Naturegraph Co., 1957. 80 pp.

FRYXELL, FRITIOF M. (ed.) *François Matthes and the Marks of Time: Yosemite and the High Sierra.* Sierra Club, 1961. 192 pp., illustrated.

HEALD, WELDON F. *Palisade Glacier Map.* New York: American Alpine Club, 1946. Large-scale map (21" x 21"), with report on reverse side. 50 cents from Alpine Club, 113 East 90th Street, New York 28.

KNOPF, ADOLPH. *A Geologic Reconnaissance of the Inyo Range and Eastern Slope of the Southern Sierra Nevada.* U. S. Geological Survey, Prof. Paper 110, 1918.

NORMAN, L. A., JR., and RICHARD STEWART. *Mines and Mineral Resources of Inyo County.* California Journal of Mines and Geology, 47:1, 1951. 206 pp. Comprehensive; separate map. State Division of Mines and Geology, Ferry Building, San Francisco. $1.00.

POUGH, FREDERICK H. *A Field Guide to Rocks and Minerals.* Boston: Houghton Mifflin, 1960. 349 pp. Part of the authoritative Field Guide Series, widely used by beginners and experts alike.

Plants

THE SIERRA NEVADA DOMINATES THE land and life not only of Owens Valley, but also of the desert far beyond. Permitting few clouds to escape eastward, the Sierra barrier has made this a Land of Little Rain, with low humidity and no fog. With little moisture, eastern Sierra flora is quite different from the lush growth of the western slope.

The height and steepness of both mountain ranges make rainfall and temperature vary tremendously between valley floor and mountain crests. Air is colder at high altitudes because it is thinner, absorbing less heat from the sun. Plants growing on the crests may be subjected to freezing temperatures in midsummer; those in the valley have frost-free days most of the year. Soil, too, varies greatly. Some valley plants must tolerate highly alkaline conditions; mountain plants must grow in seemingly sterile granite; streamside plants have acid soils. Exposure to wind and sun makes additional differences.

Here, then, there is an astonishing variety of climates; extreme heat and extreme cold occur within a few miles of each other. From Los Angeles, one would have to travel thousands of miles along the coast to reach the arctic tundra. From Owens Valley, one need travel only a few miles to reach the mountain crests where arctic conditions prevail.

How plants have evolved to cope with such varying environments is one of the great wonders. Naming the process *evolution,* and trying to find out a little about the process, our wonder only increases. There is a tendency, known as natural selection, for slight differences among individuals to be perpetuated, if the differences are advantageous. A lowland plant may produce offspring which differ slightly. Those which are shorter stemmed and fuzzier leaved, for instance, may prosper better at the upper limits of the plant's normal range. Over thousands of years, these differences may be exaggerated until there are two distinct species, one descended from the other. The four-inch alpine willow, for example, is related to the twenty-foot willow of the valley, both probably descended from a common ancestor. Many mountain plants are so changed in size and shape that they scarcely resemble their lowland relatives.

Desert plants must endure months of 100-degree temperatures, and perhaps a year without rain. They are widely spaced, each with a generous share of earth from which to draw precious moisture. They have developed ingenious ways to discourage evaporation from their leaves. Many have very small leaves; some have the edges rolled under. Some are hairy, others scaly. Some have minute glands that exude sticky or oily substances to protect the leaf surface. Some solve the problem by having thick or fleshy leaves, such as the Anderson thornbush, whose leaves resemble fat grains of rice. Some shrubs, such as shadscale and creosote bush, drop their leaves early if it is unusually dry; others, such as the *Ephedras,* have no leaves at all. It is no accident that desert plants are light colored; they reflect heat rather than absorb it. They

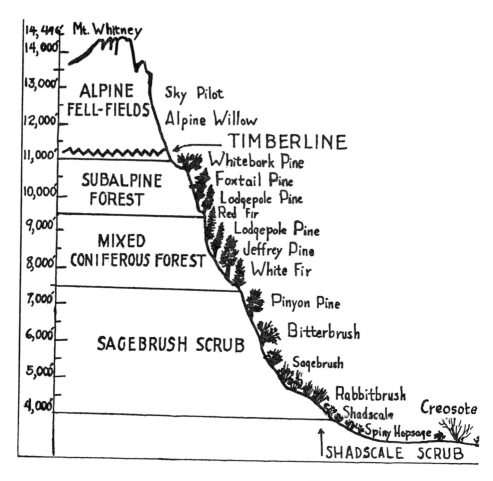

Plant Communities

(Sierra on left; Inyo-White mountains on right)

Plants adapted to the same conditions of moisture, temperature, and soil make up plant communities. In mountainous regions the communities form a pattern of horizontal bands.

usually grow low and compact, with little growing energy wasted in long branches. Root systems are developed to reach far for water. The little-leaf mahogany, growing in the Inyos, is a low, very compact bush, with short intricate branches. The edges of its quarter-inch leaves are tightly rolled under, almost to the center. Its relative living under milder conditions, the mountain mahogany, grows tall, with long upright branches. Its leaves are an inch long, with barely rolled edges.

In the middle elevations, life is easier. There are more kinds of plants, and

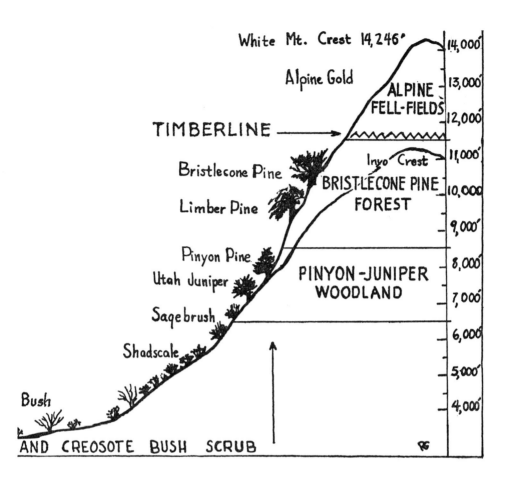

White Mt. Crest 14,246'

Alpine Gold

14,000'

13,000'

ALPINE FELL-FIELDS

12,000'

TIMBERLINE ➔

11,000'

Bristlecone Pine

Inyo Crest

BRISTLECONE PINE FOREST

10,000'

Limber Pine

9,000'

Pinyon Pine

8,000'

Utah Juniper

PINYON-JUNIPER WOODLAND

7,000'

Sagebrush

6,000'

Shadscale

5,000'

Bush

4,000'

AND CREOSOTE BUSH SCRUB

of Owens Valley

However, the lines of nature are seldom rigidly drawn. Some plants appear in more than one community; many straggle over into adjacent communities. The elevations indicated above are general guides, but exposure and drainage make great differences. For instance, bristlecone pine may grow on a shaded north slope, while at the same elevation across the canyon, pinyon and juniper grow on the sunny south slope.

they need not be so specialized. They can afford to grow large and close together.

Just as desert plants are adapted to extreme heat, high-mountain plants are as marvelously adapted to extreme cold. Toward timberline, species decrease. Few have solved the problems of growth and reproduction during the short alpine summer and survival during the winter. At high altitudes tall fir and Jeffrey pine give way to twisted sprawling whitebark pine. The three-foot flowers of moist meadows are replaced by inch-high cushion plants and "belly-flowers," so named because they are so small one must lie down to see them. On the ridges living conditions are incredibly harsh—ferocious winds, bitter cold, wildly fluctuating temperatures, nine-month winters, rocky soil. In the thin air, the sun's rays are more penetrating, the light more intense.

Alpine plants have adapted to their harsh environment in a number of ways. Since the seeds of few plants can germinate and mature in the short alpine summer, which may be only eight weeks, most alpine plants are perennials. Some do not bloom every year, but must store up energy for several years to produce seeds. Many have very long roots, which enable them to cling to windswept rocky slopes and to obtain moisture. Most are only inches high, concentrating the little growth they are capable of into producing flowers and seeds. A typical cushion plant, studied in the Rockies, gains only two tiny leaves a year, and grows but a third of an inch. Some seem ridiculously small for their large flowers. Most alpine plants have dark green leaves that are highly heat-absorbent. Some are thick, some finely divided, hairy, fuzzy, or glandular, each designed to resist evaporation or cold. A tiny algae secretes a red gelatinous covering for protection, causing the pink snow of high altitudes.

The Owens Valley region is one of the richest in plant variety. There are more than 2,000 species and there are endless variations within the species. Newcomers will find their favorites in different forms, as well as many unfamiliar species adapted to the unusual conditions here.

We can make order out of this bewildering variety by grouping plants according to the communities where they are usually found. Each community has certain indicator plants which distinguish it. Plant classifications and the plant-community concept is based on Philip Munz' *A California Flora.* After you learn to recognize the communities, then you may begin to notice small differences in terrain, soil, and exposure, and the plants that favor each. There is little enough time to become acquainted with this earth, but you will be on your way.

BRISTLECONE PINE FOREST 8500–11,500 feet

Open forests of trees 15–50 feet high, on rocky slopes and ridges of the Inyo and White mountains, and the higher desert ranges eastward. Moderate rain and snow; 50–90 frost-free days.

Indicator plants (those marked * are described in this guide): bristlecone pine (*Pinus aristata*) *, limber pine (*Pinus flexilis*) *, mountain mahogany (*Cerocarpus ledifolius*) *, little rabbitbrush (*Chrysothamnus viscidiflorus* ssp. *pumilus*), low sagebrush (*Artemisia arbuscula* ssp. *nova*), slender bluegrass (*Poa incurva*), Inyo Mountain parsley (*Lomatium inyoense*), alpine paintbrush (*Castilleja nana*), cushion phlox (*Phlox Covillei*), white globe gilia (*Ipomopsis congesta* ssp. *montana*), prickly locoweed (*Astragalus Kentrophyta* vars. *implexus* and *elatus*).

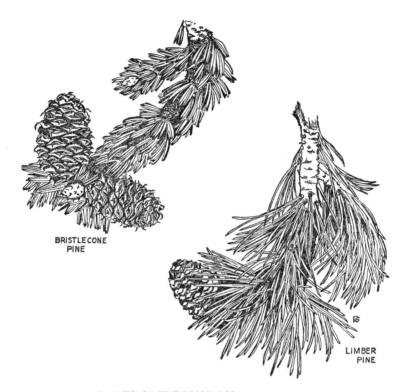

BRISTLECONE
PINE

LIMBER
PINE

PLANTS OF THE BRISTLECONE PINE FOREST

Bristlecone pine (*Pinus aristata*). Pine family. Needles in fives; immature cones purplish, with conspicuous slender prickles, turning green to brown as they mature, 3–4 inches long; bark thin, shallowly ridged, and scaly, grayish in dense forests, reddish in open stands; branchlets thickly clothed with needles toward the ends, resembling bottle brushes. Trunks often divided at base, trees bushy, 15–50 feet high. On north and east slopes, prefer limestone formations. Their dark green color and drooping branchlets give them a somber funereal appearance. The Aqueduct and Tonopah power lines used bristlecone for poles in the early 1900s; some are still standing. Though the wood is soft, its high resin content makes it durable.

Limber pine (*Pinus flexilis*). Pine family. Needles in fives; cones heavy, thick scales without prickles, 3–6 inches long, basal end rosette-like; young branches smooth, light honey color; bark of mature trees thin-scaled; branches limber. Tree 20–60 feet high; one or more very long branches give it an irregular shape; lighter warmer green than bristlecone.

PINYON-JUNIPER WOODLAND above 6500 feet

Large areas in the desert ranges, a trace along the base of the Sierra; favored by Indians for campsites. Trees 10–30 feet high; open stands with shrubs between. 12–20 inches precipitation, some snow; 150–250 frost-free days; 5–8 months growing season.

Indicator plants: pinyon pine (*Pinus monophylla*) *, Utah juniper (*Juniperus osteosperma*) *, desert bitterbrush (*Purshia glandulosa*) *, mountain mahogany (*Cercocarpus ledifolius*) *, little-leaf mahogany (*Cercocarpus intricatus*), desert snowberry (*Symphoricarpos longiflorus*) *, Inyo locoweed (*Astragalus inyoensis*), Pursh locoweed (*Astragalus Purshii* var. *longilobus*), big-podded locoweed (*Astragalus oophorus*), golden forget-me-not (*Cryptantha confertiflora*), Inyo Mountain penstemon (*Penstemon scapoides*), Stansbury phlox (*Phlox Stansburyi*) *.

Pinyon pine (*Pinus monophylla*). Pine family. One needle; cones 2–3 inches long. Tree gray-green, somewhat bushy, rounded when young, flat-topped in age. The plump sweet pinyon nuts were the Indians' staple food. Valley people go pine nutting in fall, after frost has opened the cones.

Utah juniper (*Juniperus osteosperma*). Cypress family. Leaves scalelike; fruit a berry, covered by whitish bloom; bark shreddy. Tree small, rounded when young, irregularly shaped in age; yellow-green.

Desert snowberry (*Symphoricarpos longiflorus*). Honeysuckle family. Deciduous shrub 1½–4 feet high; flower pink; berry white; branchlets short. Blooms May–June. A similar species, Mountain snowberry (*S. vaccinoides*), is common in the Sierra mixed coniferous forest. Its leaves are larger and flowers shorter.

Paper-podded loco (*Astragalus lentiginosus* var. *Fremontii*). Pea family. Plant more or less reclining, 4–10 inches high; flower purple; leaflets gray-green. Inflated pods thin and papery, usually mottled, about ¾ inch long. Shadscale scrub to pinyon-juniper woodland.

Locoweed is a specialty of the Owens Valley area. There are numerous species, many of them rare or of limited distribution. The pods come in a variety of forms and textures, papery and inflated, plump and fleshy, leathery and rigid, round and furry, plain and smooth, or other combinations of these characteristics. The flowers are just as varied. There is the beautiful scarlet loco (*Astragalus coccineus*) of the desert ranges, with showy flowers 1½ inches long, and the dainty Alpine loco (*Astragalus Ravenii*) so small and modest that it was discovered only recently on a high Sierra pass, and many others in assorted colors and sizes between these two extremes.

Stansbury phlox (*Phlox Stansburyi*). Phlox family. Perennial 4–8 inches high. Flowers rose-pink to whitish. Blooms late May–June.

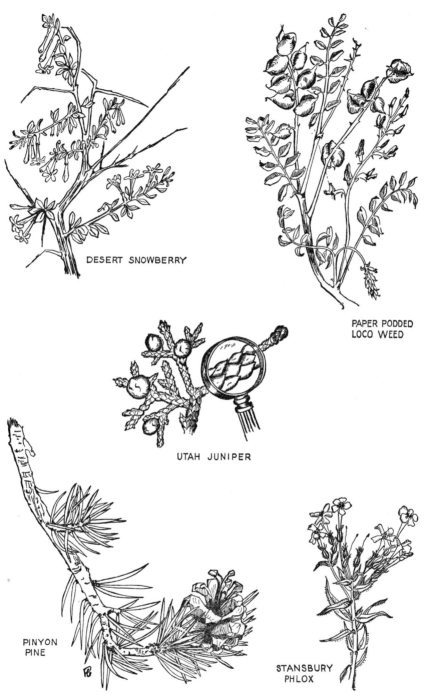

DESERT SNOWBERRY

PAPER PODDED
LOCO WEED

UTAH JUNIPER

PINYON
PINE

STANSBURY
PHLOX

PLANTS OF THE PINYON-JUNIPER WOODLAND

SHADSCALE SCRUB 3,000–6,000 feet

Heavy soil, often with underlying hardpan, of flats and slopes. Plants mostly 1–1½ feet high, shallow-rooted. Large monotonous areas with little variation in size, shape or color of shrubs. 3–7 inches of precipitation; 150–250 frost-free days; growing season limited by lack of water.

Indicator plants: shadscale (*Atriplex confertifolia*) *, spiny hopsage (*Grayia spinosa*) *, lamb's tail (*Eurotia lanata*), bud sage (*Artemisia spinescens*), spiny menodora (*Menodora spinescens*), desert alyssum (*Lepidium Fremontii*), saucer plant (*Oxytheca perfoliata*), bird-nest buckwheat (*Eriogonum nidularium*).

Shadscale (*Atriplex confertifolia*). Goosefoot family. The predominant species of saltbush in this plant community. Low, rounded shrub with woody base, spiny, 8–30 inches high; whitish branches, light gray leaves; often grows in alkaline soils. Although an indicator plant of the community named for it, shadscale may be found in lesser amounts in the bordering sagebrush scrub and creosote bush scrub.

Spiny hopsage (*Grayia spinosa*). Goosefoot family. Shrub 1–3 feet high; leaves somewhat fleshy, about 1 inch long, often tinted pinkish; female plants bear scalelike rosy-tinted fruits thickly clustered at the ends of twigs. An attractive note of color in the gray scrub, and a good browse plant for cattle and sheep.

CREOSOTE BUSH SCRUB usually below 3500 feet

Shrubs widely spaced, largely dormant between rainy periods; can endure extremely dry but not saline conditions. 2–8 inches precipitation; 180–345 frost-free days; well drained soil.

Indicator plants: creosote bush (*Larrea divaricata*) *, burrobush (*Franseria dumosa*), cheese-bush (*Hymenoclea Salsola*), brittlebush (*Encelia farinosa*), California dalea (*Dalea californica*), Anderson thornbush (*Lycium Andersonii*), apricot mallow (*Sphaeralcea ambigua*) *, beavertail cactus (*Opuntia basilaris*).

Creosote bush (*Larrea divaricata*). Caltrops family. Evergreen shrub, 3–10 feet high; flowers yellow, the petals twisted; furry seed capsules appear silvery when back-lighted; leaves olive-green, coated with a substance which retards evaporation. Widely spaced, often the only plant. This hardy shrub keeps a safe distance from saline Owens Lake and its dust, finding favorable spots along the base of the Inyos and up the washes. Blooms April–May.

SAGEBRUSH SCRUB mostly 4,000 to 7500 feet

Silvery-gray shrubs, 2–7 feet high, interspersed with greener plants. Deep, pervious soil along the base of the Sierra. 8–15 inches precipitation, partly snow; 70–130 frost-free days; growing period 3½–6 months. Deer winter on these lower slopes where bitterbrush is plentiful.

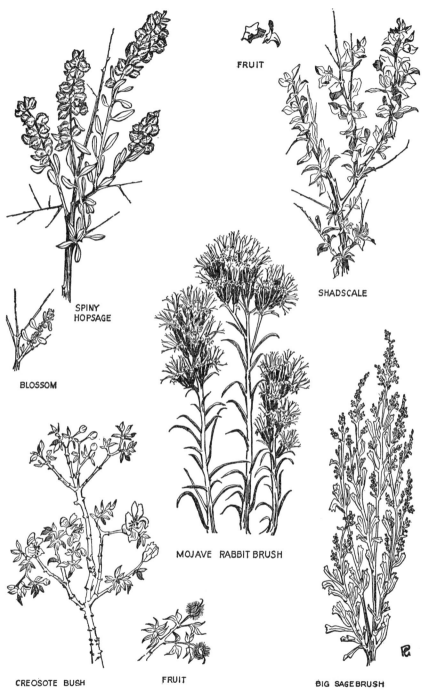

FRUIT

SPINY
HOPSAGE

SHADSCALE

BLOSSOM

MOJAVE RABBIT BRUSH

CREOSOTE BUSH   FRUIT   BIG SAGEBRUSH

PLANTS OF THE VALLEY FLOOR AND LOWER MOUNTAIN SLOPES

Indicator plants: big sagebrush (*Artemisia tridentata*)*, low sagebrush (*Artemisia arbuscula* ssp. *nova*), black brush (*Coleogyne ramosissima*), rabbit-brush (*Chrysothamnus nauseosus* ssp. *speciosus* and *mohavensis*) *, sticky rabbitbrush (*Chrysothamnus viscidiflorus*), cottonthorn (*Tetradymia spinosa*), bitterbrush (*Purshia tridentata*) *, Adonis lupine (*Lupinus excubitus*) *, desert peach (*Prunus Andersonii*) *, desert ceanothus (*Ceanothus Greggii* var. *vestitus*).

Big sagebrush (*Artemisia tridentata*). Sunflower family. Silvery gray evergreen shrub, 1½–8 feet high; aromatic; bark shaggy; leaves 3-toothed at apex; flowers yellowish, inconspicuous; upright flowering shoots laden with pollen in the fall. A dominant shrub of the Great Basin, an example of that influence in Owens Valley. In open forests, sagebrush mingles with forest trees on ridges and south slopes, wherever the soil is deep and loamy, up to 9,000 feet or more. Indians used the plant for medicinal purposes. Its seeds were a staple food.

Sagebrush sometimes grows amazingly large. One hardy specimen discovered in Wyman Canyon is 11 inches in diameter and 15½ feet tall. A sagebrush study in the White Mountains revealed specimens approximately 200 years old.

Mojave rabbitbrush (*Chrysothamnus nauseosus*). Sunflower family. Broomlike shrub, 2–5 feet high; upright branches and stems flexible, light gray-green, often almost leafless; flowers yellow, conspicuous in the fall as masses of golden color. Sometimes called rubberbrush, owing to its high rubber content.

VALLEY WILDFLOWERS

Flowers are where and when you find them. The rains set the seasons and every year is different. Desert flowers at the southern end of the valley begin blooming in April. In May look for them in the Alabama Hills and the Blackrock area near Aberdeen. Desert annuals depend on fall rains coming at just the right time to germinate their seeds and spring rains to enable them to mature. Seeds may lie dormant for years; only when conditions are right will they burst forth in a carpet of color. Perennials and shrubs are less showy than annuals, but are more reliable in dry years. In late May—but only in favorable years—the Tableland and the washes along Mazourka Canyon and Westgard Pass roads are particularly beautiful. But even in poor years, anyone who really looks will find many flowers somewhere throughout the summer. Sierra canyons begin their blooming in June. From then on, it is simply a matter of following spring up the mountainsides. The following grow from the valley floor to the lower mountain slopes, in the scrub communities.

Desert dandelion (*Malacothrix glabrata*). Sunflower family. Spring annual, 4–16 inches high; flower clear yellow; foliage mostly toward the base. Produces masses of color on the open desert and beautifies streetsides and vacant lots in valley communities.

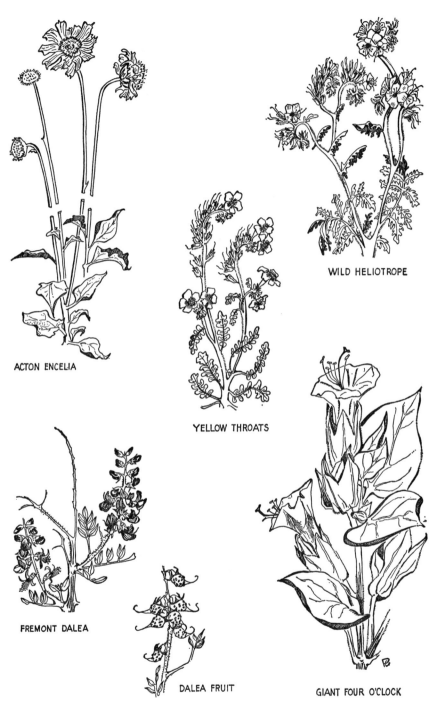

ACTON ENCELIA

WILD HELIOTROPE

YELLOW THROATS

FREMONT DALEA

DALEA FRUIT

GIANT FOUR O'CLOCK

PLANTS OF THE VALLEY FLOOR AND LOWER MOUNTAIN SLOPES

Acton encelia (*Encelia virginensis* ssp. *actoni*). Sunflower family. Low grayish shrub; flower heads solitary at tops of naked stems, 2–3 feet high; flowers yellow, showy and handsome, often blooming before other flowers appear. Usually in shadscale scrub. Blooms April–July.

Wild heliotrope (*Phacelia distans*). Waterleaf family. Annual with upright stem 8 inches to 2 feet high, finely hairy; flowers bluish. A rather tender plant, usually found growing in shrubs to escape grazing animals. Blooms March–June.

Yellow throats (*Phacelia Fremontii*). Waterleaf family. Spreading annual, 2–12 inches high; flower blue to lavender, with yellow tube, all in pastel shades. Common over a wide range and has a long flowering period.

Broad-flowered gilia (*Gilia latiflora*). Phlox family. Slender-stemmed annual, 4–16 inches high; flowers violet to lavender, white and yellow in throats. Leaves mostly basal. There are several similar species of gilia, all dainty plants but often plentiful enough to show as washes of color on the open desert.

Fremont dalea (*Dalea Fremontii*). Pea family. Intricately branched shrub, 1–3 feet high, with smooth whitish bark; flowers deep blue-purple; leaves divided into small leaflets; pods short, grandular-spotted.

Adonis lupine (*Lupinus excubitus*). Pea family. Bush 2–5 feet high with shrubby base; flowers blue to lilac (yellowish center on banner) in widely spaced whorls on stem; foliage gray-green, silvery. This lupine has several growth habits and is divided into subspecies accordingly. The showiest form is found along streams on the outwash slopes of the Sierra, where clumps may be 6 feet in diameter and almost as tall.

Apricot mallow (*Sphaeralcea ambigua*). Mallow family. Perennial, 18 inches–3 feet high; somewhat shrubby at base; erect stems; foliage harsh to the touch, tends to be yellowish with fine hairs. Plant has the appearance of a small hollyhock. Mostly shadscale scrub and creosote bush scrub.

Desert trumpet (*Eriogonum inflatum*). Buckwheat family. Perennial, 8 inches–3 feet high; flowers yellow, minute; smooth green stems inflated in upper portion, as are the main branches; divided repeatedly from top of stem, usually in threes, to form a thread-fine canopy; leaves in a basal tuft, silvery, drying early. This plant has a wide range.

Inyo County is a popular place for buckwheats (*Eriogonum* species). They are numerous and have exceedingly interesting forms. A few, such as sulphur flower (*Eriogonum umbellatum*), have showy blooms, but most species gain attention by their unusual forms and the fact that they endure so well after the blooming season is over. They do not shrivel upon aging, but hold their original shapes and mellow to rich shades of rosy browns. They come in many shapes and sizes, from minute dainty annuals to spreading shrubs. Because of their lasting qualities, they are popular for dried plant arrangements. Varieties of *Eriogonum deflexum* are used for flat-top effects,

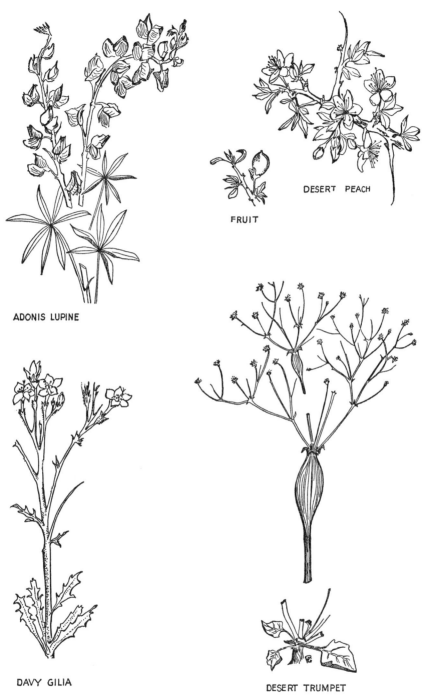

FRUIT

DESERT PEACH

ADONIS LUPINE

DAVY GILIA

DESERT TRUMPET

PLANTS OF THE VALLEY FLOOR AND LOWER MOUNTAIN SLOPES

bird's-nest buckwheat (*Eriogonum nidularium*) is excellent for small trees, and the attractive little saucer plant (*Oxytheca perfoliata*) is a favorite because of its interesting structure.

Desert paintbrush (*Castilleja chromosa*). Figwort family. Perennial, 6–16 inches high; flower bright red; stems leafy throughout. Common in the desert country, this paintbrush is appreciated as the only brilliant accent among the gray shrubs.

Giant four-o'clock (*Mirabilis Froebelii*). Four-o'clock family. Spreading perennial with stems 1–3 feet long; forms loose round mats, often quite large; flowers bright rose-purple, open in the evening; foliage sticky-hairy in the species, which grows in the sagebrush scrub and pinyon-juniper woodland; but the variety *glabrata,* found on the valley floor, has smooth leaves and is even more handsome. Flowers are the same in both types. Especially beautiful in the Blackrock area.

Desert peach (*Prunus Andersonii*). Rose family. Shrub 2–6 feet high, with short, spiny branches; flowers rose-pink, fading to light pink, thickly clustered on the branches; very fragrant; a favorite of bees; blooms early, before the leaves appear; showy in mass effects. Lower canyons and mesas along the Sierra; higher in the desert ranges.

Bitterbrush (*Purshia tridentata*). Rose family. Shrub 3–8 feet high, grayish; flowers cream or pale yellow; leaves small, wedge-shaped, 3-cleft. Ranges from the slopes of sagebrush scrub up into the mountain forests.

Desert bitterbrush (*Purshia glandulosa*) is more prevalent in the desert ranges. It is usually lower, and has smaller, narrower leaves which are green above. Bitterbrush is an essential winter browse plant for deer. Its depletion by fire and overgrazing has become a serious problem. Deer may find other food to eat, but without enough bitterbrush they will die of malnutrition or become subject to disease.

MIXED CONIFEROUS FOREST 7500–9500 feet

True forests with a variety of tall conifers, streamside trees, shrubby areas, and small meadows. Here we leave the narrow stream-cut canyons and enter the glaciated country, with mountain meadows in the broad U-shaped canyons, with 30–60 inches precipitation, heavy snows, 40–70 frost-free days, and growing season 2½–3½ months.

Indicator plants: lodgepole pine (*Pinus Murrayana*) *, Jeffrey pine (*Pinus Jeffreyi*) *, red fir (*Abies magnifica*) *, white fir (*Abies concolor*) *, quaking aspen (*Populus tremuloides*) *, snow bush (*Ceanothus cordulatus*), bush chinquapin (*Castanopsis sempervirens*), Brewer cinquefoil (*Potentilla Breweri*), meadow paintbrush (*Castilleja Culbertsonii*), corn lily (*Veratrum californicum*), western monkshood (*Aconitum columbianum*), Sierra blue gentian (*Gentiana holopetala*), shooting star (*Dodecatheon redolens*), tall angelica (*Angelica lineariloba*) *, blueballs (*Nama Rothrockii*) *, grass of Parnassus

DESERT PAINTBRUSH

APRICOT MALLOW

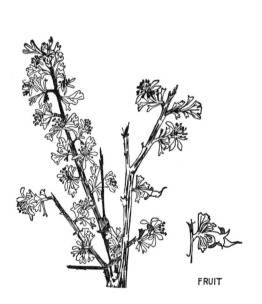

FRUIT

BITTER BRUSH

DESERT DANDELION

PLANTS OF THE VALLEY FLOOR AND LOWER MOUNTAIN SLOPES

(*Parnassia palustris* var. *californica*) *, dwarf daisy (*Erigeron pumilus* ssp. *concinnoides*) *.

We have avoided duplicating plants described in *The Mammoth Lakes Sierra,* in favor of adding new ones. Many of those named above are described in that book.

Lodgepole or **tamarack pine** (*Pinus Murrayana*). Pine family. Most common of our forest trees; its slender, straight trunk was used for log cabins. Needles in twos; bark thin, flaky, smooth, light brownish to reddish; cones the smallest of any pine in the area. The true tamarack is the eastern larch; pioneers applied the term loosely to lodgepole, and here also to foxtail pine. Tamarack Canyon in the Inyos, where bristlecone were cut for aqueduct power poles, was probably thus loosely named.

Red fir (*Abies magnifica*). Pine family. A mighty tree, 60–180 feet tall; branches tend to be short and rigid, in horizontal sprays; young trees beautifully symmetrical; needles curved upward, especially on upper branches; bark of mature trees thick, dark red-brown, roughly ridged and fissured; cones upright, do not fall whole; trunks are brittle and many older trees have been shattered by storms. Usually between 8,000 and 9,000 feet.

White fir (*Abies concolor*). Pine family. 15–70 feet tall; branches tend to be longer, with flatter sprays than those of the red fir; needles twist at base; bark ashy gray, rough, hard and furrowed. As in red fir, the cones do not fall whole, but may be seen standing upright on the upper branches. White fir adapts to a wider range than does red fir. It is not so brittle and has a better chance of enduring mountain storms. It likes sheltered canyons where soil is deep but, surprisingly, it is sometimes found along streams almost out on the desert. Usually between 6500 and 8,000 feet.

Jeffrey pine (*Pinus Jeffreyi*). Pine family. Our most stately pine, 60 to 180 feet high; needles in threes, blue-green, usually 6 inches or more long; bark thick, reddish brown, roughly ridged or in beautiful broad smooth plates on large trees; crevices in bark have a vanilla or pineapple odor; cones large and heavy, 6 inches long or more, with prickles turning inward; trunks sturdy and straight. Scattered in canyons or in solid stands, but never dense, on benches or flats.

Being large and straight, Jeffrey pine was in great demand by early sawmills. Stumps of large trees may still be seen in Sawmill Canyon.

Mountain mahogany (*Cercocarpus ledifolius*). Rose family. Evergreen shrub or small tree, 6–20 feet high; flowers inconspicuous but the silvery-feathery tails of its fruits are distinctive; leaves rigid, dark green above, slightly curled under at edges; foliage has sweet spicy fragrance on warm days. Dry, rocky slopes.

Tall angelica or **Sierra soda straw** (*Angelica lineariloba*). Parsley family. Hardy perennial, 20 inches–5 feet high; flowers white, in large umbels, the stems spreading from a central axis, 3–4 inches across; main stems hollow.

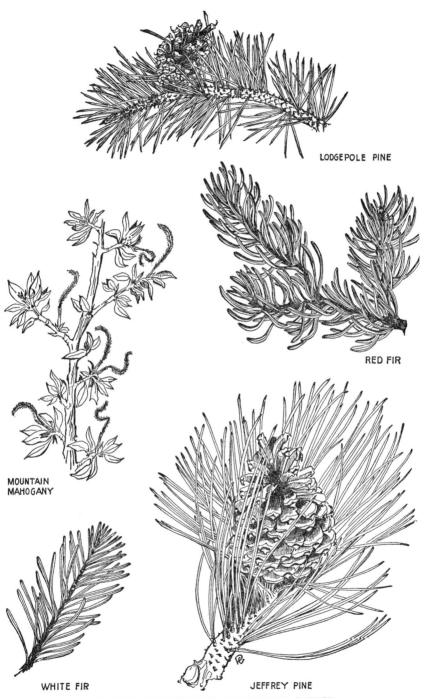

LODGEPOLE PINE

RED FIR

MOUNTAIN
MAHOGANY

WHITE FIR

JEFFREY PINE

PLANTS OF THE MIXED CONIFEROUS FOREST

Gravelly slopes as well as moist places. Dry stems of the previous season, broken between the joints, make excellent drinking straws.

Blueballs (*Nama Rothrockii*). Waterleaf family. Perennial from running rootstocks; stems 6–12 inches high, flowers in dense ball-like heads, blue to lavender; leaves coarsely toothed, glandular and finely hairy. Grows in colonies on sandy slopes or flats.

Grass of Parnassus (*Parnassia palustris* var. *californica*). Saxifrage family. Perennial, with slender, usually naked stems 10–20 inches high; flowers creamy white, veined. Wet places. Blooms July–October.

Bigelow sneezeweed (*Helenium Bigelovii*). Sunflower family. Biennial or perennial; flowers have yellow petals and large brownish ball-shaped centers; leaves long and slender; stems rise leafless, 16–32 inches high, from basal clumps of foliage. Moist places.

Dwarf daisy (*Erigeron pumilus* ssp. *concinnoides*). Sunflower family. Compact little perennial; stems 2–5 inches high; petals purple, numerous and fine; leaves gray, narrow, crowded at base. Dry gravelly slopes.

SUBALPINE FOREST 9500–11,000 feet

Open forests to scattered trees; dwarf wood to trees 40 feet tall; contains some low or prostrate shrubs and a large variety of perennial herbs. A country of broad glacial basins, high mountain lakes and rocky ledges. 30–50 inches of precipitation; killing frost possible throughout the year; growing season 7–9 weeks.

Indicator plants: whitebark pine (*Pinus albicaulis*) *, foxtail pine (*Pinus Balfouriana*) *, limber pine (*Pinus flexilis*) *, lodgepole pine (*Pinus Murrayana*) *, Sierra buckwheat (*Eriogonum marifolium* var. *incanum*), mountain gooseberry (*Ribes montigenum*) *, alpine columbine (*Aquilegia pubescens*) *, western roseroot (*Sedum rosea* ssp. *integrifolium*) *, shrubby cinquefoil (*Potentilla fruticosa*), red heather (*Phyllodoce Breweri*), Labrador tea (*Ledum glandulosum* var. *californicum*) *, mountain penstemon (*Penstemon Newberryi*) *, meadow mimulus (*Mimulus primuloides*) *, alpine gentian (*Gentiana Newberryi*), shooting star (*Dodecatheon redolens*), golden aster (*Happlopappus apargioides*).

Whitebark pine (*Pinus albicaulis*). Pine family. Prostrate to 45 feet tall; needles in fives, dark green; bark thin, smooth and whitish when young, fissured and scaly on mature trees; cones up to 3 inches long, but seldom found entire after maturity; seeds a favorite food of Clark's nutcrackers. The tree adjusts to timberline conditions by hugging the slopes "with its back against the wind," but in more protected locations it is inclined to grow broomlike, with several trunks and branches spreading upright toward the top. It offers the best in sleeping accommodations—snug protected nooks and a generous collection of dry needles. The common tree of timberline.

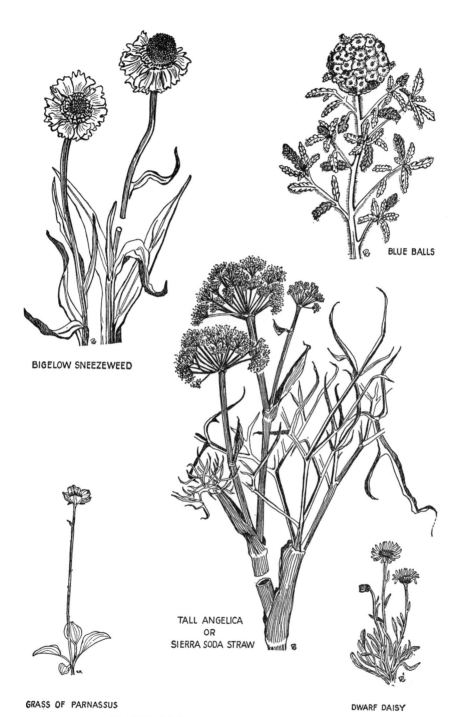

BLUE BALLS

BIGELOW SNEEZEWEED

TALL ANGELICA
OR
SIERRA SODA STRAW

GRASS OF PARNASSUS

DWARF DAISY

PLANTS OF THE MIXED CONIFEROUS FOREST

Foxtail pine (*Pinus Balfouriana*). Pine family. 18–45 feet tall; needles in fives, dark blue-green; young trees slender, with very short branches; mature trees stout and spreading, with conical trunks; bark a rich cinnamon color in open stands, divided into rectangular plates; branchlets pendulous, densely clothed with needles toward the tips, like a bottle brush or fox's tail; cone scales tipped by slender prickles. Dry rocky slopes and ridges. This tree is much like the bristlecone pine.

Alpine columbine (*Aquilegia pubescens*). Buttercup family. Perennial 8–30 inches high; flowers in all pastel shades, large with long slender spurs. Rocky places.

Western roseroot (*Sedum rosea* ssp. *integrifolium*). Stonecrop family. Fleshy little plants, 2½–6 inches high; young ones resemble tiny cabbages; flowers minute, dark purple, at summit of leafy stem. Moist rocky places, often on rocky islands in streams.

Mountain gooseberry (*Ribes montigenum*). Saxifrage family. Scraggling shrub, 1–2 feet high, very spiny; flowers saucer-shape, inconspicuous; berries red, good flavor. Moist rocky places, often where streams run through tumbled rocks.

Labrador tea (*Ledum glandulosum* var. *californicum*). Heath family. Evergreen shrub, 1½–4 feet high, rounded and rather stiff; flowers white in terminal cymes; leaves have a turpentine odor when crushed. Lake borders and boggy places. Sometimes mistaken for rhododendron or azalea to which it is closely related.

FOXTAIL PINE

WHITEBARK PINE

PLANTS OF THE SUBALPINE FOREST

ALPINE COLUMBINE

MOUNTAIN GOOSEBERRY

MOUNTAIN PENSTEMON

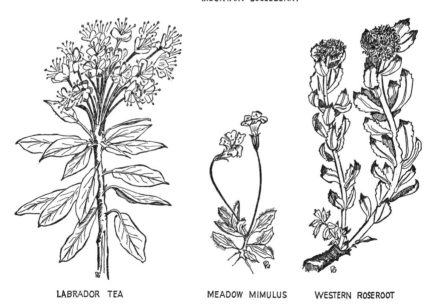

LABRADOR TEA

MEADOW MIMULUS

WESTERN ROSEROOT

PLANTS OF THE SUBALPINE FOREST

Meadow Mimulus (*Mimulus primuloides*). Figwort family. Stems delicate, 2–6 inches high; flower yellow; leaves in a tiny basal rosette, often frosty on upper surface due to hairs which hold moisture. Wet places.

Mountain penstemon (*Penstemon Newberryi*). Figwort family. Low shrubby plant, 4–12 inches high; flowers rose-red, tubular, about 1 inch long; leaves somewhat leathery. Grows along base of rocks.

ALPINE FELL-FIELDS mostly above 10,500 or 11,000 feet.

Almost entirely perennial herbs, forming low turf or scattered among rocks; many cushion plants. High basins, ridges and mountaintops. A place of heavy snows, swept by gales; growing season 4–7 weeks.

Indicator plants: timberline bluegrass (*Poa rupicola*), darkies (*Carex Helleri*), mountain sorrel (*Oxyria digyna*), Shockley ivesia (*Ivesia Shockleyi*), alpine bluegrass (*Poa Suksdorfii*), granite buckwheat (*Eriogonum Ovalifolium* var. *nivale*), Brewer cushion-cress (*Draba Breweri*), Lemmon cushion-cress (*Draba Lemmonii*), prickly locoweed (*Astragalus Kentrophyta* var. *danaus*), alpine paintbrush (*Castilleja nana*), alpine willow (*Salix anglorum* var. *antiplasta*) *, Sierra primrose (*Primula suffrutescens*) *, alpine loco (*Astragalus Ravenii*), sky pilot (*Polemonium eximium*) *, whitestem goldenbush (*Haplopappus macronema*), silver mat (*Raillardella argentea*), alpine gold (*Hulsea algida*) *.

Alpine willow (*Salix anglorum* var. *antiplasta*). Willow family. Creeping shrub, forming mats; erect branches 2–4 inches high, easily identified by upright catkins 1–2 inches long; leaves ¾–1½ inches long, dark green above, paler beneath. Moist places.

Sierra primrose (*Primula suffrutescens*). Primrose family. Stems rather woody, branched, creeping, 4–6 inches high; flowers magenta, fading to pinkish, with yellow throat, usually in showy masses; leaves smooth, crowded. Usually under overhanging rocks or in crevices between them. The only real primrose native to California.

Rose epilobium (*Epilobium obcordatum*). Evening primrose family. Stems from a tufted base 2–6 inches high; flowers rose-purple, fragrant; leaves small, crowded. Rocky places.

Sky pilot (*Polemonium eximium*). Phlox family. Stems 6–10 inches high; flowers blue, in dense heads, fragrant; leaves finely dissected, sticky-glandular, odorous, basal. Rocky ledges and slopes.

Alpine gold (*Hulsea algida*). Sunflower family. Leafy stems 4–12 inches high; flowers like a robust yellow daisy, showy; leaves up to 6 inches long; entire plant sticky-glandular with strong odor. Slopes of peaks. Food for mountain sheep.

The following trees and shrubs grow only along streams or where some underground moisture is available. They are listed, roughly, in order of the elevation at which they are found, beginning on the valley floor.

Fremont cottonwood (*Populus Fremontii*). Willow family. Deciduous tree, 35–90 feet high; leaves 2–3 inches long, yellowish green, alike on both sides; bark whitish, roughly cracked; broad open crown. Usually below 5,000 feet.

Arroyo willow (*Salix lasiolepis*). Willow family. Common deciduous shrub, 6–20 feet high; bark smooth, yellowish to brown; catkins appear before the leaves; leaves 2–4 inches long, dark green and smooth above, lighter be-

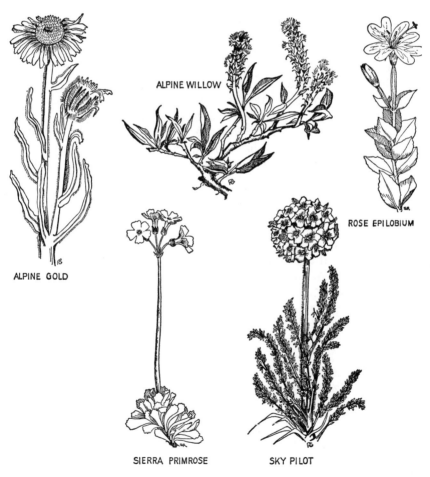

ALPINE WILLOW

ROSE EPILOBIUM

ALPINE GOLD

SIERRA PRIMROSE   SKY PILOT

PLANTS OF THE ALPINE FELL FIELDS

neath. Usually below 7,000 feet. There are many other streamside willows; this one is most common at lower elevations.

Water birch (*Betula occidentalis*). Birch family. Deciduous shrub up to 24 feet tall; leaves 1–2 inches long; bark shining bronze; many trunks from base, usually spreading or leaning outward. Up to 8,000 feet.

Canyon oak (*Quercus chrysolepis*). Oak family. Evergreen spreading tree, 18–60 feet high; leaves vary in shape and size, some spine-toothed; acorns thick, about 1 inch long; cup shallow and thickened, scales hidden by felt-like covering; bark gray, rather smooth, scaly. Usually below 6500 feet.

Black oak (*Quercus Kelloggii*). Oak family. Deciduous tree, 30–75 feet high; leaves bright green above, paler beneath. Acorns about 1 inch long, scales on cup thin, more or less ragged on margins. Trees grow in groups or circles. Groves common along lower base of Sierra and in lower canyons.

Black cottonwood (*Populus trichocarpa*). Willow family. Deciduous tree, 40–60 feet high; leaves 3–5 inches long, dark green above, light beneath; bark grayish, furrowed in age; broad, open crown. Usually between 6,000 and 9,000 feet. Between the black cottonwood and the Fremont cottonwood is a belt of lanceleaf cottonwood (*Populus acuminata*) on some of the valley streams. This tree resembles the former in size and shape of leaf, but those of the lanceleaf are a yellower green and the same on both sides.

Quaking aspen (*Populus tremuloides*). Willow family. Deciduous tree, 6–60 feet tall; leaves ¾–1½ inches long, quake with the slightest breeze; bark smooth, greenish white, showing black scars in age. Usually above 8,000 feet. In fall aspen turn a glowing golden color.

LICHEN

Up the canyons, especially on north slopes, you may notice patches of rust, chartreuse, or black which appear to be colors in the rock itself. Close examination reveals it to be a scaly growth, actually a partnership of organisms known as lichen. An alga and a fungus are the partners in this intimate, mutually beneficial relationship. The fungus extracts its food from the alga, since fungi are not capable of manufacturing their own food from nature. In turn, the fungus protects the alga from drying up. Joined together, these two organisms can live on sun-baked rock slopes where neither could survive alone.

The nondescript lichen is of basic importance to all other plant life. A lichen patch a few inches across may be several hundred years old. It works so slowly, breaking down rock grains and catching particles of dust, it may take a hundred or a thousand years to prepare enough dust-like soil to support larger lichen. They continue the soil-building process; centuries may be needed before there is a tiny pocket of soil capable of supporting grass or a flowering plant.

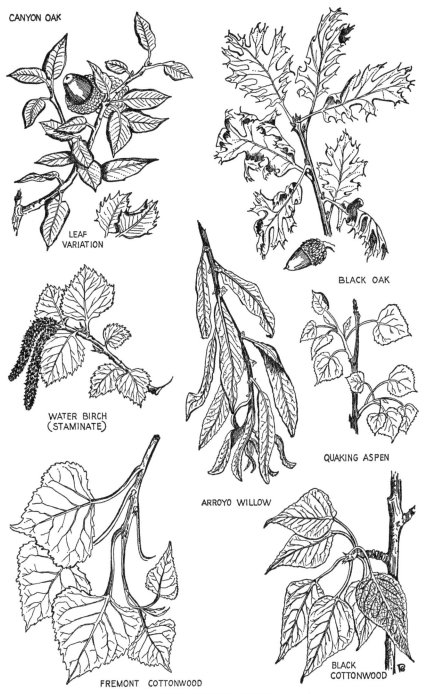

CANYON OAK

LEAF
VARIATION

BLACK OAK

WATER BIRCH
(STAMINATE)

ARROYO WILLOW

QUAKING ASPEN

FREMONT COTTONWOOD

BLACK
COTTONWOOD

STREAMSIDE TREES

Selected Reading

JAEGER, EDMUND C. *Desert Wild Flowers.* Stanford: Stanford Univ. Press, 1950. 322 pp. An excellent handbook.

McMINN, HOWARD E. *Illustrated Manual of California Shrubs.* Berkeley: Univ. Calif. Press, 1959. 663 pp. Useful in Inyo County since so much of the area is in shrubs. For laymen as well as professional botanists.

MUNZ, PHILIP A. *California Desert Wildflowers.* Berkeley: Univ. Calif. Press, 1962. 122 pp. *California Mountain Wildflowers.* Berkeley: Univ. Calif. Press, 1963. 122 pp. Beautifully illustrated handbooks, many color plates and line drawings. Cloth- and paper-bound.

PEATTIE, DONALD C. *A Natural History of Western Trees.* Boston: Houghton Mifflin, 1953. 751 pp.

STORER, JOHN H. *The Web of Life.* New York: Devin-Adair, 1953. 144 pp. Simply written, well illustrated book on one of the most fascinating concepts, the interdependence of all living things. Available also as a 50-cent Mentor paperback, MD288.

STORER, TRACY I. and ROBERT USINGER. *Sierra Nevada Natural History.* Berkeley: Univ. Calif. Press, 1963. 408 pp. A pocket guide identifying common fungi, lichens, mosses, ferns, flowers, trees, insects, fishes, amphibians, reptiles, birds, and mammals. Many illustrations, over 220 in color. Cloth- and paper-bound.

Mammals and Birds

JUST AS PLANT LIFE HAS EVOLVED species adapted to differing climates and environments, so has animal life. To each its own niche. The valley quail, white-tailed ground squirrel, and black-tailed jackrabbit live in the lower parts of Owens Valley; their relatives—mountain quail, golden-mantled ground squirrel, and white-tailed jackrabbit—dwell only in the mountains. There are desert specialists, and still others that live only close to water. A very few, such as the deer, coyote, deer mouse, and raven, are unusually adaptable and range from Valley floor to mountain crests.

However, an individual animal is not restricted to a one-spot habitat as is a plant; an animal need not spend its whole life enduring wind or scorching sunlight on a single exposed slope, but can seek shelter. Some can leave an area entirely—but not so freely as might at first appear, for another individual of the same species (or a competing one) may already have the adjoining region staked out as private territory and be ready to fight to the death for it. Few animals can travel as far as a willow can—in the form of a downy seed in a high wind!

Winter brings serious problems to mountain animals—lack of food and bitter cold. Warm-blooded animals solve these problems in three ways: by migrating, by burrowing, and by hibernating. Some migrating birds travel long distances, such as the western tanager, which breeds in the mountains here and winters in Mexico. Most birds perform vertical migrations, flying to nearby lowlands to pass the winter. Marmots, Belding and golden-mantled ground squirrels, and chipmunks adapt to winter by hibernating. The body temperature of a hibernating animal drops almost to freezing, usually about 40° F. In addition, its heart rate, blood circulation, and other body functions slow down. Most important, probably, is the pronounced decline in metabolic rate, enabling it to survive the long period of food scarcity on a relatively small supply of stored food or fat. Small mammals such as mice escape the cold by burrowing under the snow, where temperatures are rarely below freezing even when it is 20° below zero above the snow.

A few mammals, such as the marten and white-tailed jackrabbit, are able to find sufficient food in winter and are active year round; but in order to survive the rigorous winter, they have bodies well adapted to cold. Winter insulation—layers of fat and thicker fur—enables them to withstand temperatures they could not endure in their summer coats. They are often larger and more chunky than their relatives living in the warmer lowlands. They also have shorter legs, ears, and tails. A large round mammal can keep warmer than a small one because the ratio of its skin surface (by which body heat is lost) to total body weight is less. The white-tailed jackrabbit differs in these ways from its black-tailed desert relative.

[149]

High mountain animals have also had to adapt to a lower concentration of oxygen. They have more red blood cells and hemoglobin, larger hearts and lungs, to utilize the limited oxygen supply better.

Just as some species have evolved adaptations to mountain conditions, so have others evolved equally marvelous adaptations to the harsh desert environment of heat and aridity. Most desert birds migrate from the desert in late spring after nesting. The mule deer migrates in the same way. Other mammals survive the summer's heat and lack of food by going into a summer sleep called estivation, a condition similar to hibernation, with reduced temperature and metabolism. Small mammals burrow, coming out only at night when it is cooler. Those species which are active during the day above ground—such as the white-tailed ground squirrel, coyote, and the birds—get relief by finding shade, by panting, and by licking their fur. Just as the mountain species are larger with shorter extremities, desert species are generally smaller with longer ears and legs, a shape that permits more loss of body heat.

The most extreme adaptations to water shortage are found in the small mammals. The kangaroo rat has gone nearly as far as can be imagined in conserving water. It never drinks water at all, but gets its water from the process of metabolism carried on in its body. Other desert species which drink no water at least eat succulent vegetation, but the kangaroo rat eats dry seeds only. In addition, it neither perspires nor salivates, and its urine is concentrated so that it is semisolid.

The great variety of animal life found in the Owens Valley region, then, is here not in spite of, but *because* of the great variety of climates and habitats. In fact, this region is one of the richest in North America in variety of animals. Since it is on the boundary of three great animal and plant communities—the Mojave Desert, the Sierra Nevada, and the Great Basin—species from all three occur here. There are about one hundred species of mammals, and one hundred species of birds in summer.

As you camp and hike the Sierra, you are sure to see many animals, for the roads and trails are along creeks where animals are concentrated. In contrast, as you drive the Valley floor or the Bristlecone Pine Road, you may see very few. But don't conclude that the desert country has no life. In the Valley you see fewer animals simply because many are nocturnal. In the White Mountains there are few animals on the bare ridges where the road lies. You may be surprised that there are almost as many varieties in the "barren" desert as in the Sierra. There are 66 species of breeding birds listed for Owens Valley, 65 for the Sierra, and 49 for the Inyo and White mountains. There are about 58 mammal species in the Valley, 62 in the Sierra, and 42 in the Inyo-Whites.

Because the big-eared kit or desert fox is nocturnal, you will rarely see it. Unfortunately, its numbers have been markedly reduced by poison bait set out for coyotes. It is more common in the southern half of the Valley, rarely occurring near Bishop.

The small ball of fur that scampers across roads in daytime, with tail held over the back so its white underside is nearly all that is visible, is the white-tailed ground squirrel. It is often mistaken for a chipmunk. This squirrel is found up to at least 7,000 feet, at Westgard Pass. Since these active little mammals do not hibernate, they may be seen throughout the winter, although they are inactive during bad weather.

The California or Beechey ground squirrel estivates in June or July, then passes into the more profound state of hibernation, and does not emerge until February. Thus it escapes from adverse conditions for eight months of each year.

While you may seldom see the woodrats, you may find their large jumbled nests in trees, rocks, or cactus. The desert woodrat characteristically occurs in the Valley. Woodrats are not like rats; they are very clean, and make fine pets, except that they are active only at night. The dusky-footed woodrat, a much larger form, is oddly distributed. It is found on the Valley floor south of Aberdeen, particularly along the banks of the river; but it does not seem to occur in the Valley near Bishop, nor in the White Mountains, though it is found to 10,000 feet in the Sierra.

The enormous ears of the common black-tailed jackrabbit led to his being named after the jackass. This hare ranges to at least 9,000 feet in the mountains. (Hares differ from true rabbits in that they nest above ground rather than in burrows, and have young which are active when born.)

The desert cottontail is a true rabbit, and may be distinguished from the jackrabbit by its shorter ears, white tail, and smaller size.

The area's unique mammal is the tule or dwarf elk, native to the Central Valley, and there hunted almost to extinction. Tule elk were introduced here in 1933. They range the Valley from Lone Pine to Bishop, and up to about 8,000 feet in the mountains on both sides. Elk are often found along the Owens River and in the Poverty Hills–Red Mountain area.

Recently there has been considerable controversy over the elk. Some cattlemen would like to see the elk herd either eliminated or drastically reduced. Other people want the elk completely protected. Between these two views are the sportsmen who want some elk to hunt. The crux of the controversy is that elk compete with cattle for food. Whatever the elk eat is just that much less for cattle. In addition, elk often bolt through fences, rather than jumping them, and feed on and trample ranchers' alfalfa fields. The policy of the Fish and Game Commission is to maintain 250–300 elk in Owens Valley, and to allow controlled hunts when the number approaches the upper limit. They wish to perpetuate the rare species, yet keep its numbers down so that it does not overgraze its range nor interfere unduly with ranching. The Committee for the Preservation of the Tule Elk believes that until there has been a thorough study, it is premature to say whether the herd is too large or too small. It hopes to see an elk refuge established. (For a copy of its free booklet, "History of the California Tule Elk," write 5502 Markland Drive, Los Angeles 22.)

WIDELY DISTRIBUTED MAMMALS

The **deer mouse,** California's most abundant mammal, has the widest altitudinal distribution of any North American small mammal. The local subspecies is found from Death Valley to the top of White Mountain Peak. You will see the deer mouse most often at night as it scurries across roads, appearing all white in car headlights.

The **Inyo mule deer** is another species that may be found at nearly any altitude and in any plant community. In spring, deer move into the mountains, and stay until snow drives them down. However, some deer remain in the Valley in summer. In winter, deer occur only at low elevations, below the snow line.

The Fish and Game Department manages the deer herds, their goal being to maintain healthy herds in balance with available feed. Usually there is plenty of summer range, but winter range is the key to the size of the herd. If there are too many deer, they will overgraze the plants, causing permanent damage to the range; in addition some deer will starve and others will be malnourished. When herds are out of balance with their range, the Commission recommends late-season doe shoots (after fawns are weaned) and issues a limited number of permits.

Fish and Game personnel believe that in the absence of former predators the deer herds in certain parts of Owens Valley can get too large. They cite the badly overgrazed winter range in the Buttermilk Country, Swall Meadow, and south of Cottonwood Creek, where the bitterbrush is not thrifty and there are too few young and middle-aged plants. Some local groups support doe shoots, believing they will benefit the deer in the long run. Others oppose them. Among the reasons given by those opposed are: (1) there used to be many more deer in the region than there are now; (2) there are too few, rather than too many deer; (3) Fish and Game deer counts are too high; (4) killing does will only reduce the herds further; (5) there is plenty of winter range, even in the dry years. The crux of the matter is whether the winter range is or is not overgrazed. Evidence of overgrazing seems compelling. If it is indeed overgrazed, then we have a choice either of supplying additional range for deer or of finding some appropriate way of keeping deer numbers in balance with the existing range capacity.

KIT FOX

COYOTE

WOOD RAT AND NEST

DEER MOUSE

LEAST CHIPMUNK

DESERT COTTONTAIL

WHITE TAILED GROUND SQUIRREL

TULE ELK

MULE DEER

WHITE TAIL BLACK TIP

BIGHORN MOUNTAIN SHEEP

OWENS VALLEY MAMMALS

It is important not to bother baby animals, particularly fawns, that appear to be lost. Usually the mother is nearby, waiting to resume care of her baby. If you fondle it, the mother may desert it because of the human scent.

The coyote too may be found at any altitude, usually in more open country. You can hear the yelping chorus of the coyotes anywhere away from the towns, especially on moonlight nights. The chief food of the coyote is the jackrabbit, plus other smaller rodents. Strangely, coyotes are often called cowardly because their refuge from danger lies in their speed.

The coyote is another animal over which there is repeated controversy. Some claim there are too many coyotes. Sportsmen and cattlemen (by no means unanimously) have been the chief proponents of coyote control in Owens Valley recently. One group cites the damage coyotes do to game—pheasant, duck, quail, and fawns—and proposes a bounty to reduce their numbers. Ranchers and farmers, citing the loss of chickens and newly born calves, propose that a professional trapper be hired. They fear that a bounty would result in too many coyotes being eliminated and consequent rodent damage to crops and fields.

MOUNTAIN MAMMALS

There are several species of chipmunks in the mountains on either side of the Valley. The only species found in both mountains is the least chipmunk, restricted to the pinyon-juniper woodland, above 6,000 feet.

The golden-mantled ground squirrel is found on both sides of the Valley, and ranges in the Inyo-Whites from 7,000 to 14,000 feet. It can be distinguished from the chipmunks by the two stripes on its sides (rather than four) and the lack of striping on its head. These commonly seen mammals are active from April until October, when they hibernate.

The yellow-bellied marmot is a close relative of the woodchuck of the east. From May until September you are likely to see it running across a meadow or basking on a rock, above 10,000 feet in the Inyo-Whites, above 8,000 feet in the Sierra.

The bushy-tailed woodrat, one of the fabled pack rats of western lore, is related to the valley woodrats.

The white-tailed jackrabbit (Sierra hare) replaces the black-tailed above 9,000 feet. This hare, erroneously called snowshoe rabbit because it turns white in winter, has been seen on the very summit of White Mountain Peak. After loss of its white coat, it can be identified by its white tail and large size. The mountain cottontail occurs at about 10,000 feet. These two animals have the same relationship as the black-tailed jackrabbit and the desert cottontail in the Valley.

The pine marten is found in the Sierra, but not in the Inyo-Whites. An arboreal weasel, it lives mainly on tree squirrels (chickarees), which are not found east of the Valley. It sometimes robs fishermen's creels and catches left to cool on snowbanks, though it is cautious and rarely seen.

The wary, seldom-seen **bighorn** or **mountain sheep** live in both ranges, the Sierra bighorn in the Sierra, the desert bighorn in the Inyo-Whites. Once widely distributed in California, sheep are now found only in a few of the ranges. The bighorn is a wilderness animal that cannot tolerate human disturbance. The decrease in their numbers is due to several factors: heavy and uncontrolled livestock grazing in high mountain areas, which severely depleted the forage; infectious diseases and parasites from domestic livestock; human disturbance, particularly the appropriation of desert springs; and poaching. In summer sheep occur only near the mountain crests. In winter they migrate below the deep snow. Sierra sheep may be seen in the foothills near Independence.

The following additional mammals are described in our companion book, *The Mammoth Lakes Sierra:* Panamint kangaroo rat, striped skunk, porcupine, Belding ground squirrel, lodgepole and alpine chipmunks, chickaree, Shasta beaver, and pika (cony).

VALLEY BIRDS

The large **black-billed magpie** is one of the most conspicuous Valley birds, and a valuable one for his scavenging. You will see many of these long-tailed black and white birds perched on fences or eating car-killed animals on the highway.

The gurgling song of the **western meadowlark** is so penetrating you can hear it great distances across open fields, even as you whiz by in your car. This chunky brown bird has a bright yellow breast crossed by a black V.

When spring brings abundant insects, the **Texas nighthawk** appears. On summer evenings you may often see it foraging with bats, feeding entirely on the wing, and flying low and swiftly over open country. Slim tapered wings, white-barred at their tips, identify it easily.

Almost anywhere in the Valley, particularly in the brushy foothills near water, one may see coveys of **valley quail** scurrying along, their feathered topknots bobbing as they go. The forward-tipped topknot distinguishes this lowlander from the forest-dwelling **mountain quail,** which has a slender upward-pointing plume.

The glossy black **raven** is one of the most widely distributed birds; the same species occurs around the world. Here you will find ravens from the Valley floor to at least 12,500 feet, though it rarely goes so high in winter. Ravens are often confused with their smaller relatives the **crows,** which are extremely rare east of the Sierra. You can distinguish the two by their calls and their manner of flight. Crows have a raucous caw and fly with continuous, vigorous flapping. Ravens have a deep throaty croak, a longer tail, and alternate flapping with soaring.

Smallest of the hawk family, the brightly marked **sparrow hawk** commonly perches on power lines, good vantage points for hunting. In summer this swift falcon can also be found in the mountains up to 12,000 feet, where it seeks grasshoppers and mice in the meadows.

The **horned lark** is a year-round resident which nests on the Valley floor in spring, moves to higher brush country in summer, then returns ahead of advancing snows to winter on the desert. It also nests higher, in the White Mountains. Its head and throat are marked with black and white; unique black ear-tufts give it its name.

The comical **roadrunner,** a ground dwelling cousin of the cuckoo, prefers the sparsely vegetated creosote plains, where it hunts for lizards and snakes, using the skins of victims to line its rude nest of sticks and cactus thorns.

MOUNTAIN BIRDS

The large, striking **chukar partridge,** native to southeast Europe and Asia, has been introduced as a game bird. It competes with native quail for habitat and food. Adaptable to both desert and mountain climates, it ranges from 4,000 to about 13,000 feet, though it seems to prefer rocky canyons. Chukars winter in the lower snow-free canyons and throughout the Valley. Black-barred flanks and a striking red bill accent its slate gray plumage.

A large woodpecker with an appetite for ants, the **red-shafted flicker** ranges from creosote deserts in winter to pine forests in summer. In flight, vermilion underwings contrast brightly with its salt-and-pepper plumage.

In the Sierra, the black-hooded **Oregon junco** outnumbers any other bird. White outer tail feathers flash conspicuously as a flock flies off. Juncos nest in the mountains. In winter mixed flocks of several kinds of juncos occur in the Valley.

There are several kinds of hummingbirds in the area. In desert and brush habitats the magenta-throated **Costa hummer** predominates. At higher elevations you will find the tiny **calliope hummer,** with flashing reddish throat feathers.

In the pinyon-juniper woodland of the drier mountain slopes you will find the **piñon jay,** a bluish gray, crowlike bird with a peculiar mewing call. In winter noisy bands scatter in search of ripe pine nuts. In the mixed coniferous forests, campers will see the crested, cobalt blue **Steller's jay.** Higher yet lives another crowlike bird, the gray and white **Clark's nutcracker.** Both are noisy, inquisitive scavengers around campsites, and have earned the name of "camp robbers" for their bold tactics. The nutcracker is one of the truly alpine birds of the area. In summer you will hear its harsh rattling call among the timberline pines. The better you get to know the high country, the less harsh the bird sounds. You may see it whacking pine cones open with its stout black bill; it also feeds on the abundant grasshoppers of high meadows.

RED-SHAFTED FLICKER

WHITE RUMP

SALMON RED

PIÑON JAY

BLACK

OREGON JUNCO

RUSTY

CHUKAR PARTRIDGE

RED
WHITE

CALLIOPE HUMMINGBIRD

NUTCRACKER

MOUNTAIN BIRDS

SPARROW HAWK

VALLEY QUAIL

MEADOW-LARK

MAGPIE

WHITE WING BARS

RAVEN

NIGHTHAWK

VALLEY BIRDS

[157]

For pictures and descriptions of other common mountain birds—hermit thrush, chickadee, bluebird, tanager, white-crowned sparrow, finches, water ouzel—see *The Mammoth Lakes Sierra.*

MIGRANT BIRDS

Many species are only seasonal visitors, annually flying through the Valley on their way to and from distant nesting grounds. Among the first spring tourists are the warblers, small, active, yellow insect eaters: the tiny **Wilson's warbler,** bright yellow with a velvety black cap; the **yellow-throat,** distinctively marked with a black mask across its eyes; and the gray-hooded MacGillavray's warbler. A flock of the sleek, tawny, crested **cedar waxwings,** birds with red-tipped wings and yellow-edged tails, might go unnoticed as they perch motionless in a leafless tree, but their high-pitched lisping call gives them away. In fall they reappear on their southward flight, frequenting garden shrubs to feed on berries.

WATER BIRDS

When Owens Valley had many swamps and lakes, it was an important flyway for migrating water birds. Still, wherever open water affords a resting place for tired travelers, there is a steady succession of ducks and geese flying thousands of miles to and from their northern nesting grounds. Most stop only briefly in the Valley. Look for them at Little Lake, Haiwee and Tinemaha reservoirs, Dirty Sock, Klondike Lake, Fish Slough, in the willow thickets along the Owens River, and in irrigation canals. A few stay over and nest, so that any permanent body of water has its **mudhens** and **ruddy ducks.** Some water birds winter in the area.

Among the migrants are the handsome **pintails,** with white necks and chocolate brown heads. Usually with them are numbers of dumpy **shovelers,** the sportsman's spoonie, with black and white plumage, orange feet, and a very broad bill. The familiar **mallard** is often outnumbered by its half-size cousins of the teal family. **Green-winged teal,** with bright cinnamon heads and white rump patches, usually predominate, but there are also large numbers of the unmistakable red-brown **cinnamon teal.** Most female ducks are an unpretentious mottled brown, and difficult to identify.

The first appearance of the flight formations of Canada **geese** in autumn and spring is always a thrilling sight. These dark, heavy-bodied birds, with white bands across their throats, seek marshy grasslands and cultivated fields for daytime foraging.

Two often confused species are the **white pelican** and the rare **whistling swan,** large white birds with broad wingspans which resemble each other in flight. Their resemblance is detrimental to the swan, for although it is protected, the pelican is not. On the water, however, the pelican's profile— short neck and satchel-size bill—is unmistakable.

Shallow marshes provide ideal nesting environments for wading birds. The striking black and white **avocet** places its nest wherever standing water permits it to keep eggs moist during incubation. Avocet colonies often adjoin nesting grounds of the **black-necked stilt,** similar in build and color, but marked with bright red legs. A special treat is the occasional sight of the **snowy egret.** Adults are pure white, with black legs and bill, and in spring have long backward-curving plumes on their heads.

Selected Reading

ALLEN, DURWARD. *Our Wildlife Legacy.* New York: Funk and Wagnalls, 1954. 422 pp. The intricate and vital relationships animals have with all that surrounds them.

BROWN, VINSON. *The Sierra Nevadan Wildlife Region.* Healdsburg: Naturegraph Co., 1962. Handbook of plants and animals, arranged by communities.

BROWN, VINSON and H. G. WESTON, JR. *Handbook of California Birds.* Healdsburg: Naturegraph Co., 1961. 156 pp. 368 birds. Helpful diagrams of bills, feet, patterns of flight, foraging behavior.

BURT, W. H. and R. P. GROSSENHEIDER. *A Field Guide to the Mammals.* Boston: Houghton Mifflin, 1952. 200 pp. Widely used by experts as well as beginners.

CALIFORNIA DEPARTMENT OF FISH AND GAME. *Big Game.* 56 pp. *Upland Game.* 40 pp. *Waterfowl.* 32 pp. Concise, well-illustrated booklets. 25 cents each from Documents Section, North Seventh Street at Richards Blvd., Sacramento 14.

INGLES, L. G. *Mammals of California.* Stanford: Stanford Univ. Press, 1954. 396 pp.

PETERSON, ROGER T. *A Field Guide to Western Birds.* Boston: Houghton Mifflin, 1961. 365 pp. The most widely used bird guide, for beginner and expert.

SUMNER, LOWELL, and JOSEPH S. DIXON. *Birds and Mammals of the Sierra Nevada.* Berkeley: Univ. Calif. Press, 1953. 484 pages.

Fish

WHEN IT COMES TO FISHING IN INYO COUNTY, things aren't what they used to be. And it's a lucky thing, too! Before the coming of white men, the Owens River drainage contained no trout and only a few species of rough fish: suckers, chubs, dace and pupfish. The majority of the waters were devoid of fish life. The Kern River drainage, however, contained native rainbow trout in the lower areas and golden trout in the upper tributaries. Early settlers began transplanting these fish to barren waters, usually scattering a few fish here and there from buckets or coffee pots. Lahontan cutthroat were among the first trout to be transplanted into this region. Supposedly they were brought in water barrels hung on freight wagons from the Walker River drainage, where they are native. Rainbow, eastern brook, and brown trout were first introduced around 1900, by consignments from the state and federal governments.

Construction of the Mount Whitney State Fish Hatchery in 1917 was the first major step in the establishment of large-scale stocking programs throughout the eastern Sierra. Operations there have continued to expand; it is now one of the state's most important trout-rearing facilities. Later, rearing facilities were constructed at Hot Creek, Fish Springs, and Black-rock Springs. Ideally located on excellent water supplies, they produce well over 200 tons of trout annually.

When fishing pressures on roadside waters increased to a point where satisfactory angling could no longer be maintained by planting fingerling trout, it became necessary to rear and plant larger-sized trout. Thus evolved the catchable trout program. Changes in bag limits reflect the human population expansion: 50 trout could be legally taken in 1919, but only 10 may be taken today. Highly developed broodstocks of spring- and fall-spawning strains of rainbow trout are kept at Mount Whitney and Hot Creek hatcheries. These fish have been selectively bred to provide rapid growth and resistance to disease. Eggs from both strains provide catchable trout, which average eight inches long. Catchable rainbows are expensive (about 17 cents each to produce and stock), but they are efficiently utilized—and anglers spend far more than that to get them out of the stream. Studies in Inyo-Mono reveal that from 75 to nearly 100 per cent are caught.

Back-country lakes are still planted with fingerling trout, now mostly by air. Mortality of trout planted by air is light, and planting costs are much less than by pack train. Air-planted fish are usually released "free-fall" several hundred feet above the water, and drift down like falling leaves. Upon hitting the water, the fish quickly seek cover in the shoreline areas. In some lakes, spawning conditions are sufficient for a fish population to maintain itself entirely by natural spawning, and planting is unnecessary. In others, natural spawning must be supplemented by planting. Where no spawning areas exist, the entire population consists of planted trout. Goldens, browns, and brookies are planted only as fingerlings; rainbow are planted as fingerlings as well as catchables.

Eastern Sierra fishermen are fortunate in having dozens of lakes and streams accessible by car, where they can take the planted catchables. They are doubly blessed to have, in addition, countless back-country waters within a few hours' ride or hike. The "out-of-this-world" fishing—where you may catch larger, natural-spawned fish—is, of course, not accessible by car. Fish in the back country maintain their populations and grow large for the very reason that they *are* less accessible; fishing pressure is less because fewer fishermen take the time and trouble to travel far by trail. Next time there are plans to build new roads to make the back country "more accessible," sportsmen may well ponder this paradox. No lake or stream can produce enough fish naturally to supply the crowds that come with roads. They have to be planted with hatchery catchables, and then offer no more variety or thrill than other roadside waters.

NATIVE RAINBOW IN BACK-COUNTRY LAKES

Shortly after the breakup of ice in springtime, adult fish enter tributary streams to spawn, depositing their eggs several inches deep in the gravel of the stream bottom. These eggs develop slowly in the cold water, generally hatching within a couple of months. The young trout are nourished for a short time by the yolk sac attached to their bodies, but soon learn to feed on small organisms. As they grow, their main diet consists of terrestrial and aquatic insects. Some of these trout remain in the stream, but the majority enter the lake. Here their main diet consists of immature forms of a mosquito-like midge, which abound in most high mountain lakes. Only a small percentage of young trout survive to adulthood. Various predators take their toll, the principal one being larger trout. By the end of the first growing season, a young rainbow may be several inches long. By the end of the second season, if food is adequate, it will be over six inches. If it survives into its third year, it may be nine inches or more.

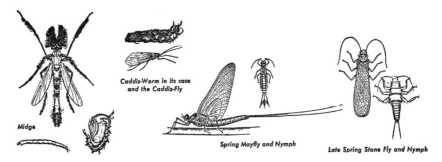

Midge

Caddis-Worm in its case
and the Caddis-Fly

Spring Mayfly and Nymph

Late Spring Stone Fly and Nymph

Favorite Trout Food (courtesy American Nature Association)

Habitat exerts a great influence upon trout growth. Whereas a two-year-old trout in the high country may be six inches, a trout of the same age in a lower, richer habitat (such as Crowley Lake) may be twelve inches long and weigh over a pound. Because food is less available in the wintertime, and cold decreases the trout's activity, most growth occurs during the warmer summer season.

The mountain lakes generally freeze during the winter. Freezing occurs only on the surface, usually to a depth of a foot or so. It is a common misconception that lakes "freeze solid" during winter. Snowfall on top of the ice acts as an insulator, preventing further freezing. Water temperatures range from slightly above 32° F. to 39° F. Trout, being cold-blooded, are not active during this cold period. They will, however, feed if organisms are available. Occasionally winter kill will occur, and many dead fish will be observed on a lake bottom after the ice breakup. Ordinarily this is the result of oxygen depletion in the water, usually caused by the decomposition of organic matter.

FISH OF THE OWENS RIVER AND FISH SLOUGH

The fishery of the Owens River is unique in that various warmwater species, in addition to trout, can be taken. More than one hundred miles of river exist between the mouth of the Owens River Gorge and the Aqueduct intake near Aberdeen; this section is open to year-round fishing. Brown and rainbow trout abound in the Owens, providing the bulk of the fishery, although an occasional largemouth or smallmouth bass, bluegill, channel catfish, or carp is also taken. Brown bullheads are common particularly below Bishop. None of these species is native to the Owens River drainage; all have been introduced.

The Department of Fish and Game has made experimental plants of smallmouth bass and channel catfish in the hope that these species will sustain good natural fisheries in the lower portion of the river.

The completion of Pleasant Valley Dam in 1954 blocked off areas in Rock and Pine creeks which were formerly utilized by spawning brown trout. To compensate for this, in 1962 the Los Angeles Department of Water and Power completed an artificial spawning channel below the dam, immediately adjacent to the river. The channel was designed to provide ideal water flows and gravel and was utilized for the first time by spawning brown trout in the fall of 1962.

Fish Slough provides good angling for largemouth bass and brown bullheads. Supplied by springs of about 65° F., the stream provides a more suitable habitat for the bass than does the Owens River.

It is presently legal to fish for black bass and catfish year-round. In addition, you may fish for catfish at night in Inyo County. To keep up-to-date, consult current California Sport Fishing Regulations.

TROUT SPECIES

There are approximately 200 lakes in Inyo County. Of these, 99 contain eastern brook, 98 rainbow, 40 golden, 7 brown trout, 7 cutthroat, and 49 contain two or more species. Of 46 streams, 20 contain eastern brook, 45 rainbow, 3 golden, 32 brown trout, and 40 contain two or more species. For descriptions of the distinctive markings of the various species, see *The Mammoth Lakes Sierra*.

Golden trout (*Salmo aguabonita* Jordan). The golden trout, California's state fish, is unique and native to the southern Sierra, specifically to certain tributaries of the upper Kern River. Prized for its unbelievably brilliant color, this gold-sided, scarlet-bellied trout was among the first to be transplanted to other High Sierra waters.

The various tributary streams of the upper Kern were originally inhabited by the Kern River rainbow trout (*Salmo gairdnerii gilberti* Jordan). Natural barriers (waterfalls created by lava flows) on certain of these streams isolated the fish populations from the parent stocks, the isolated fish gradually evolving into the golden trout of today. Many factors undoubtedly were involved in the evolutionary processes. The similarity in the coloration of riparian geological formations (especially the brilliant white and yellowish sand beds of their native streams) to the trout's colors suggests that this may have exerted much influence in the development of the golden's unparalleled beauty. Although fish taxonomists differ, golden trout are now generally classified as *Salmo aguabonita* and are differentiated into two subspecies: *Salmo aguabonita aguabonita* Jordan, from the South Fork of the Kern, and *Salmo aguabonita whitei* Evermann, from the Little Kern drainage. The greater number of black spots, especially the presence of spots below the lateral line, is said to distinguish the latter from the former.

Golden trout are well adapted to high, cold waters. When transplanted to lower, warmer habitats, their gleaming colors fade to dull grays and reds. One of the most significant golden trout transplants occurred in 1876, when thirteen fish from Mulkey Creek (tributary to the South Fork of the Kern) were transported in a coffee pot to Cottonwood Creek in Inyo County. These fish became well established, and in 1891 about a hundred were taken past impassable waterfalls and transplanted upstream in the Cottonwood Lakes. With completion of the Mount Whitney Hatchery, facilities were available to rear goldens; beginning in 1918, the Cottonwood Lakes were utilized as a source of golden trout eggs. They continue to be the state's primary source. Golden trout throughout the west are all descendants of the original Cottonwood Lakes stock. Each spring (generally by early June) crews from Mount Whitney Hatchery go on horseback to Cottonwood Lakes. When the fish are ready for spawning, eggs are stripped from the females, fertilized, and loaded onto pack mules for the trip down to the roadhead. Much of this trip is usually made over deep snow, and early June can still bring rugged weather.

About six weeks after the eggs reach the hatchery, the young trout begin to hatch. In two months, usually early September, they are ready for planting.

Goldens hybridize readily with rainbows. Where these two species occur together, fish are found ranging from pure golden to pure rainbow. Although hybrids are generally sterile, progeny of two closely related species sometimes produce offspring with sufficient fertility to maintain a self-sustaining population; this is believed to occur in golden-rainbow crosses.

Golden trout are generally found above 9,000 feet. The Cottonwood Lakes are famous for their goldens; they also occur in some lakes of the Pine, Bishop, Big Pine, and Independence creek drainages.

Rainbow trout (*Salmo gairdnerii* Richardson). The rainbow trout is a very game fish, in back-country waters generally a better fighter than the eastern brook. During the height of the vacation season, hatchery trucks usually plant catchable-size rainbow at weekly intervals in most Inyo roadside waters. Another strain of rainbow, the Kamloops, prized by fly fishermen for its fighting qualities, has been introduced into Long, Sabrina, and South lakes in the Bishop Creek drainage.

Brown trout (*Salmo trutta* Linné). When brown trout were first introduced into California waters, two subspecies were recognized, the Loch Leven and the German Brown, since the original stocks came from Scotland and Germany. Because of extensive crossing, both in the hatchery and in the wild, all such trout in California are now properly referred to as brown trout.

Browns are generally able to sustain their populations through natural reproduction, and stocking is necessary only in lakes without suitable spawning conditions. Because brown trout are wary, they are hard to catch. Frequently they grow large and, to sustain themselves, feed largely on smaller fish. This is not because they are more predaceous than other trout, but because the wary brown lives long enough to reach a size where it can no longer subsist on insects alone. Brown trout are abundant in the Owens River and in the lower reaches of tributary streams. Good populations also exist in Pleasant Valley Reservoir, and in the various forks of Bishop Creek as far up as the reservoirs. North Lake has some real tackle busters in it; browns up to ten pounds have been taken there.

Lahontan cutthroat trout (*Salmo clarkii henshawi* Gill and Jordan). The cutthroat trout is a beautiful fish, heavily spotted over the entire body. In the spring spawning season the males turn a brilliant rosy color. Its name was derived from the red slash marks on the membrane between the jawbones. It interbreeds readily with rainbow. Although this species was at one time abundant in the Bishop Creek drainage, it has been replaced by brown, rainbow, and eastern brook trout. The cutthroat seems to do best in waters where it is not forced to compete with other species. Cutthroats are scarce in Inyo County, but may be found in a few lakes in the headwaters of Pine, Bishop, and Williamson creeks.

Eastern brook trout (*Salvelinus fontinalis* Mitchill). Although technically the eastern brook is a char and not a trout, the "brookie" will be considered a trout for this discussion. It is well adapted to mountain lakes and streams. Very prolific, in some lakes it becomes so abundant that there is not enough food, and stunting results. In some overpopulated eastern brook lakes, ten-year-old fish may be only six inches long. When this happens, the species is removed by chemical treatment of the water and the lakes replanted with a less prolific species. Because of its prolific nature, eastern brook may occasionally crowd out other species, generally in lakes where adequate spawning conditions are not available for the other fish. The brookie is unique among eastern Sierra trout in that it spawns successfully in lakes, where other species require flowing streams; it spawns in streams also, when they are available. Eastern brook and brown trout spawn in the fall; other trout here spawn in spring. The brookie is one of the most flavorful of all trout. It is found commonly throughout the back country and in the upper reaches of many roadside streams.

FISHING HINTS

There seem to be as many theories on how to catch fish as there are fishermen. Fishing is best generally in early morning or late evening hours, when trout tend to feed. Artificial flies are especially effective at these times. If you have trouble fishing with conventional fly tackle, use a spinning outfit and a plastic bubble, with about six feet of light leader between the bubble and fly; you will be amazed at the distance you can achieve. Carry several patterns of flies (light and dark) of different sizes; keep trying them until you find one the fish like.

For mid-day fishing, lures and bait are the best bet. Cover your hook carefully with bait, and *move* it occasionally by giving your reel handle a couple of turns. If you keep losing your bait on snags, try a cork or plastic float to lift your bait a few inches off the bottom. If you use lures, carry a varied assortment, and practice your retrieve to simulate the movement of a small fish. A lure retrieved too rapidly will attract nothing but sore muscles in your reeling arm.

In fishing for browns in a lake, use lures and spinners, for as a rule the big fish are always taken trolling. Some rigs are: 1) a big spinner with a couple of polished attractor blades followed by a gob of worms about eighteen inches behind the second blade; 2) your favorite lure, or a plastic minnow; 3) a lure with a spinner. Troll slowly and deep enough so you will reach the lunkers. It may be necessary to place several ounces of weight on your line to get the lure deep enough. For bait fishing, since browns generally do not take salmon eggs, a gob of worms completely covering the hook is best. Worms are hard to beat for stream fishing, also—if you can withstand the disdain of anglers who see you using worms. Use a leader hookup which is just heavy enough to play and land the fish; if you use too heavy a leader, the big browns won't give you a tumble. If the current is swift, weight your leader with a couple of shot about eighteen inches ahead of the hook to get the bait to the bottom where the browns hang out. With lures, try to drop them beneath undercut banks, where the browns are likely to be resting. Plastic minnows are your best bet for getting a really big brown in a stream.

Fishing success seems to drop off during a full moon. One theory is that then trout feed at night. However, there are always a few hungry fish available, regardless of the phase of the moon. For good fishing with a minimum of competition and a maximum of scenery, try the fall months after Labor Day crowds have dispersed and the leaves begin to turn. The mountains are not ready for winter yet, but they are quite ready for you.

Selected Reading

CURTIS, BRIAN. "The Golden Trout of Cottonwood Lakes," *Transactions of the American Fisheries Society*. Vol. 64, 1934, pp. 259–265.

EVERMANN, BARTON WARREN. "The Golden Trout of the Southern High Sierras," *Bulletin of the Bureau of Fisheries*. Vol. XXV, 1905, pp. 1–51.

WALES, JOSEPH H. *Trout of California*. Sacramento: Department of Fish and Game, 1957. 56 pp. Authoritative, well-illustrated booklet. 25 cents from Documents Section, North Seventh St. at Richards Blvd., Sacramento 14.

History

THROUGHOUT OWENS VALLEY, RE-minders of long-gone people will surprise you in unlikely places: stone foundations beside dry stream beds; rusted ore buckets and caved-in tunnels high up a small canyon; obsidian chips on ridge tops; bits of brown pottery in the sagebrush; splintered timbers overgrown with brush; holes in the ground; bones bleached white; low mounds, the length of a man. They whisper of forgotten hearts and minds. Of struggle, of hopes that came true, and of broken dreams. They are yesterdays that can flavor your todays, with wistfulness perhaps, and fascination too.

That people lived in Owens Valley 3,000 years ago is certain. But where they came from, how long they lived here, why they left (if they did)— all are riddles with yet no answers. Evidence is scant; perhaps we never will know much. But we can clothe our wonderings about ancient peoples in the fabric woven by Paiute storytellers in the shadows of a flickering fire on winter evenings in the deep valley. How much did a storyteller remember having heard from his father or grandfather, and how much did he add to make the story better? We can surmise that in a day of fewer distractions, when the only way history could be passed along was with frequent storytelling—in that day reporting by word of mouth may have been more accurate than ours. The capacity to learn was there, and to remember too. And perhaps, because the Indian was closer to his world, he had a sensitivity we *could* have retained.

One other thing we won't know is what the *real* stories were that the Indians told each other, with none of the language difficulty interposed that had to get in the way when white man attempted to capture their symbolism with his own, quite possibly missing a great deal in the process. And then there were probably some Indians who, being gentle and considerate when given a chance, told the white scholar what they thought he wanted to hear.

These are vagrant musings. Add your own as you read the translations of what the Indian storytellers said. And bear in mind that in almost all mythologies you'll find an account of a flood.

Birth of the Land.—Long, long ago many beings lived on the peak of How-wah-nee (Mount Tom) when this country was under water. They pleaded for land, and dived in the water to find soil. Coyote, distrusted and hated by most everyone, took an active part. He would plunge in and bring up a grain or two of sand, offering it as proof that he had dived to the bottom, while there was no doubt he had placed it under his fingernails before making the plunge. Finally, they called on the Helldiver. He plunged into the deep blue water and stayed under longer than anyone else. When he came up he assured them it was no use. But others pleaded with him to try again, so he did. He was gone for a long time. At last he popped up, worn out, and refused to dive any more. After several days of coaxing, the little Helldiver promised to make his last dive at dawn the following day.

As the morning star peeped over the horizon, the Helldiver pleaded for strength and endurance. When the star ascended high into the sky, he plunged straight into the deep water. It was near noon when the anxious crowd concluded that the Helldiver had drowned. Coyote cried and sang funeral songs; they carried on a regular funeral ceremony. Suddenly the diver came to the top and made his way to shore. He offered a handful of fertile soil, and distributed it over the great water a little at a time, as if sowing grain. Soon the water began to lower. Islands and valleys here and there popped up as water pooled into lakes, rivers, and creeks. The mountains and the whole country seemed to turn green overnight. (Condensed from *Story of Inyo.*)

Birth of the People.—Once there was a woman, Korawini, who lived on the other side of Long Valley. All men fell in love with her, and she killed them one by one until only Coyote was left. Coyote brought a big feast of ducks to Korawini and her mother. They said, "He is a good husband and provider." They had a big feast of ducks because now there was a man to furnish plenty of food. Korawini and her mother were satisfied with Coyote, although he was very homely.

After they had lived there a while, Coyote decided to go back to his home in Round Valley. The woman was pregnant and complained of a pain in her stomach. She said, "Make me a cutiavita [a hole warmed by fire]." When it was done, she said, "Go to the stream and get me some water." When Coyote went to get the water, he saw a big flat sloping rock by the creek. He began to slide down it and play. Coyote was clever and smart, but often he acted like a child.

While Coyote was sliding down the rock, he looked back toward his wife and saw many people—all the people in the world at that time, dressed in different ways. There were Miwok, Shoshoni, Modoc, and so on—all the Indian tribes.

Coyote hallooed, "Wait! I am your father. I want to pick my people. I have to make my own tribe." But they paid no attention to him, and went away. Coyote hurried over to his wife, but when he got there only some homely Indians were left. They stayed in Round Valley. When Coyote came to where his wife was, she said, "Well, Coyote, why did you go over there to

---

Map of Owens Valley Paiute camps, seed lands, trails

For the most part, Valley Paiutes clustered along the streams flowing from Sierra canyons. Each group had a slightly different dialect. The Paiutes traded with other Indians both east and west. From Bishop there were many trails east, including one up Silver Canyon to Fish Lake Valley. From Big Pine there were several, to Deep Springs and Eureka Valleys. South of Mount Whitney, many trade trails led west across the Sierra, over what are now Walker, Olancha, Army, and Cottonwood passes, and Ninemile Canyon. North of Mount Whitney trails led over Taboose, Kearsarge, and Piute passes.

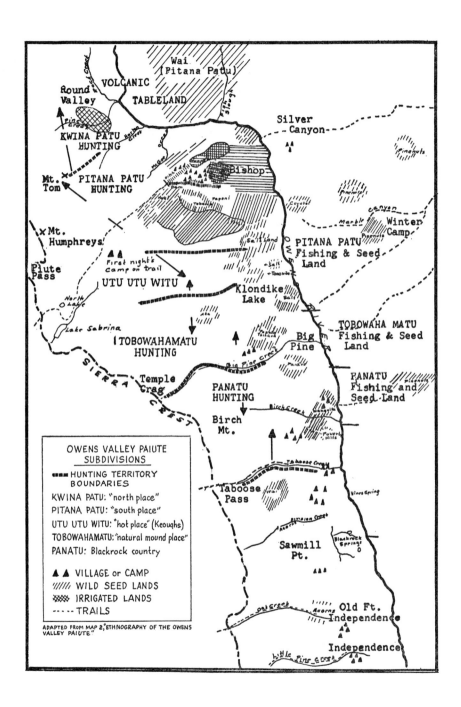

Wai
(Pitana Patu)

VOLCANIC
Round
Valley
TABLELAND

Silver
Canyon

KWINA PATU
HUNTING

Pinehuts

Bishop

Mt.
Tom

PITANA PATU
HUNTING

Mt.
Humphreys

Winter
Camp

PITANA PATU
Fishing & Seed
Land

Piute
Pass

First night's
Camp on trail

UTU UTU WITU

Klondike
Lake

North
O Lake

Lake Sabrina

TOBOWAHAMATU
HUNTING

TOBOWAHA MATU
Fishing & Seed
Land

Big
Pine

Temple
Crag

PANATU
HUNTING

Birch Creek

PANATU
Fishing and
Seed Land

Birch
Mt.

Taboose Creek

Taboose
Pass

Vines Spring

Division Creek

Blackrock
Springs

Sawmill
Pt.

OWENS VALLEY PAIUTE
SUBDIVISIONS
━━━ HUNTING TERRITORY
    BOUNDARIES
KWINA PATU: "north place"
PITANA PATU: "south place"
UTU UTU WITU: "hot place" (Keoughs)
TOBOWAHAMATU: "natural mound place"
PANATU: Blackrock country

▲ ▲ VILLAGE or CAMP
///// WILD SEED LANDS
▨▨▨ IRRIGATED LANDS
----- TRAILS

ADAPTED FROM MAP 2, "ETHNOGRAPHY OF THE OWENS
VALLEY PAIUTE."

Old Ft.
Independence

Independence

Little Pine Creek

play when you should be here attending to me? Now here are your children. Take care of them."

Coyote said, "Very well, these are my poor children here. But I say to the world, no matter what my children do, whether it is in fighting or hunting or anything, they shall be better than you." (Condensed from *Myths of the Owens Valley Paiute,* told by Jack Stewart of Big Pine, a Paiute about 100 years old.) These are but two brief versions of several Paiute stories of creation; a gifted narrator might spend several evenings developing his story.

The Paiutes.—We do not know how many hundreds of years Paiute Indians have lived in Owens Valley. Paiute (probably derived from páh-yah, water) is a White man's term that mapmakers of the early 1800s applied loosely to Indians living in the Great Basin. Spellings varied: Pah-Ute, Pahutah, Pa U Teh, Paiuches. The accepted spelling of the Indian name for the past hundred years has been Paiute. Geographers, however, have simplified the spelling of most of the places named for the Indians to Piute (Piute Pass, Piute Creek, *but* Paiute Monument). We follow this inconsistency consistently. Paiute now refers to the Indians living just east of the Cascades and the Sierra in Oregon, Nevada, and California. They are related by language and culture not to Indians west of the mountains, but to Great Basin peoples.

Owens Valley was the southernmost permanent home of the Northern Paiute. North of them lived the Washo; south and east, the Shoshoni. Early white men estimated there were a thousand Paiutes in Owens Valley; there

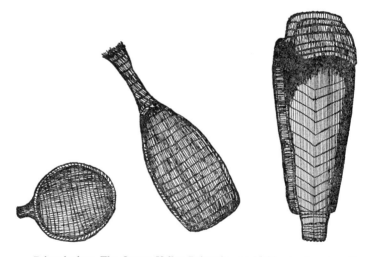

Paiute baskets. The Owens Valley Paiutes' most highly developed craft was basket-making. From willow they wove food containers, cooking baskets, hats, cradles, winnowing trays, and water bottles. From left to right, seed beater from Round Valley, seed beater from Fish Springs, boy's cradle from Bishop.

Paiute tule house. Paiute summer houses were basically sun shades, brush or grass roofs supported by upright willow boughs. Winter houses were more substantial. A shallow pit was dug and a cone of poles erected and covered with whatever was at hand —willow, aspen, brush, grass, skins, or tules.

may have been twice that many. They are a stocky people, with dark straight hair.

The Valley abounds with evidence of the Paiutes—acres of obsidian chips, dozens of petroglyph sites, many "house rings" (circles of rocks which may indicate shelters), endless clusters of mortars worn deep into bedrock by years of seed-grinding, and "drying circles" (rock rings three to six feet across used for drying pinyon cones). Their valley camps were located where food, seeds, and small game were most abundant. They diverted some of the streams to irrigate natural wild seed lands. In good pine-nut years, many spent the winter at mountain camps in the pinyon forests.

Owens Valley natives called themselves nóo-muh, "people." Their neighbors, the Shoshoni, called them pah-nah-gwet-too, "western people"; they in turn called their neighbors west of the Sierra the same name. Too loosely organized to be called tribes, Paiute communities were simply collections of families living near each other. They were generally peaceful; what squabbles there were arose from trespassing on pine-nut or hunting territory.

Living was first of all a struggle for food. Paiute welfare depended completely on the moods of nature. Few of the old and weak could survive winters following poor pine-nut crops. Mush made from pine-nut and seed meal was their staple; a handful of dried insects or meat might be added. Owens Valley Paiutes traded with Indians across the Sierra, who were particularly eager for obsidian. To the Yokuts of the southern San Joaquin Valley fifty pounds of obsidian was worth about fifty tanned deer skins.

Besides games and storytelling, the favorite Paiute pastime was gambling. Most popular of all was the hand game, something like "Button, button, who has the button?" played with four small bone sticks, two of them marked.

There are no Paiutes now living who remember the days before White men changed their valley. Fortunately, in 1927 Julian Steward wrote down the life stories of two men about 100 years old. The following is condensed from the story of Sam Newland, of Bishop Creek.

We were camped on a mountain called tupi mada (near Glass Mountain) when my father became sick and died. They buried him and then moved our camp. We spent the rest of the winter here, and ate pine nuts. In spring we returned to Bishop. In fall there was a big dance and people gambled a great deal. They bet shell bead money and great sums were won and lost. They frequently got into fights over their games. People had come from all over Owens Valley. The Fort Independence men are always good dancers, so we invited them to do the totsoho dance, performed by four men in feathers and eagle-down skirts. We danced for five days and nights and then the people went home.

It was a hard winter with so much snow that the sagebrush was buried and you could not even see the tops of it. We ate seeds my mother had gathered. There had been no pine nuts that fall but we had some left at tupi mada from the year before, and made several trips to bring them down. I spent many nights in the sweat house with the other boys my age. The men gave us a corner to sleep in. Those who had families stayed at home with them. The men talked a great deal and I heard many stories told.

When spring came, the people got together for a big feast and elected the irrigator for the coming summer. The large villages split up and went out after food. Some went to their seed places in the hills, others went to the river to catch fish, and some went north after other seeds. We always got as many seeds as we could to keep ahead on food.

In the spring I went on a trading trip. I had put salt up in balls because the people across the mountains like them better that way. Six of us started out late one afternoon. When we reached the other side, the Indians took us in and gave us food. While we were eating with one family, someone else would come in and say, "When you get through, come to my place," so we would go over and eat another meal. We could talk with these people in our own language, although they were a little difficult to understand. The next morning we began to trade. A man picked up a flat cake of salt and said, "This is no good, it will be used up too fast." Then he looked at my balls and said: "This is the kind! This has a heart and will last." He put a red woolen blanket on a rock and said, "Whoever owns this salt come and get it."

On the way back we found a porcupine and clubbed it on the nose. We cleaned its inside, burned off the hair and quills, and covered it with coals and dirt. The next morning we had a fine breakfast. We also had some acorn flour which we made into a mush by boiling with hot rocks in a basket.

The Petroglyph Makers.—Throughout Owens Valley and on the Tableland there are acres and acres of Indian petroglyphs, mysterious designs pecked into rock. Some of the carvings are half an inch deep, others barely scratched on. Some look fresh; others are so weathered and covered with lichen you can scarcely make them out.

Whose hands chiseled the thousands of petroglyphs found east of the

Sierra? Were they the ancestors of the Paiutes, or an unknown people who lived here long before and then wandered elsewhere? Are the designs meaningless doodlings, or are they maps, signposts, or symbols to appease angry spirits? Despite more and less educated guesses, no one really knows. Local Indians disclaim any knowledge of their origin or their meaning. This leads to speculation that the petroglyphs must be more than a few generations old, otherwise stories about them surely would have been handed down. Most archeologists agree that petroglyphs are meaningful. They know of no living people who devote much time and work to making pictures with no significance. The meaning and the age of the Owens Valley petroglyphs may be determined someday after patient archeological detective work.

The Pinto People.—Four or five thousand years ago, people who made dart and spear points quite unlike the Paiutes lived in the region. Those who made these distinctive points are called the Pinto people because their traces were discovered and recognized as a distinct culture in Pinto Basin, Riverside County.

Pinto sites are found throughout the Valley, as far north as Montgomery Pass, and particularly on the high beaches on the north shore of ancient Owens Lake. Traces of the Pintos are found south into Lower California. The Southwest Museum, excavating a Pinto site at Little Lake (the oldest open-site dwellings yet found in the United States), discovered scrapers, stone tools, house sites, and nearly five hundred projectile points.

No one knows what became of the Pinto people. As the climate became more arid, did they drift away? Did earthquakes or volcanic explosions frighten them away? Or did they gradually change the pattern of their points and, lingering in the region, become the ancestors of the later Paiutes?

There is even evidence that people lived in this region many thousands of years before the Pinto people. The evidence is not abundant, but it is there—from the White Mountains, Owens Lake, Little Lake, and Walker Lake. This evidence so far consists of large weapon points—Clovis, Folsom, and Sandia —which may be ten to twenty thousand years old. The evidence also suggests migration into Owens Valley from the east and northeast at a very early date.

Selected Reading

HARRINGTON, MARK R. *A Pinto Site at Little Lake, California.* Southwest Museum Papers No. 17. Southwest Museum, Highland Park, Los Angeles, 1957. 91 pp. A true detective story about the Pinto people. How archeologists found thousand-year-old clues and pieced them together.

MALLERY, GARRICK. *Picture-Writing of the American Indians,* in Tenth Annual Report of the Bureau of Ethnology to the Secretary of the Smithsonian Institute, 1888–1889. Gov't Printing Office, Washington, D.C., 1893. A classic, detailed study, including many illustrations of eastern California petroglyphs.

STEWARD, JULIAN. *Ethnography of the Owens Valley Paiute.* Univ. Calif. Publ. Amer. Arch. and Ethn., 33:3, pp. 233–350. Berkeley, 1933. A wealth of information on Paiute customs and habits.

Myths of the Owen Valley Paiute. Univ. Calif. Publ. Amer. Arch. and Ethn., 34:5. Berkeley, 1936. Legends collected from local Indians.

Two Paiute Autobiographies. Univ. Calif. Publ. Amer. Arch. and Ethn., 33:5. Berkeley, 1934.

UNDERHILL, RUTH. *The Northern Paiute Indians of California and Nevada.* Bureau of Indian Affairs, 1941. Available for 60¢ from Haskell Institute, Lawrence, Kansas (make checks payable to U. S. Bureau of Indian Affairs).

Ancient obsidian Pinto points   Recent Paiute points

Pinto points have distinctively shaped bases, besides being larger, thicker, and cruder than the delicate Paiute points. Such small differences, perhaps not obvious to the untrained eye, enable archeologists to distinguish one people from another.

DISCOVERY AND EXPLORATION

1834—Exploring for beaver, Joseph R. Walker leads the first white men over Walker Pass and through Owens Valley.

1843—Walker guides the first wagon train, a group of the Chiles party from Missouri, over his Owens Valley route.

1845—Walker guides the first official party to map and explore Owens Valley, Captain John Frémont's third expedition.

1855—A. W. von Schmidt makes the first survey east of the Sierra, from the Mount Diablo Base Line near Mono Lake south beyond Owens Lake.

1859—Colonel Beall, looking for hostile Indians, leads a military force from Fort Tejon to Owens Valley.

Joseph Walker discovers Owens Valley.—Barricaded by the massive Sierra Nevada from the Franciscan missions and Spanish ranchos of coastal California, the Paiutes lived undisturbed for three hundred years after Cabrillo discovered California in 1542. Fur traders and trappers, enticed by the fortunes to be made from beaver pelts, were the first to break through the desert barriers isolating California from the frontier towns along the Missouri. Known as Mountain Men, these hardy adventurers pushed westward into the Rocky Mountains and across the Great Basin deserts. It was they who guided later wagon trains, explorers, and military expeditions. Among them was Jedediah Smith, first white man across the Sierra (west to east) in 1826.

You may read that Smith was the first white man to visit Owens Valley, and that he also found gold at Mono Lake. Since Smith was killed by Comanches when he was only thirty-two, and his maps and journal disappeared, until recently his route across the Sierra was debatable. Just a few years ago, however, historian Carl I. Wheat discovered what amounts to a copy of one of Smith's maps, which sheds new light on his travels and achievements. There is now little doubt that Smith never entered Owens Valley, but crossed the Sierra farther north, near the present Ebbetts Pass.

Though others may have wandered through the Valley, they left no record. As far as we know, it was Joseph Walker, one of the most respected and capable Mountain Men, an experienced trapper and trail blazer, who discovered Owens Valley. Captain Benjamin Bonneville, who was organizing a large trapping party, employed Walker to command a group and explore west of Salt Lake to California. Traveling unknown, unmapped, and unnamed country, Walker successfully followed the Walker River to its headwaters, crossed the Sierra in 1833, and wintered at Monterey. The following February, with 52 men, 300 horses, and 400 cattle, Walker set out to return to Salt Lake. From the San Joaquin Valley he followed the Kern River up its South Fork, crossed the mountains over the pass named for him, turned north, and eventually reached Owens Valley. His general route is commemorated by markers on Highway 6, at Olancha and Indian Wells. From the head of the Valley, Walker went east through the mountains and then north, circling back to his trail on the Humboldt.

[175]

Walker found no beaver, but this was one of the great explorations. He achieved many "firsts"—pioneering the Salt Lake–Humboldt trail, which later became the most important emigrant route, making the first western crossing of the central Sierra, discovering Yosemite Valley, and finding the Walker Pass–Owens Valley route.

Captain John Frémont, having led two western expeditions, was sent again in 1844–45 to find a shorter route to Oregon. He employed Walker to guide his largest group south from Walker Lake to map and explore. In the course of a winter trip of great hardship—low food supplies, little game, snow, bitter cold—Walker led the men down Owens Valley, over Walker Pass, and finally rejoined Frémont at San Jose. Surveyor von Schmidt, who mapped during 1855–1856, made the following comments about the Valley and its natives: "This valley contains about 1000 Indians, and they are a fine looking set of men. They live principally on pine nuts, fish, and hares, which are very plenty. On the western edge of this valley I found great quantities of grouse, other game very scarce. On a general average the country forming Owens Valley is worthless to the white man, both in soil and climate.

"But with all this they are in poor condition. The families being divided off and each having his own hunting ground causes some to go without food for days. One chief told me that sometimes he had nothing to eat for six days at a time. They are in a state of nudity, with the exception of a small cloth about their loins." (Adapted from *Story of Inyo.*)

Another source of information is the reporter who accompanied Colonel Beall to Owens Valley in 1859. During the 1850s settlers west of the Sierra, warring with local Indians, drove them into the mountains. Owens Valley was thought to be one of their strongholds. Beall was sent to Owens Valley to find these hostile Indians and to recover stolen stock. But according to the August 27, 1859 *Los Angeles Star,* he found only frightened Paiutes:

"The Indians fled, having been told they would be killed, until we reached Pine Creek, where the interpreter found a poor woman attempting to escape with her crippled child. She having been assured that the people would not be injured soon became the means of reassuring the Indians.

"The Wakopee or Owens River Indians appear to be both morally and physically superior to any of their race in California, for in point of probity and honesty I certainly have never met their equal. Captain Davidson informed them that so long as they were peaceful the government would protect them. Their reply was that they had at all times treated the whites in a friendly manner, and intended to do so in the future. He further informed them that should they resort to murder and robbery, they would be punished with the sword. The old head man turned with a smile to the interpreter and said: 'Tell him that we fear it not; that what I said, I have said. I have lain my heart at his feet; let him look at it.'" (Condensed from *Story of Inyo.*)

THE LURE OF COSO SILVER

1860—Dr. Darwin French discovers the Coso ledges, the first strike in the future county of Inyo. Colonel Russ and Dr. George locate claims in the Inyos and organize the Russ Mining District, the first district in Owens Valley.

1862—The San Carlos Mining and Exploration Company of San Francisco locates the Romelia claim in the Inyo Mountains, and starts the camp of San Carlos.

Following the discovery of gold, the fame of the Mother Lode on the Sierra's west slope sped around the world. But for ten years, few thought to prospect east of the mountains. Then in 1859 "Old Virginia" Fennimore and "Old Pancake" Henry Comstock (so nicknamed because he was too lazy to make bread) discovered rich silver ore east of Lake Tahoe. Thousands of hopefuls who had only recently crossed the plains to the Mother Lode feverishly retraced their trails back across the Sierra to the fabulous Comstock Lode. That same year Cord Norst discovered gold in a wash near Mono Lake. The next summer prospectors located rich quartz veins northeast of Monoville; the wildly speculative camp of Aurora (Esmeralda District) mushroomed into a community with 17 mills and 5,000 people. Hopelessly infected with "Washoe fever" and "Esmeralda excitement," men surged on into the other desert mountains.

With a small party, Dr. Darwin French left Visalia in 1860 to search for the legendary Gunsight Mine. (Supposedly a 49er picked up a chunk of metal somewhere to make himself a gunsight; it proved to be pure silver.) Instead, French discovered silver ledges in the Coso Range southeast of Owens Lake. After he returned to Visalia with a few samples and glowing accounts, Coso zoomed into prominence, San Francisco and Visalia newspapers printing reports of silver ore assaying over $2,000 per ton. Small mills and arrastras produced a little gold, but none of these early strikes proved important. Colonel Russ of San Francisco and Dr. George located the Union, Eclipse, and Ida claims in the mountains southeast of Independence. When they inquired about names of the region, Chief George told them the mountains were called Inyo, "dwelling place of a great spirit."

CATTLEMEN, THE FIRST SETTLERS

1859—L. R. Ketcham, of Visalia, drives the first cattle into Owens Valley. Ketcham leaves his stock near Lone Pine and rides on to the Mono Diggings. Finding possibilities poor, Ketcham backtracked and sold his cattle at the Coso camps.

1861—Allen Van Fleet drives a herd of cattle from Carson Valley, and builds the first cabin (of stone and sod) on the Owens River near Laws.

The McGee and Summers families drive cattle from Tulare Valley over Walker Pass to Monoville. Two McGee boys decide to winter on Lone Pine Creek.

Charles Putnam builds a stone cabin and starts a trading post at Little Pine (now Independence).

Samuel Bishop brings in 500 cattle and 50 horses from Fort Tejon; Mrs. Bishop is the first white woman to live in Owens Valley.

Tales of silver first sparked interest in the land east of the Sierra; the new mining camps, in turn, drew stockmen. Looking for new markets, cattlemen from the San Joaquin and Carson valleys drove their herds to Coso, Monoville, and Aurora, supplying them with horses and beef. Attracted by the virgin rangeland and natural meadows, a few decided to winter in Owens Valley.

SETTLERS AND PAIUTES AT WAR

Winter 1861–1862—Hungry Paiutes kill cattle. A cowherd shoots an Indian taking an animal; Paiutes retaliate by killing a white.

January, 1862—Piutes and cattlemen sign first peace treaty.

February–March—As the settlers drive stock south down the valley, during the night at Keough Hot Springs, Indians drive off 200 head. The men at Putnam's kill four Indians. Near Benton, a prospector kills ten Indians before they kill him. Settlers attack a camp near the Alabama Hills, destroying a ton of dried meat, and killing several Paiutes.

April—The battle of Bishop, about fifty settlers against over five hundred (possibly fifteen hundred) Indians. Settlers retreat to Big Pine, with three dead. The first soldiers arrive, Colonel George Evans and troops from Camp Latham near Santa Monica, and Lt. Herman Noble with fifty men from Fort Churchill, Nevada. Colonel Evans commands an unsuccessful attack north of Round Valley; the whites retreat to Putnam's. Most settlers drive their animals (4,000 cattle, 2500 sheep) south out of Owens Valley.

May–June—Indians control Owens Valley, and attack isolated parties.

July 4—Colonel Evans and 201 men establish Camp Independence.

October—Responding to Indian Agents, Paiutes gather at Camp Independence and agree to a treaty. Chief George remains as hostage.

March 1863—Chief George escapes. Indians attack four men on Big Pine Creek, ransack two cabins near San Carlos, kill a prospector. Soldiers attack Indians unsuccessfully at Blackrock Springs. Indians burn the camp at the Union Mill, and attack the Summers-McGee party at Charlies Butte. Soldiers and settlers fight Indians near Cottonwood Creek, driving them to the shore of Owens Lake. Indians attempt escape by swimming. Whites pick them off by moonlight, killing more than 30.

April–May—Companies D, E and L, Second California Cavalry, reinforce Camp Independence, successfully attack Indian camps, and destroy 300 bushels of pine nuts and taboose.

June—400 Indians surrender at Camp Independence.

July—Lured by food and promises, 998 Indian men, women and children gather at Camp Independence. Commanding Officer McLaughlin orders them to a reservation near Fort Tejon, south of Bakersfield. Camp Independence abandoned. The northern part of Owens Valley, Joaquin Jim's territory, remains dangerous.

The explorers and first prospectors, who disturbed the Indians little, found them generally friendly. But when stockmen moved their herds into the Valley, killing game, grazing and trampling the best seed lands, the Paiutes asked them to move on their cattle and demanded tribute. When the stockmen refused, the Indians began stampeding the cattle. Life for the Paiutes, always a struggle against starvation, became even more precarious during the severe winter of 1861, when it rained and snowed for fifty-four days straight. Just as hungry white men did, the Paiutes helped themselves to cattle. And just as naturally, the stockmen tried to stop them—first with threats, then with bullets.

With the score even, one Paiute and one white dead, the worried settlers conferred at the San Francis Ranch and proposed peace. Bishop, Van Fleet, and nine others signed a treaty dated January 31, 1862; Chief George, Chief Dick, and Little Chief Dick made their mark. It read in part: "After talking over all past grievances, we have agreed to let what is past be buried in oblivion. The Indians are not to be molested in their daily avocations by which they gain an honest living. And it is further agreed that they are not to molest the property of the whites, nor to drive off or kill cattle that are running in the valley, and for both parties to live in peace." (*Story of Inyo.*)

Since the Paiute groups scattered throughout the Valley were not united under one chief, when Chief George signed the treaty, other head men felt no obligation to observe it. The most determined enemy of the whites was Joaquin Jim, a west slope Indian whose own people had outlawed him, and who had become headman of the Indians north of Big Pine Creek. A capable leader, who hated white men fiercely and never accepted their domination, he kept his men hostile long after most others submitted. At first it was guns against arrows, with few white deaths. But as the Indians obtained guns, casualties mounted. As Indian and white became more fearful and bitter, provoked and unprovoked outrages occurred on both sides. Both white and Paiute called on their brothers for help. Soldiers came to reinforce the settlers; Indians came from the north and west to aid the Paiutes.

Indians and whites battled for a year and a half. The Indians gradually weakened during the months of fighting; with the whites destroying their seed and meat caches, unable to gather nuts and conduct rabbit drives, some of them were driven by hunger to surrender. Here, in the words of a Paiute, is how Indian resistance ended.

"The white men proposed peace and arranged a big feast at Fort Independence for all the Indians in the region. The Indians arrived, Panatubiji among them, and were at once deprived of their arms. The following morning the soldiers drove them down Owens Valley and then across the Sierra Nevada to Fort Tejon, a journey of many days. Many people escaped en route and returned home." (As told by Tom Stone, of Bishop, grandson of Panatubiji, to Julian Steward.)

SETTLEMENT RESUMES

1863—Mining companies resume operations, small mills at the Ida and Union mines. A camp begins 3 miles from San Carlos, Bend City. Bell starts a sawmill on Big Pine Creek. Small settlements at Lone Pine and Owensville.

1864—San Carlos Company starts a 5-stamp mill. Pugh and Spear build a sawmill on Bishop Creek. Kearsarge claims discovered west of Independence; the mining camp of Kearsarge City begins the next year. California State Geological Survey party under William Brewer visits Owens Valley, after discovering and naming Mount Whitney.

1865—Indians kill Mrs. McGuire and 6-year-old son at Haiwee Meadows. Whites retaliate by killing 41 Paiute men, women, and children. Company C, 94 men, reëstablishes Camp Independence, which remains active until 1877. The Jones brothers sow 4½ acres, the first wheat in Round Valley.

1866—$40,000 10-stamp mill built near Kearsarge claims. The last killings; soldiers fight Indians east of Owens Lake; estimated dead during five years of fighting: 60 whites, 200 Indians. California legislature establishes Inyo County, from the eastern part of Tulare County; County seat, Independence (boundaries changed in 1870 and 1872 to present locations); school districts organized; total vote, first election: 91. Thomas Edwards lays out the first townsite, Independence, and receives the first land patent. The first flour mill; John Jones builds a water wheel to run his hand mill in Round Valley.

1867—A. N. Bell completes his flour mill on Oak Creek.

1869—The first church. Rev. Andrew Clark starts the Baptist Church in Bishop.

1870—Chalfant and Parker print the first newspaper, *The Inyo Independent*. Regular mail service twice a week inaugurated.

1871—Total votes cast in county election: 586. The 60 soldiers and scientists of the Wheeler expedition, exploring and mapping west of the 100th Meridian under Lieutenant George M. Wheeler, visit Owens Valley.

By the summer of 1863 the worst of the fighting was over, although scattered incidents continued to occur. As Indians ambushed isolated settlers and killed stock, Valley people repeatedly sent petitions begging for troops. Their requests were answered when Captain Kelley and 94 men reëstablished Camp Independence in 1865. The last fight between soldiers and Indians took place in August 1866. Joe Bowers, a headman, helped quiet his people, warning that if they fought again, the white men would slaughter them. Though some remained sullen and defiant as long as they lived, many Indians went to work on the ranches.

With order restored in the Valley, once more prospectors explored the hills and pioneers came to settle. During the great drought of 1862–64, stockmen drove their herds to the mountain meadows and the Valley's grasslands. Sheepmen, too, brought their animals for summer range. Leaving Bakersfield in April, they drove their flocks over Tehachapi or Walker Pass, feeding them on the way and arriving in the Valley two months later.

William H. Brewer described Owens Valley as he led his geological party through it in July 1864: "Tens of thousands of the starving cattle of the state have been driven here this year, and there is feed for twice as many more.

"We camped on the river near Bend City and went into town for fresh meat and to get horses shod. It is a miserable hole, of perhaps 20 or 25 adobe houses, built on the sand in the midst of the sagebrush. . . .

"We wanted some fresh meat, so two of the boys (soldiers) went out and shot a fine heifer and brought in the beef. They assumed that she belonged to a Secessionist and confiscated her. It is very common here for men traveling to supply themselves with beef from the large herds. . . .

"At the north end of the valley there are nine or ten square miles of the best grass I have seen in the state. Three or four settlers have come in this year with cattle and horses, but there is feed for ten times as many. One has started a garden to sell vegetables in Owensville and Aurora." (Adapted from *Up and Down California,* Francis P. Farquhar, ed.)

During the 1860s, living in the isolated Valley was not easy. Pioneer families often lived in tents until they could build rock or sod cabins. Lumber was too scarce and expensive. Since cattle roamed at will, farmers had to watch their fields all day and often slept in them at night. "Beef straight," was their diet, with beans when they had them; some gathered taboose and pine nuts. For weeks at a time, they might have no vegetables or grain. Fifty pounds of flour sold for as high as $25. A bucketful of potatoes, carrots, or beets would trade for a huge chunk of beef. Some lived through a winter without any white flour, but only cornmeal for bread. Salt could be scraped up in Saline Valley; soap could be made from fat. Tallow candles or rags in bowls of grease gave a little light. Wood was free, though it might take several days to haul it down the mountains.

Typical of many who came to prospect and then stayed to farm was the Shuey family. The following is adapted from the scrapbook of John Shuey, whose family came to the Valley in 1864 when he was six years old:

"Father Shuey caught the mining fever but by the time we got to the Inyo Range miners had not found much gold. After working for a few months at the Eclipse Mine, the mill shut down and father went on a prospecting tour, leaving the family comfortably located near the mill.

"Along in January 1865 a horseman came rushing up and reported that Indians had killed a woman and her son about fifty miles south of Lone Pine, and were coming up the valley. A team and wagon from Bend City moved mother, the children, and furniture into a small adobe house in Bend City, built in a horseshoe bend of Owens River. The only two men left in the town took turns as patrol guards.

"Father finally heard of the trouble and came down, and later decided to raise stock and do a little farming. He bought an old wooden frame house in Bend City and moved it to the ranch five miles south of Independence. He went into the mountains and cut birch and cedar posts, and built a fence around about eighty acres. He got three yoke of oxen to plow the wire grass. Some of it was impossible to break up with the harrow, so he cut a hole with the edge of an axe, put four grains of corn into it, and closed it with the hoe handle. The land was rich and the corn came up quickly.

"Several times Indians broke out and we had to keep a man patrolling around our houses at night, but they were generally good and we employed many of them during the years. We paid the Indian men and squaws 50¢ a day and had them do hoeing, husking corn, and shelling it. We sold all we could produce to the Eclipse mill for mule feed.

"About once a year the Indians would gather at our rancharee and have a two weeks pow-wow and dance. They kept things lively day and night. Every fall they would have a rabbit hunt, with nets 3 feet high and half a mile long, made from grass and set in a semicircle. They would go off a mile and drive the rabbits into the net. I have seen them come home at night with their horses packed with as many as they could carry. They dried the meat for food and the skins for clothing."

CERRO GORDO

Total production: lead, silver, and zinc worth $17,000,000.

1865—Pablo Flores discovers ore in the Inyo Mountains, northeast of Owens Lake.

1866—Lone Pine Mining District organized.

1868—Victor Beaudry, half-owner of the Union Mine, builds a small furnace. Mortimer Belshaw and partners organize the Union Mining Company, build a smelter at Cerro Gordo and a tollroad from Owens Lake.

1869—The rival Owens Lake Silver-Lead Company builds a smelter at Swansea. Total claims filed: 999.

1870—Beaudry and Belshaw together produce 9 tons per day.

1871—Output for the year: 2200 tons.

1872—James Brady builds the *Bessie Brady* to ship bullion across Owens Lake.

1873—Colonel Sherman Stevens builds a sawmill and flume in Cottonwood Canyon to supply fuel, mine timbers, lumber, and charcoal. Water becomes scarce and expensive; 100 burros pack in 6,000 gallons per day; smelters must curtail production in the dry season.

1874—Cerro Gordo Water and Mining Company builds an 11½ mile pipeline, bringing 90,000 gallons per day from Miller Springs. Belshaw and Beaudry increase their output to 18 tons (400 bars) per day. Output for the year: 5290 tons of bullion worth $2,000,000.

1876—Belshaw's furnace shuts down permanently.

1877—Known deposits are becoming exhausted; the price of lead and silver declines.

1879—Union Mine abandoned; Beaudry's smelter stops production.

1911—Louis Gordon discovers zinc ore. Cerro Gordo produces zinc, besides silver and lead, until 1915.

Newspaper reports of the silver strikes are amusingly monotonous: assays of $1200, $2000 per ton; ledges several thousand feet long; mining stock leaping in value; "the richest mine in all California," "a ledge that will rival the Comstock." Most reports proved to be no more than reflections of the prospectors' dogged optimism or the promoters' glib tongues. But one in a thousand—or was it one in ten thousand?—did uncover a bonanza. Such a one was Pablo Flores. Familiar with the ores of their 300-year-old Mexican silver mines, Mexicans made a number of the early silver discoveries in Nevada and eastern California. Cerro Gordo's silver was tremendously important to the growth of the small pueblo of Los Angeles, and for eight lusty years the camp brought excitement and prosperity to Owens Valley.

Most supplies for the mushrooming town came from Los Angeles. Since freight charges from Los Angeles ranged as high as twelve cents a pound, Owens Valley settlers could get high prices for their beef, chickens, eggs, flour, butter, vegetables, hay, and grain. The gleaming metal that passed in ever-increasing quantities from the smelters drew the honest and the hard-working, as well as the tough and the crooked. Dr. Hugh McClelland, a physician at Cerro Gordo, wrote his memories of the roaring days:

"Here were men who had fled from the vigilantes of Montana and Idaho, horse thieves . . . renegade Mexicans who had been driven out of Sonora. What few tenderfeet came from the eastern states found the place too strenuous. There were good people as well.

"One evening I met a young man who said he would like to visit the dance halls, and asked me if I would accompany him. The dance hall girls all had fictitious names, and some very odd ones. The Horned Toad, a fiery high-tempered Mexican girl, was on the floor cutting up some high and fantastic stunts when the young man asked me her name. I told him she was the Horned Toad, and she overheard me and came at me like a flash with stiletto drawn, and would have plunged it into me had not the Fenian, a beautiful Irish girl, caught her by the wrist. A Mexican who was a friend of hers came running toward me with a knife in his hand, and George Snow, who saw that something serious might happen to me, shot the Mexican dead. This resulted in a general shooting, and the lights were extinguished at once.

"Gun fights were common . . . and houses were few that did not have bullet holes. One man was killed in bed in Boston's hotel, a bullet having gone through the ceiling during an altercation in the barroom below. I was called to see Mr. Cohen, who had pneumonia, and found him in bed surrounded by sandbags four feet high. I had to ascend a stepladder to reach the patient. Mr. Cohen told me he would not take any chances, as bullets were flying too thick and fast and were penetrating houses all over the town.

"The Fenian . . . was the reigning belle of the camp; her besetting sin was drink. Many houses were built on the hillsides, with terraced paths leading close to the roofs of cottages beneath. One starry night when the Fenian had on a large cargo of whisky she went for a stroll along one of the paths, lost her footing and fell through the roof of a shack just below, where ten or twelve Chinamen were playing fantan. The commotion and sudden fright of the Chinamen may well be imagined. One of the Chinamen in his hurried exit fell over an embankment and broke his leg." (*The Quarterly,* Historical Society of Southern Calif. June 1940, 22:2.)

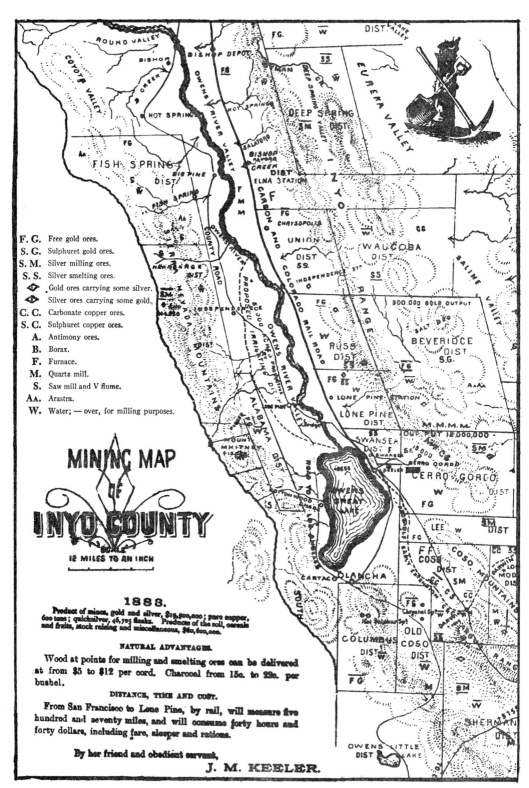

Legend

F. G. Free gold ores.
S. G. Sulphuret gold ores.
S. M. Silver milling ores.
S. S. Silver smelting ores.
◆ Gold ores carrying some silver.
◆ Silver ores carrying some gold.
C. C. Carbonate copper ores.
S. C. Sulphuret copper ores.
A. Antimony ores.
B. Borax.
F. Furnace.
M. Quartz mill.
S. Saw mill and V flume.
Aa. Arastra.
W. Water; — over, for milling purposes.

MINING MAP OF INYO COUNTY

SCALE
12 MILES TO AN INCH

1888.

Product of mines, gold and silver, $2,500,000.00; pure copper, 600 tons; quicksilver, 46,725 flasks. Produce of the soil, cereals and fruits, stock raising and miscellaneous, $60,600,000.

NATURAL ADVANTAGES.

Wood at points for milling and smelting ores can be delivered at from $5 to $12 per cord. Charcoal from 15c. to 23c. per bushel.

DISTANCE, TIME AND COST.

From San Francisco to Lone Pine, by rail, will measure five hundred and seventy miles, and will consume forty hours and forty dollars, including fare, sleeper and rations.

By her friend and obedient servant,

J. M. KEELER.

Map adapted from the original in the library of Francis Farquhar

MINING CAMPS AND FARMERS

AURORA, 10 miles east of Bodie: gold, silver; peak activity, 1859–1869; total production: $31,000,000.

CANDELARIA, 60 miles north of Bishop: gold, silver; discovery 1863; peak activity 1870–1890; estimated total production: $15,000,000.

PANAMINT, west slope of the Panamint Mountains: silver, copper; boom days, 1874–1877; estimated profits to the silver senators (Jones and Stewart of Nevada, organizers of The Panamint Mining Company): $1,000,000.

DARWIN, 30 miles east of Olancha: lead, silver, zinc; peak population late 1870s, 5000; estimated production (intermittent), 1874–1952: $29,000,000.

BODIE, north of Mono Lake: gold, silver; boom days, 1877–1881; peak population, 8000; estimated total production: $30,000,000.

TONOPAH, 80 miles northeast of Bishop: silver, also gold, lead, copper; active 1901–1940; estimated peak population, 20,000; total production (peak 1910–1914): $149,000,000.

GOLDFIELD, 28 miles south of Tonopah: gold, also silver, copper, lead; active 1903–1940; estimated peak population, 20,000; total production (peak 1906–1915): $87,000,000.

Mining was most important to Owens Valley's growth. Most of the desert camps raised no food, for water was often scarcer than whiskey. The large mining camps paid good prices for all the produce and livestock Valley settlers could produce, spurring them to irrigate more land, raise larger crops, and increase their herds. Valley sawmills supplied lumber. But by 1880, most of the early camps had passed their peak, and for the next twenty years there were no new rich strikes. Moreover, the price of silver declined drastically, from $1.34 per ounce in 1866 to sixty-two cents in 1900.

Then in 1900 another lucky one, Jim Butler, discovered gold and silver near Tonopah Springs, starting a new boom that lasted through World War I. Two years later ore was found at Goldfield, then in other nearby hills. Rhyolite, Silver Peak, Manhattan, and Round Mountain were among the large camps that flourished, bringing a second wave of prosperity to Owens Valley.

The Inyo Mountains and the desert ranges farther east abound with diggings, tunnels, shafts, dumps, and jeep roads. (Watch out for half-hidden, open shafts.) Those fascinated with old mines can find books full of details from the California Division of Mines, Ferry Building, San Francisco, beginning with the first report on Inyo County, *The Eighth Annual Report of the State Mineralogist, 1888*. The most recent report is *Mines and Mineral Resources of Inyo County*, 1951 (see Selected Reading, Geology Section).

Besides the familiar farmer in bib overalls and the rancher in hip denims, Owens Valley towns knew many a prospector. Usually on foot, often with a burro or two, he wandered in from whichever hills claimed him at the moment. These were the men with sand in their boots and sun in their eyes, who chose to spend their lives wandering after rainbows and the pot of gold that lay just under the next shovelful of dirt. In an unpublished manuscript, Lorin Ray tells of this almost-vanished breed: They were kindly little men with eyes faded from the sun. They patched their pants with bits of pillow ticking and sewed them with sacking needles, half-soled their shoes with bits of belting and inner tube. They never knew a sleeping bag or air mattress, but drew long-unwashed blankets and canvas over their heads and slept soundly through the night winds. Their socks were sour, and they smoked corn cob pipes that gurgled, or rolled their own. They came to town when they were broke and needed a grubstake, or supplies, and women, and whiskey. They didn't ask for pity, only the chance to be disappointed again. Others got rich on their findings; usually the county buried them.

With prospectors constantly bringing in ore samples, and with the newspapers reporting the promoters' newest bonanzas in every issue, many a Valley settler contracted a serious case of mining fever. Some acquired claims by purchase; others through debts or grubstaking (providing a prospector with food in return for a share of whatever he might find). Here is one forecast, in the 1908 *Inyo Magazine,* of the wealth aching to be tapped: "From Mt. Whitney to Telescope Peak, range after range, like hurdles in a giant's race-course are there, gray as ashes, silent as death, yet richer than the treasures of the Incas. The mines of Ophir, the gravels of Klondyke's frozen wastes, or the dazzling richness of Africa lie buried in duplicate."

Mines that never pay are the butt of many jokes. One experienced investor, telling of the Long Chance Mine, said he considered it a very successful venture. It sold for $25,000 and cost only $26,000. Then there was the sun-baked desert rat who took $25,000 from his Deep Secret Mine, but said there was too much overhead to make it worthwhile. He had to spend $5000 for supplies and $25,000 for whiskey.

THE 1872 EARTHQUAKE

On March 26, 1872, at 2:30 A.M. a major earthquake killed 29 people and injured many. The worst damage occurred at Lone Pine, where many homes were built of crude adobe—blocks of dried mud piled on top of each other, the cracks plastered with more mud. The adobe huts fell to pieces, walls and roofs crushing the sleeping occupants. A letter from John McCall of Lone Pine pictures the plight of many. "My wife and little daughter, as well as myself, were buried in the ruins for an hour and a half; there were four feet of adobe upon us. We were living a mile and a half from anyone, and were nearly dead when taken out. . . . Everything lost." Camp Independence and the County Courthouse were shattered.

The tragedy also produced some cherished stories. When his home collapsed, Burkhardt and his neighbor Lubken could hear the screams of Mrs. Burkhardt, but no sound came from his son who was buried too. "Hell," cried Burkhardt, "the Old Lady's screaming, so she's all right. Let her lay. We'll get the boy first." After they dug out young Fred and revived him, they exhumed his mother, undamaged but considerably riled, having heard what her husband had said. (*Up in Our Country,* G. P. Putnam.)

The *Inyo Independent* reported that a young gentleman of Bishop Creek was "setting up" with his young lady when the shock came. She fainted into

THE GREAT INYO EARTHQUAKE.

ANTONIA MONTOYA'S TRAGIC DEATH. DEATH OF MEYSAN'S CHILD. MUZINGER & LUBKEN'S BREWERY

LONE PINE DURING THE CONVULSION.

San Francisco Chronicle, April 21, 1872 (Courtesy Eastern California Museum).

After a 6-day trip over Walker Pass, a *Chronicle* correspondent reached Lone Pine. His report tells of the Meysan family's escape, and their horror on discovering that the seventh child was caught under their crumbling house. He tells also of Antonia Montoya, "a misguided young Mexican woman [left] . . . to perish miserably in the ruins."

his arms, and did not recover quickly. The next day he swore he would "give twenty dollars a shot for earthquakes when setting up with an offish gal."

THE SAGEBRUSH VALLEY BLOOMS

1878—The beginning of large irrigation projects. Settlers plan the McNally Ditch near Laws, the Bishop Creek Ditch, the Big Pine Canal, and a Lone Pine Ditch.

1883—The Carson & Colorado narrow gauge railroad is completed to Keeler, sending commerce north to San Francisco, rather than south to Los Angeles.

1885—The first county fair. First locations made on Owens Lake to recover salts from its brine.

1886—The Methodist church starts the first high school, the Inyo Academy in Bishop.

1887—Work begins on the Owens River Canal and the Inyo Canal.

1888—The Inyo Marble Company of San Francisco opens a quarry near Keeler.

1892—First Indian day school opens at Bishop.

1901—The "145," a citizens' organization formed to stop the contraband whiskey trade with Indians, forcibly puts the worst offender in his buggy and runs him out of the valley, besides "encouraging" six other traders to leave.

1902—The first bank, the Inyo County Bank in Bishop. The first public high school, in Bishop. The first electric plant, the Bishop Light and Power Company.

1903—The first city; Bishop people vote 63 to 36 to incorporate.

1905—The Nevada Power, Mining and Milling Company (parent of today's California Electric Power Company) completes its power plant on Bishop Creek.

1916—The State completes the first important section of paved highway, the road over Sherwin Hill; 1000 Valley people celebrate with a barbecue at Rock Creek. Peak production of the Tungsten Hills 1916–1918.

1917—Mount Whitney Fish Hatchery completed.

While rumors of ledges and nuggets kept the air filled with excitement, it was farming and ranching that brought stability to Owens Valley. The farmers who came with their families loved their land and stuck it out through good years and bad.

During the '70s, with Cerro Gordo, Panamint and Bodie at their peaks, farmers prospered. But when the big mines closed, and in addition the soldiers left Camp Independence, there were some lean years. Though the new railroad brought an outlet to Nevada and San Francisco, it also put many teams out of business, and engines ate no hay or grain. In the late 1880s, beef on the hoof went down to 2¢ a pound, the price of horses so low they were not worth feeding. Cash for taxes and mortgages was scarce. Good times returned in 1900 with the discovery of Tonopah and the growth of other large western Nevada silver camps. To them, Valley farmers shipped carloads of sheep, cattle, and hay, and quantities of produce.

Completion of the railroad to Owens Valley in 1883 added to the brightness the Valley's future seemed to promise. As the fabulous Nevada Comstock passed its heyday, the silver financiers had begun looking for other ventures. Believing the strikes near Owens Valley would prove important,

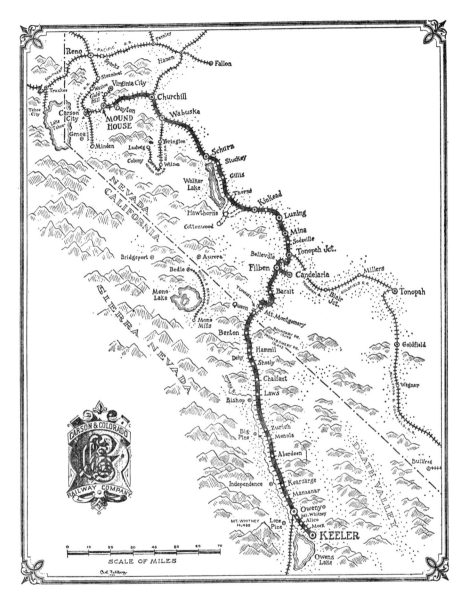

The Carson & Colorado Railroad

The railroad in its entirety, as built in 1881–1883. Added are other connecting or adjacent lines which then existed or were built in the next half century. (Courtesy John Hungerford, *The Slim Princess*.)

they thought a railroad to tap the expected flood of silver seemed a profitable investment. Organizing the Carson & Colorado Railroad, to connect
with their Virginia & Truckee near Carson City, they pushed narrow-gauge
tracks south across the Nevada desert and over Montgomery Pass into the
Valley. Plans were to continue on to the Colorado River, but by the time
three hundred miles were completed to Keeler, a slump in the price of silver
stopped all thought of extending the line farther. When San Francisco financial wizard D. O. Mills rode the train to Keeler to inspect his new railroad,
he was strangely silent. Finally, asked for his opinion, Mills is said to have
muttered, "Gentlemen, we either built it 300 miles too long or 300 years
too soon."

Mills proved right, for the mines did not materialize. In fact, Mills
thought he was doing well when in 1900 he sold the line to the Southern
Pacific for $2,750,000. Ironically, the same year rich ledges were discovered
at Tonopah; the story goes that in one year, hauling silver ore, the S.P.
earned back its investment. The western Nevada mines kept the C & C
profitably busy for some years. Later, as trucking became a more economic
means of hauling freight, bit by bit sections of track were abandoned.

Hungerford's *The Slim Princess* gives the full story of the C & C and
its casual habits—giving a lift to anyone walking the tracks, filling prospectors' water barrels, stopping while the crew took a dip in Walker Lake or
went hunting for a few hours. Indians were permitted to ride free in the
freight cars or on top, where their colorful shawls flapped in the breeze.

Their own way of life gone forever, many of the Paiutes who drifted back
from Fort Tejon went to work for the ranchers. The men became ranch
hands and cowboys; the women washed, ironed, and did garden work. While
some whites never had much use for them, real affection grew between others
and their Indian families. Some helped the Paiutes obtain land and protected
them from being cheated out of it. The Paiutes, in turn, taught the white
women some of their native remedies, were loyal to their friends, and took
the names of families they respected or worked for.

When pioneer John Shepherd died in 1908, the Paiutes wanted their own
ceremony in addition to his Masonic funeral. Two hundred of them danced
and chanted, then each passed the coffin and patted his face saying, "Goodby,
Shepherd."

A favorite story concerns Frank Shaw of Pleasant Valley, who needed
to go to town while the Indians were building fence. Worried that they would
loaf while he was away, he took out his glass eye, put it on a fencepost and
said "He lookum." During his absence there was little loafing.

Living became less harsh as frame houses replaced adobe huts. Shade
trees gave relief from the summer sun. Valley towns grew steadily, with more
churches and schools, better roads, more lodges and clubs. More farms had
substantial barns, silos, large neat farmhouses, and flower gardens.

Pioneers remember that when Bishop wanted to incorporate, the Women's Club had difficulty in listing the necessary 500 people. When someone discovered a new family just outside the limit, no time was lost in finding a place for them to live, for they had nine children. An Indian with a dozen children was promptly made a resident also.

Not all pioneer memories are happy. One wrote: "Grandmother . . . told me how very, very homesick she was and how she longed for her friends and the green wooded hills of Missouri. When she could bear it no longer she would go out in the tall rabbitbrush and have her cry out, then return with a smile . . . because for the sake of Grandpa's health they must remain in the west."

Farm families worked hard but had their fun too—Sunday visiting, picnics, and parties. Parents might take mattresses with them for the children to sleep on, while they danced until dawn and sometimes stayed for breakfast. Horse racing was a favorite sport, with tracks at Round Valley, Bishop, Wright's Place, and Independence. Clubs sponsored parades, barbecues, masquerades, and dances. The county fair was a real festivity. The Harvest Festival of 1912 boasted an Alfalfa Palace, built of eighty tons of baled hay.

The first settlers chose homesteads along the creeks and the river. Later settlers had to take land without water; but with thousands of swings of their picks and millions of shovelfuls of dirt, they carried the water farther and farther from the streams onto the parched land. With the land fertile, and a maze of canals and ditches brimming with water, the 4500 Valley settlers were turning their sagebrush desert into a pastoral paradise of orchards and hayfields.

Farm Census, 1910	*Farm Production, 1910*
43,000 sheep	58,000 bushels corn
5,000 horses	51,000 bushels wheat
20,000 cows and cattle	53,000 bushels potatoes
5,800 colonies of bees	174,000 pounds of butter
20,000 apple trees	37,000 tons of alfalfa
40,000 grapevines	100 tons of honey
	150 tons of grapes

The Valley's prospects seemed bright. The 1911 California Blue Book made these promising forecasts:

"Owens Valley is one vast sweep of tillable land, only one fourth of it as yet being under cultivation, the remainder holding forth immense opportunities to homeseekers and farmers, great and small. The amount of water for both irrigation and power is unlimited. Artesian wells have been bored successfully near Independence, artesian strata varying from 25 to 500 feet in depth, and the water flows in a steady stream. . . . Where sagebrush grows the rankest, there is the most fruitful soil if water can be put upon it, and there is plenty of water."

How that water went south to Los Angeles instead of onto alfalfa fields is a story that spanned the next twenty-five years.

LOS ANGELES BUYS THE RIVER

1892–1904—12-year drought in southern California.

1903—Engineer J. C. Clausen, of the newly created U. S. Reclamation Service, surveys Owens Valley's potential for a federal irrigation project. Settlers are enthused and back the project. As Los Angeles water tables continue to drop and stream flows to decrease, the Water Department meters factories and heavy users.

1904—Over 10 days, L.A. consumption exceeds reservoir inflow by 4,000,000 gallons.

August—Joseph Lippincott, an officer of the Reclamation Service and also consulting engineer to the L.A. Water Department, visits Owens Valley to inspect Clausen's study. Friends accompanying him include Fred Eaton, mayor of Los Angeles. Clausen gives a glowing account of the Valley's irrigation possibilities.

September—Within a week of his return, Eaton persuades his friend William Mulholland, Water Superintendent, to visit Owens Valley. The two spend over a month investigating the feasibility of tapping the Owens River. Later, to a few City officials, Mulholland outlines a plan for an aqueduct from Owens Valley to Los Angeles.

March 1905—Pretending interest in land for ranch purposes, Eaton obtains a $450,000 option on key property along the Owens River.

April—Eaton secretly shows the water possibilities to City officials, who pose as cattle buyers on their visit to the Valley.

May—Eaton turns the option over to the City. Eaton and his son secure options on other land necessary to the Aqueduct and secretly convey them to the City.

July—The *Los Angeles Times* breaks the Aqueduct story—estimated water will supply a city of two million. Los Angeles is jubilant; Owens Valley outraged. Lippincott recommends that the Reclamation Service abandon its irrigation plans and let Los Angeles take over the water project.

September—City reservoirs drop 3,000,000 gallons per day. Los Angeles votes $1,500,000 to buy Owens Valley land and water rights.

1906—Lippincott resigns from the Reclamation Service and accepts a leading post with the L.A. Aqueduct, taking with him all data on Owens Valley.

1907—The Interior Department abandons the Owens Valley reclamation project. Los Angeles votes $23,000,000 to construct the Aqueduct.

April 1913—Mulholland and a committee, meeting with Valley irrigators, agree verbally to the right of Valley ditches for a specified flow from Owens River. This agreement is never made binding nor fulfilled.

November—40,000 people at the San Fernando reservoir celebrate completion of the 233-mile Aqueduct.

1917—With abundant Owens River water, San Fernando irrigated lands multiply from 3,000 acres in 1914 to 75,000 acres of orchards and truck gardens.

1921—Another drought begins.

1923—Haiwee Reservoir drops and San Fernando is short of water. To assure more water for its aqueduct, the City begins buying land and water rights north of its Aberdeen Intake.

March—The City secretly hires William Symons, president of the McNally Ditch, to take options on all ditch property at $7500 per second-foot. Symons obtains 80 per cent of

McNally lands for $1,000,000. When the news becomes public, the Valley is furious at Los Angeles and at Symons and his assistant "traitors."

October—Big Pine Canal users sell 4400 acres for $1,100,000.

March 1924—With continued drought, Mulholland shuts off San Fernando water. San Fernando irrigators come to Bishop, trying to buy 50,000 acre feet of water. Valley leaders offer to sell all their land and water for $8,000,000, including $750,000 damages to businessmen for loss of trade.

May—Valley anger flares when Los Angeles files suit to recover McNally and Big Pine water, which upstream canals are "wrongfully diverting." Forty Valley men blow up the aqueduct north of Lone Pine.

November—City agents propose that 30,000 acres be "kept green" and free of city purchase but ignore damage claims. The Irrigation District (comprising the two big ditches left, the Owens River Canal and the Bishop Creek Ditch, Wilfred Watterson president) answers by seizing the Alabama Gates and turning all water out of the aqueduct for five days.

1925—To secure possession of the water it has already bought, but which upstream farmers are putting into their canals, the Water Commission begins buying land along tributaries of the Owens River. Bishop Creek users sell out to the city. City pays $1,000,000 for 2700 additional acres in West Bishop. Owens River Canal group holds out for higher prices.

1926—Owens River Canal users demand $2,500,000. Haggling becomes bitter. Valley men dynamite the aqueduct twice.

1927—L.A. continues to refuse damage claims. Deadlock on Canal price.

May-July—Fourteen dynamitings; City sends armed guards to patrol the aqueduct.

August—A state bank examiner arrives unexpectedly in Bishop and finds the Watterson banks short of over $2,000,000. Later the Watterson brothers are convicted of embezzlement.

1929—L.A. agrees to a 3-man board of arbiters to fix prices for remaining property, though refusing to pay damage claims.

1931—L.A. begins buying town properties.

While farmers blessed the generous river that watered their crops, four men from outside the Valley—J. C. Clausen, Fred Eaton, William Mulholland, and Joseph Lippincott—came to realize the value of that river also, but from differing viewpoints. Clausen was an engineer with the just created U. S. Reclamation Service. Mulholland was water superintendent, Eaton former water superintendent and now mayor of Los Angeles. Lippincott was employed by both, as an officer for the Reclamation Service and as consulting engineer for Los Angeles. Sent to survey Owens Valley, Clausen reported that with a dam at Long Valley and canals on both sides of Owens Valley, there would be enough water to irrigate over 100,000 acres of new land.

Among the first to hear Clausen's glowing report were his superior Lippincott, and Lippincott's friend Eaton. Both were men of vision, ardent Los Angeles boosters, and water engineers, keenly aware that recurring drought would limit their city's expansion. Eaton recognized immediately that the Owens River could provide plentiful water for a city of millions. He also knew that unless options were secured before the aqueduct news became public, land prices would soar. Masquerading at times as a rancher, other times as an agent for the Reclamation Service, he rapidly secured all the options necessary to the Aqueduct. Lippincott continued to serve two masters for a time, though early in the story he threw his lot in with the City. His high position in the Reclamation Service enabled him to spike the project in favor of Los Angeles.

Valley farmers did not object to the City's taking part of their river for city faucets, but they objected heatedly when they learned that much of the water would irrigate the dry San Fernando Valley. Los Angeles men, on the other hand, recognized that though their little city now needed but little additional water, the big city they dreamed of would need huge amounts, and that they must obtain that water quickly before others established rights to it. In the meantime, they could use the water to irrigate San Fernando.

The fight between Owens Valley and Los Angeles in the early years, then, centered on two points. First, *who* would harness the river, the Reclamation Service or Los Angeles? Second, could the City be prevented from using the water to irrigate San Fernando? When Valley farmers appealed to the Interior Department and President Theodore Roosevelt not to abandon the federal project, they were no match for the City of 200,000 with its political friendships and know-how.

Congress gave the City needed rights-of-way across federal land. Then the City found an ally in Chief Forester Gifford Pinchot, who closed the lands to homesteading by creating a huge federal forest district in the Valley, though the only trees were the poplars and locusts the settlers had planted. Pinchot also convinced his friend Roosevelt that there was no reason to prohibit Los Angeles from irrigating. Questioned on these points thirty years later, Pinchot wrote: "it is perfectly true that I did what in me lay to prevent the people of Los Angeles from being held up by a handful of people. . . . The essential fact is that I used my power . . . for the greatest good of the greatest number, and that the results have abundantly justified my action."

The Los Angeles Aqueduct, an engineering triumph.—Building the largest aqueduct in the Western Hemisphere was an engineering feat second only to the Panama Canal. Its 5,000 workmen required 57 camps, with 2300 buildings and tent houses. Needing a million barrels of cement, the City constructed a half-million dollar cement plant near Tehachapi. It built two power plants, 500 miles of roads and trails, over 400 miles of telephone and transmission lines. To move men and supplies, the Southern Pacific sent a 120-mile spur north from its main line at Mojave to Owenyo near Lone Pine. At Aberdeen, partway between Big Pine and Lone Pine, an intake diverted the river into a 60-mile canal which emptied into Haiwee Reservoir. Without a single pump, gravity pushed it the rest of the way through pipes, troughs, 12 miles of steel siphon (it took 52 mules to haul one section to the installation site), 142 tunnels, and two more reservoirs. The $25,000,000 project was completed in five years.

Though they had lost their chance for a federal irrigation project, and though the Aqueduct dried up the southern part of the Valley, most farm families had not yet been hurt. The center of agriculture lay upstream from the Aberdeen intake, along the ditches of the Big Pine Canal, Owens River Canal, Bishop Creek Ditch, and McNally Ditch.

Incredibly, the Aqueduct planners expected that a pipe stuck in the Owens River near its *mouth*, with miles of farmers' ditches taking out water upstream, would assure them adequate water. The essential that they over-looked was the pattern of eastern Sierra rainfall, several very dry years alternating with one or two very wet ones. During wet years, streams ran far out of their banks, with plentiful water for both City and Valley. During dry years, ditches took all the water, and the river bed was dry between Big Pine and Owens Lake. The next drought, beginning in 1921, made their mistake all too clear.

The 1920s started with a million dollar joke, at Los Angeles' expense, when it began buying water rights north of its intake. The plum it hoped to buy was the big McNally Ditch near Laws. Secretly hiring the Ditch president himself to act as their agent, the City purchased the Ditch for over a million dollars. To the delight of the Valley, the plum proved sour, for McNally water had no chance of reaching the Aqueduct intake thirty miles downstream. Small ditches took their share, and all that was left gurgled into the Big Pine Canal, fifteen miles upstream from the intake. A million dollars for nothing, chortled the farmers; but their hilarity was short

Water With a Kick in It!

Cartoon from the Los Angeles Times, November 23, 1924, when Valley ranchers "captured" the Alabama Gates and turned water out of the aqueduct for five days. Valley farmers posted armed guards at their head-gates, opened spillway gates, and blew up the aqueduct seventeen times. Newspapers generally condemned Los Angeles.

Will Rogers extended sympathy through his syndicated column: "Ten years ago this was a wonderful valley with a quarter million acres of fruit and alfalfa. But Los Angeles had to have more water for its Chamber of Commerce to drink more toasts to its growth, more water to dilute its orange juice. . . . So, now this is the valley of desolation."

lived. The City only stepped up its land purchases and its prices, and before the year was over bought the Big Pine Canal too.

Seeing the Big Pine people demand double the McNally price and get it, the remaining farmers held out for even fatter prices. Town merchants, seeing their trade dwindle as their customers moved away, decided they were entitled to damages. Town leaders urged the City to finish buying water rights, and in addition, to pay them damages. Arguments during the next years centered mainly on price.

Many farmers were in a poor position to bargain. With the postwar recession of 1921, many an Inyo farm was mortgaged. With Los Angeles water plans apparent, outside banks would not lend to Valley people. Now as hopelessness piled onto the bitterness engendered by years of defeat and broken promises, Valley feelings erupted. Peaceful farmers turned to dynamite. Though they knew a few explosions could not defeat the giant, they hoped to rouse public sympathy. In this they were successful.

The California legislature investigated the situation on two occasions, and both times severely criticized the City. The Senate unanimously adopted a resolution calling the episode "one of the darkest pages in our history . . . the utter destruction of one of our richest agricultural sections."

But sympathy did not change the march of events. In a manner quite unforeseen, Valley resistance ended suddenly and dramatically. A City official suspected that the Watterson brothers, owners of five Inyo banks and leaders of the Valley's fight, were in financial difficulties. At his instigation, a state bank examiner came to Bishop. The banks were in far greater difficulties than anyone supposed. When they closed and the brothers were convicted of embezzlement, the Valley was stunned. Their leaders had fallen; families' life savings were wiped out and merchants and farmers were without credit.

Hostilities over, Los Angeles finished its work—buying land, then extending the Aqueduct north into Mono County and building the Long Valley Dam. Next, to utilize the Long Valley water, it constructed power plants in the Owens River Gorge.

In justice to the City of Los Angeles, let it be remembered that no land was condemned, that water rights were purchased, and that many a rancher sold gladly for a price that made him financially independent.

The real tragedy lay with those farmers who loved their land and did not want to sell at any price. Some sold when mortgages came due and they saw no other way out. Others were tricked into selling. Checkerboard buying and planted rumors fed fear that their neighbors were selling, fear they could not maintain the ditches, fear that Los Angeles would divert their water. Some were induced to option upon being told that their neighbors had sold, only to find later that their neighbors had done no such thing. When they organized to resist scattered purchases, the City broke the pools by offering high prices to a few. Some ranchers could be fooled; others could be bought. The saddest part of the story concerns those Valley people who, for a price, broke faith with their neighbors and worked for the City as secret agents and informers.

The men of vision were devotedly ambitious for their city. To supply it with water they broke promises, masked their strategy, concealed their motives, and resorted to devious, though always legal, tactics. Had they also been men of compassion, had their vision included Owens Valley as well as their City, they might have filled their Aqueduct, watered Valley acres too, and avoided twenty-five costly bitter years.

The exciting, complex story, with its clashing personalities, broken friendships, betrayals, hidden motives, and political maneuverings, is told in Remi Nadeau's *Water Seekers*. W. A. Chalfant gives the Valley's side in *Story of Inyo*.

Sagebrush returns.—The '30s were sad years for Owens Valley. The City continued to buy, eventually owning most of the Valley floor. Pioneer families left the land their grandparents had homesteaded to earn a living elsewhere. By 1935, a third of Bishop had moved away. During dry years the City drained all surface water into the Aqueduct, besides pumping ground water. Those who leased land back had no water rights, and could irrigate only during the wet years when there happened to be extra water. Farming under such arrangements was impossible, though a few stockmen grazed cattle on land they leased from the City. Its ranches turning brown and only small mines operating, the eastern Sierra's future seemed bleak indeed. Forlorn houses and barns with dead trees, weed-grown fields, neglected fences, and empty ditches were poignant reminders of shattered hopes and plans. As one pioneer, returning for a visit, put it, "Every time we pass the old home place, my wife cries and I swear."

THE NEW VALLEY

1931—At Redrock Canyon 1,000 carloads of people celebrate completion of the paved highway between Los Angeles and Bishop.

1939—Large mill constructed at the Pine Creek Tungsten Mine.

1942-1945—10,000 Japanese live out World War II at the Manzanar Relocation Camp.

1953—Los Angeles completes the $45,000,000 Owens River Gorge hydroelectric plants.

1960—Population, 11,684 (doubled since 1930).

1961—Inyo National Forest ranks seventh among all National Forests in recreation use. Forest campground and picnic use multiplies ten-fold since 1940, Forest resort use twenty-fold.

1962—Recreation visitors, Inyo National Forest: 1,400,000.

In the hopeless years when their ranches were drying up, some Owens Valley people began to realize they still had the richest bonanza of all— their magnificent mountain and desert scenery. Today tourist business is double the value of ranching, mining, and lumbering put together. Service stations alone account for twice as many dollars as cattle. New motels, resorts, and campgrounds dot the Valley and its mountains.

Inyo County Statistics

Cattle sold (1959)	$2,000,000
Minerals produced (1960)	11,000,000
tungsten, soda products, pumice,	
talc, clay, and others	
Lumber produced (1960)	900,000
Retail trade (1958)	24,000,000

Many factors stimulated this astonishing growth of outdoor recreation, particularly the skyrocketing population of Los Angeles. As wages went up, working hours went down; automobile wheels were powered to roll faster on better roads. Rapid transportation has made the once-isolated Valley but half a day's drive from Los Angeles, a short day from San Francisco. The Inyo Good Road Club sent a lobbyist to Sacramento to make sure that far-off Inyo County would be included in highway plans and that some money would go to El Camino Sierra, now known as Highway 395. In addition, the Valley began to make itself known as a vacation land. Among the leaders who recognized the Valley's scenic assets and inspired others to begin building a new Valley, was Father John Crowley, the "Desert Padre" who helped organize Inyo Associates, an organization to develop the Valley's recreation potential. The establishment of Kings Canyon National Park and Death Valley National Monument brought national attention to the mountain and desert wonderlands nearby.

There is a new generation in Owens Valley now, which holds no bitterness about the past but accepts things as they are, which realizes that the future depends on coöperation with the City and the patronage of its outdoor-minded people. The City has sold some town property back to the people, and continues to do so when it believes demand justifies it. Scientific research in the Valley has barely begun. The unusual variety of climate, altitude, and plant and animal habitat offers scientists unique opportunities for study. Retired people are beginning to move to the Valley, in love with its space, clean air, invigorating climate, and outdoor life.

Both Inyo County and the Forest Service plan more campgrounds. The Forest Service plans additional ski areas. The State Department of Water Resources is now conducting a feasibility study of a proposed 30,000 acre-foot reservoir at Fish Slough which could provide a year-round warm water fishery. The U. S. Fish and Wildlife Service is studying the possibilities for a Federal Wildlife Management Area in the Valley which could provide feed and habitat for migratory waterfowl, serving as a refuge as well as public hunting area, and could also provide suitable habitat for pheasants. The local chapter of the Izaak Walton League is actively aiding government agencies and the City of Los Angeles in both these studies of additional recreational opportunities.

Fishermen in spring, campers in summer, hunters in fall, skiers in winter, artists, photographers, rockhounds, lovers of mountain and desert—this is the new valley. If there were somehow a way to get the water back, Owens Valley would provide the finest possible foreground—from one end to the other—for the all-year vacation land the surroundings have become. Little islands of greenness here and there suggest what might have been. But it has all worked out fairly well. For one thing, more and more people want less and less to live on farms. For another, it happens that man doesn't create water; he only uses it. He likes it best when it is fresh and cool. And he renews himself a little when he climbs up above Owens Valley to the great country to which water comes fresh and cool from the heavens, bringing quite a bit of heaven along with it. It waits there, not wanting quite to come down, nor to go back up, awaiting discovery by those who want to know the real meaning of the deepest valley.

Selected Reading.

CHALFANT, W. A. *Gold, Guns and Ghost Towns.* Stanford: Stanford University Press, 1947. 175 pp. Lively, humorous mining tales, by the late editor (for fifty-five years) of the *Inyo Register*.
   Story of Inyo. Bishop: published by the author, 1933. 430 pp. Details of Indian war and pioneer life, much of the information from local pioneers.

DOYLE, HELEN M. *A Child Went Forth.* New York: Gotham House, 1934. 364 pp. Out of print. Autobiography of Dr. Nellie, beloved doctor, who came to Owens Valley in 1887. Vivid picture of Valley life.

FARQUHAR, FRANCIS P. "The Story of Mount Whitney" in *Sierra Club Bulletin.* 14:1, 1929; 20:1, 1935; 21:1, 1936. Documented history of Mount Whitney.

HUNGERFORD, JOHN B. *The Slim Princess.* Reseda: Hungerford Press, 1958. 36 pp. Story of the Carson & Colorado narrow gauge; many illustrations. Available locally, or send $1.00 to Hungerford Press.

INYO REGISTER. Weekly Bishop newspaper, frequently publishing historical articles by Dorothy Cragen and others.

MURBARGER, NELL. *Ghosts of the Glory Trail.* Palm Desert: Desert Magazine Press, 1956. 291 pp. Tales, maps, and directory of 279 Great Basin ghost towns.

NADEAU, REMI A. *City-Makers.* New York: Doubleday, 1948. 270 pp. Out of print. Chapters on Cerro Gordo and Panamint.
   The Water Seekers. New York: Doubleday, 1950. 309 pp. Out of print. Story of the Los Angeles Aqueduct.

RAY, C. LORIN, ed. *Mementos of Bishop.* Bishop: Bishop Chamber of Commerce, 1961. 92 pp. Bishop Centennial book; many historic pictures. Available locally, or send $1.25 to Bishop Chamber of Commerce.

Groundwater Conflict 1970–

THE BITTER CONFLICT between Owens Valley ranchers and the Los Angeles Department of Water and Power ended in the 1930s, as described in the previous chapter. Many ranchers and merchants, seeing no future for their valley, moved away. Those remaining eventually realized that, although they had lost control of their water, they had not lost their dramatic mountain scenery and that a new future lay in promoting their valley and its mountains as prime vacation land.

During the next forty years, DWP continued to extend and enlarge its aqueduct system. By 1940 the system extended an additional 105 miles north, capable of gathering the waters of the Sierra Nevada tributary to Mono Lake as well as all waters tributary to the Owens River. By 1970 construction of a second aqueduct enlarged the system's capacity for export by 50 percent. To fill both aqueducts, DWP diverted four of the five streams flowing into Mono Lake and initiated large-scale pumping from wells in Owens Valley. As the consequences of pumping became evident, forty years of serenity ended abruptly. In 1972 Inyo County filed suit against Los Angeles.

Yesterday's conflict revolved around the right to use *surface water,* the right to divert running streams. Today's conflict centers on the right to use *groundwater,* which lies below the surface of even the most arid valleys. Does the owner of land have exclusive control over use of the water below? Does he have the right to drill and pump without limit—regardless of harm to plants, animals, air and people? An even broader argument questions whether anyone has the right to use *any* water without regard for the impact that use will have on other people and on the environment.

These are among the issues involved in the lawsuit filed by Inyo County against the Los Angeles Department of Water and Power. In the two chapters following, the special counsel to the County of Inyo and the chief engineer of water works and assistant manager, Los Angeles DWP, interpret the critical issues as they see them. Today's battle has been waged in the courtroom, and Inyo has looked to the law—not dynamite—for relief. The final outcome of this suit will have far-reaching implications for water use throughout the arid West.

June 1978   GENNY SMITH

Water for the Valley

HOW MUCH MORE OWENS VALley water shall go to Los Angeles? This is the question fundamental to one of the most significant environmental disputes of our time. The history of this dispute—of legal attack and counter-attack—is an exciting story in itself. The ultimate significance of *Inyo* v. *Los Angeles,* however, goes beyond the immediate struggle between county and city. For what we witness today, within our Deepest Valley, foreshadows even larger and more difficult controversies in the coming years: the efforts of regions with massive populations and immense appetites for material and energy, to extract the last resources of regions with small populations.

What right does one group of people, concentrated at the social and productive "center" of society, have to use up the resources of the sparsely populated regions? What right do the people in those regions, few in number, have to keep what nature has given them—not just to protect their environment, but to preserve their own options for future growth and development? These are questions that we all will face in our lifetimes on this planet.

1970: LOS ANGELES COMPLETES SECOND AQUEDUCT; STATE ENACTS ENVIRONMENTAL QUALITY ACT (CEQA)

This story begins in 1970. Two landmark events occurred that year, apparently separate at the time, entwined ever since. The Los Angeles Department of Water and Power (DWP or department) completed construction of its second aqueduct from the Owens Valley to Los Angeles, enlarging by 50 percent its capacity to export Owens Valley water to the city. To fill this "second barrel," the city for the first time implemented a systematic program of extracting the valley's groundwater. But just as DWP was putting its second aqueduct into operation, the state legislature enacted the California Environmental Quality Act (CEQA), in response to public demands that government agencies pay heed to environmental values when making decisions. As a starting point, the act required each agency to prepare an environmental impact report (EIR) on any project it proposed that might have a significant effect on the environment.

Antonio Rossmann, author of this chapter, is special counsel to the County of Inyo and one of California's leading public interest attorneys. Following his graduation with honors from the Harvard Law School in 1971, he served as law clerk to Justice Mathew Tobriner of the California Supreme Court. In 1975 he became California's first ombudsman when he was appointed Public Adviser to the California Energy Commission.

Los Angeles DWP increases groundwater pumping in Owens Valley.—
Los Angeles, in deciding to build the second aqueduct in 1963, originally
visualized a moderate program of groundwater extraction to supplement
natural runoff from the Sierra in dry years. Based on its projected needs and
on a simultaneous commitment to provide Inyo County ranchers who lease
DWP land with a firm supply of water in dry as well as wet years, the department stated its intention to pump in an average year 89 cubic feet per
second (cfs) of Owens Valley groundwater.* At the time the department
announced this intention, approximately 31,000 acres of its Owens Valley
holdings were irrigated and leased to Owens Valley ranchers.

Beginning in 1970, however, DWP constantly increased both its planned
extraction of groundwater, and its actual pumping. In 1970 the actual pumping exceeded 90 cfs. Two years later, pumping exceeded 200 cfs. Subsequently
the department proposed an average extraction rate of 180 cfs, with a dry
year maximum of 376 cfs.

Effects of more pumping.—Valley residents, whether aware or not of
DWP's plans, soon became aware of their effect. By 1972 two years of
heavy pumping had dried up the valley's most popular and ecologically
significant springs. The artesian wells along Mazourka Canyon Road, from
which Independence townfolk had for years taken fresh water, stopped
flowing; and the vibrant plant and animal community at Little Black Rock
Springs was destroyed. This loss was not compensated for by DWP's creation
of an adjacent artificial habitat at the discharge of one of its largest pumps.

The people of Inyo also noticed a dramatic increase in the frequency and
intensity of dust storms during the windy winter months. This exacerbated
dust level, with its attendant discomfort and aggravation of respiratory
conditions in older valley residents, seemed to be generated by DWP's
groundwater pumping. Prior to the pumping, the relatively high water table
in the valley supported water-loving plants which gave color and protection
to the valley's desert soils. But as the pumping drew down the water table,
many of these plants died off, leaving the soil susceptible to wind erosion.

In an effort to placate valley concerns and to show that its pumping
program would benefit the people of Inyo as well as Los Angeles, DWP in

---

* A cubic foot per second (or second-foot) is a measure of water flow: one cubic foot
of water flowing past a particular point each second. Pumping at a rate of one cfs for
one year will produce a total volume of approximately 236,000,000 gallons, or 724 acre-
feet. Equivalents for some of the pumping rates referred to in this chapter are as follows:
89 cfs equals 57,500,000 gallons per day; 315 cfs equals 203,000,000 gpd; 666 cfs equals
430,000,000 gpd. Flowing at full capacity, the aqueduct in one year can transport at
least 157 billion gallons from the eastern Sierra to Los Angeles. To complicate matters,
reliance on *average* extraction rates is generally not meaningful. In California water
seldom runs off in average amounts, but more often in extremes. Thus an average rate
of 89 cfs could anticipate no groundwater pumping at all in wet years and more than
double the average rate in dry years—at the very time when pumping might cause the
most environmental damage.

1972 circulated a draft water management plan describing the intentions and effects of the plan. Although DWP assured them that the increased pumping would bring a more reliable supply of water to the valley, valley residents found little comfort in those representations. They were quick to observe that whereas DWP now promised to irrigate 11,000 valley acres with a "firm" supply, DWP had actually irrigated three times that much acreage a decade before. Moreover, the 1972 report confirmed the city's intentions to increase the intensity and scope of groundwater extraction. New wells would be drilled, and the 89 cfs long-term rate projected in 1963 had grown to 180 cfs.

1972: INYO COUNTY SUES LOS ANGELES CLAIMING IRREPARABLE DAMAGE AND CLAIMING CEQA MANDATES AN ENVIRONMENTAL IMPACT REPORT

When confronted with similar unilateral decisions by the city in the past, Owens Valley people had appealed to the state legislature for assistance and, by forceful actions such as dynamiting the aqueduct in the 1920s, appealed to public sympathy. In 1972, however, the people of Inyo believed that the legislature had already provided the relief they needed by enacting CEQA. So for the first time in their history, Inyo people through their county government appealed to the courts to enforce the law for their protection.

On November 15, 1972, District Attorney Frank Fowles filed a lawsuit in the Inyo County Superior Court. In that action, entitled *County of Inyo* v. *Yorty* (Inyo County Superior Court No. 9365) the county claimed that the department's groundwater pumping project was producing an irreparable environmental impact on the Owens Valley and that the department had failed to prepare an EIR on that project. On behalf of the county Fowles demanded (1) that Los Angeles be enjoined from extracting any more groundwater from the Owens Valley; (2) that DWP be ordered to prepare an EIR; and (3) that the court retain jurisdiction over the county's claim to ensure that no groundwater pumping would take place that would cause environmental damage in the valley.

Narrowly, then, the county demanded an EIR. More broadly, however, the county asked the court to prohibit any groundwater pumping that would harm the environment. The former claim drew upon the letter of the law in CEQA; the act clearly required EIRs on new projects with potentially adverse effects. But the county's latter claim—that the law substantively prohibited environmental damage to the valley—was not clearly authorized by CEQA. Five years would pass before the county's basic plea—that its environment not be destroyed—matured as a claim that the courts would recognize.

Superior Court rules against Inyo.—In response to the county's lawsuit, Inyo County Superior Court Judge Verne Summers issued a temporary restraining order against any increased pumping. But Judge Summers never had the opportunity to decide whether that injunction should continue or to adjudicate the county's claim and the city's defenses. Less than two weeks after the suit was filed, Los Angeles invoked a provision of state law which enabled the city as defendant to demand that the case be tried in a separate county. Judge Summers granted the department's motion to change venue, and the parties agreed to remove the case to Sacramento County, a neutral location that was reasonably accessible to both sides.

In January 1973 the matter came before Sacramento Superior Court Judge William White (Sacramento County Superior Court No. 228928). The county sought to obtain a preliminary injunction that would remain in effect until the trial was completed. On January 19 Judge White denied that injunction, concluding that the city's principal defense was meritorious: because the second aqueduct was completed and placed into operation prior to the effective date of CEQA, no EIR could be required on either the aqueduct or on the pumping that was initiated to fill the aqueduct.

Court of Appeal assumes jurisdiction.—The county now faced a turning point. By order of the Superior Court, the groundwater pumping and its adverse effect on the valley would continue. While the county could proceed with a trial in this court, Judge White's preliminary ruling did not offer Inyo much promise that its claim—that an EIR was legally necessary—would prevail. So District Attorney Fowles took the best route open to protect the county's position. On January 26, 1973, he submitted a petition to the Third District Court of Appeal in Sacramento, asking the appellate court to order Judge White to halt pumping until completion of the trial in his court. Such an unusual petition would be granted by the appellate court only if it believed the county's claim to be substantial.

The court of appeal did not issue the injunction that the county requested. Instead on February 26 it took an action of far greater magnitude and significance: the appellate court elected to treat the county's request for an injunction as a claim for final relief on the merits, and boldly assumed the duty of adjudicating that claim on its own, without trial in the superior court. In so acting, the court of appeal followed a rarely invoked but well-established procedure that allowed it to assume original jurisdiction over a claim of great public importance, whose significant issues must be resolved as soon as possible.

Thus the court of appeal in Sacramento became the primary forum in which have been resolved the county's claims for relief from DWP's groundwater pumping in the Owens Valley. Over the next five years that court would write for itself, the people of Inyo, and the people of our state one of the most distinguished chapters in the history of judicial response to an intense public controversy. The court's eloquent wisdom, expressed first through its Justice Frank Richardson (now a justice of the California Supreme Court) and subsequently through Justice Leonard Friedman, not only balanced and adjudicated the claims and interests of Inyo and Los Angeles. It also charted a course for all Californians to heed in meeting human needs from diminishing and remote natural resources.

1973: COURT SUSTAINS INYO CLAIM THAT LOS ANGELES MUST PREPARE EIR ON PUMPING

Following the court's assumption of original jurisdiction, Inyo and Los Angeles in March 1973 submitted briefs restating and refining their positions. Inyo claimed that notwithstanding the completion of the aqueduct in June 1970, the city's continued and expanded extraction of groundwater since that time formed a "project" under CEQA for which an EIR was required. The county cited specific examples of destruction of the valley's environment, such as the drying of natural springs, to dramatize the need for an EIR. Los Angeles, on the other hand, argued that in 1970 its second aqueduct was already completed and, as early as 1963, was approved and financed on the premise that systematic groundwater extraction would take place in the valley. Thus CEQA should not now be retroactively applied to determine if that which was already approved should be reapproved.

On June 27, 1973, the court of appeal issued its decision. In that opinion (*County of Inyo* v. *Yorty* (1973) 32 Cal. App. 3d 795) the court sustained Inyo's claim. Noting that CEQA required decision makers in government to identify and evaluate environmental factors and to prevent irreparable harm before it is too late, the court emphasized that an EIR was at the core of this now-mandatory process. In order to carry out the law's intent, the court held, the completed project of the second aqueduct should be separated from the ongoing project of groundwater extraction. An EIR should be prepared on this ongoing project so that its potential to harm the environment would be revealed.

Three-year dispute over the rate of interim pumping, 89 cfs or 211 cfs.—The court then turned to the difficult task of determining the rate of groundwater pumping during preparation of the EIR. The court noted the county's claim of perceptible damage caused by pumping. At the same time, the court recognized DWP's vital role as supplier of water to the state's largest city and the city's need for a reliable and adequate source of water. Weighing these considerations, the court declared a temporary pumping rate of 89 cfs— the pumping rate in November 1970 when CEQA became applicable—and directed the Sacramento Superior Court to conduct further hearings to determine an interim pumping rate that represented an average of extraction for the wettest and driest years between 1970 and 1973.

Although the court of appeal may have anticipated that its orders would be carried out with dispatch, three full years were devoted to disputes over the interim pumping rate and over the scope of the EIR. When the superior court in October 1973 conducted its first proceeding to refine the pumping rate, DWP over the county's strenuous objection convinced the court to permit pumping up to 221 cfs on a fiscal year (July to June) average. The county brought its objections to the court of appeal; that court in a brief order of September 4, 1974, set aside the 221 cfs rate, re-established the 89 cfs rate temporarily, and ordered the superior court to attempt a more equitable application of the 1970–1973 average.

Three-year dispute over the scope of EIR: should it encompass only pumping for use in Owens Valley, or pumping for aqueduct export too?—In its preparation of the EIR, the department proceeded on the following premise: because the court of appeal required an EIR for the pumping program but not for the second aqueduct, groundwater pumping for aqueduct export was not part of the project; instead, the EIR would only evaluate the project of increased pumping for use in the Owens Valley. Thus, not only would the EIR address pumping of a much smaller scope, but also the *alternatives,* which CEQA required to be identified and considered, would only embrace alternatives of less water left in the Owens Valley. In a nutshell, Los Angeles proceeded with these strong convictions: that in 1963 the total export of water from the valley—from groundwater as well as surface sources—was planned to maintain a level of 666 cfs; that DWP had already approved a groundwater extraction plan to maintain that level; and therefore DWP need not evaluate in its EIR any change of that export level.

Dispute over irrigation supply for valley ranchers.—Until September of 1974 the county objected, with little efficacy, to what it viewed as a deliberately truncated definition of the groundwater pumping project. In that month an unfortunate decision by Los Angeles brought this issue to a dramatic head. As related above, on September 4 the court of appeal had set aside the superior court's 221 cfs rate and temporarily reinstalled the 89 cfs rate. In response, DWP announced on Friday September 20 that it would terminate the Owens Valley ranchers' irrigation supply the following Monday. In justifying this move, which the department's aqueduct engineer later characterized as "educational," the department claimed that it was forced to cut back because of the district attorney's success in rolling back the 221 cfs rate.

The department's precipitous action immediately brought the county's new district attorney, L. H. "Buck" Gibbons, back into Judge White's Sacramento courtroom. Gibbons sought and obtained on September 27 a temporary restraining order against cutting back irrigation supplies. He also sought to enjoin further processing of the EIR on grounds that it purposely misdefined the scope of the groundwater pumping project. Once the temporary restraining order was issued, however, the other matter never came to hearing. Instead, the department agreed to withdraw its draft EIR and prepare a revised draft and, in preparation of that draft, to consult system-

atically with the government and citizens of Inyo. The county and DWP also
agreed to a total groundwater extraction of 68,000 acre-feet for the winter
of 1974–75, to govern instead of the 89 cfs annual rate that the court of
appeal installed, pending the superior court's resetting of the rate. In May
1975 the superior court reset the pumping rate at 178 cfs, again over the
county's objection.

In its subsequent EIR preparation the DWP did establish formal mech-
anisms for receiving county input. Not only did it provide the county with
advance copies of its draft, but it also established an EIR task force of
Owens Valley citizens with whom it met regularly. Despite these gestures,
however, Los Angeles never succeeded in overcoming the valley's general
distrust for the process and substance of DWP's efforts. More often than not,
it seemed to the valley folk, DWP was using the public meetings not to
receive comments or criticism, but instead to sell its preconceived assumptions
and judgments. Despite repeated valley objections to DWP's assumption
that its EIR did not have to address groundwater for export, DWP insisted
that the only project for which the court ordered an EIR was that of
groundwater extraction for Owens Valley uses.

DWP certifies EIR and approves large-scale pumping program.—In May
1976 the controversy fully matured. Just as the briefing had been completed
in the court of appeal on Inyo's claim that the superior court had erred again
in setting an excessive pumping rate of 178 cfs, the department published
its final EIR and announced its intention to certify it within the month.
These actions meant that DWP would shortly approve the expanded groundwater pumping program. In response to the comments on its EIR, DWP had
modified its program somewhat. Rather than a long-range average pumping
rate of 180 cfs and a maximum of 376, DWP now proposed a long-range
average rate of 140 cfs with a maximum of 315 cfs. No new wells were to be
drilled. Nonetheless, aqueduct export remained fixed at 666 cfs.

In its three-volume report justifying these decisions, the department
devoted but a handful of pages to discussion of the alternatives that meant
most to Inyo county: conserving water in Los Angeles and obtaining more
water from its other historic source, the Colorado River. Despite the county's
strenuous objections, the city showed no intentions of altering either its EIR
or its groundwater project. With no relief apparent to the county short of a
major court battle, District Attorney Gibbons recommended to the Inyo
County Board of Supervisors that it engage special counsel to meet the
demands of litigation, and on June 1, 1976, the board adopted the recom-
mendation.

Los Angeles' formal approval of the project and certification of the EIR
were scheduled for June 3. The district attorney and special counsel obtained
a brief postponement in order to address personal appeals to the Los Angeles
Board of Water and Power Commissioners, Mayor Thomas Bradley and

City Attorney Burt Pines—asking each to exercise responsibility and avoid a legal fight that, in the county's view, the city could only lose. Bradley and Pines never responded, and the Water and Power Commissioners on July 15 certified the EIR and approved the full groundwater pumping project.

1976: DISPUTES OVER
ADEQUACY OF EIR AND INTERIM PUMPING RATE

Anticipating that DWP would certify the EIR and then ask the court of appeal to dismiss Inyo's suit because the EIR had been completed, the county had one week earlier seized the initiative in that court. Urging the court to reassert the original jurisdiction that it had assumed in 1973, the county asked the court not to discharge Los Angeles' responsibilities until it had evaluated the adequacy of the department's EIR. The law not only required an EIR, claimed Inyo, it required an adequate one. In addition, until such adequacy was determined, the court must continue to restrain groundwater pumping in the valley. Furthermore, the county asked the court of appeal to set the interim pumping rate itself. In response the city argued that, by completing its EIR, it had discharged its duty to the court and that no need remained for the court to establish pumping rates.

Court rules it will evaluate EIR.—At the extraordinary oral argument of July 21, 1976, the court of appeal resolved some of these claims and established the framework for resolving them all. Departing from its accustomed pattern of hearing formal argument for 30 minutes at most and of announcing its decision weeks or months later in a written opinion, the court in this instance devoted more than two hours to reach this immediate conclusion: that its 1973 mandate required not only an EIR, but an *adequate* EIR. Furthermore, that adequacy must be judicially reviewed; the court established a process for that evaluation.

Court sets interim rate at 149 cfs.—In its subsequent written opinion of August 17 (*County of Inyo* v. *City of Los Angeles* (1976) 61 Cal. App. 3d 91), the court of appeal reaffirmed its original jurisdiction over Inyo's claims and determined itself the pumping rate to govern pending review of the city's EIR. It accepted Inyo's claim that the superior court's rate was too high and that it should have been set on a water-runoff year (April to March) rather than a fiscal-year basis. Nonetheless the court rejected Inyo's claim that the court abandon the 1970–1973 average and constrain DWP to the 89-cfs rate that coincided with CEQA's effective date. Taking judicial notice of the dry condition prevailing, the court fixed the rate at 149 cfs, subject to the significant condition that DWP provide valley users their customary supply.

1976: INYO REVIVES THE MAJOR ISSUE: DOES CEQA PROHIBIT HARMFUL PUMPING IF DWP HAS A LESS DAMAGING ALTERNATIVE?

For Inyo, the opportunity was now ripe not only to void the EIR, but also to revive its original claim that the law under CEQA prohibited Los Angeles from unnecessarily harming the environment of Owens Valley. Thus in late 1976 Inyo urged the court (1) not only to reject the EIR because of its faulty project definition and failure to assess meaningful alternatives; (2) but also to reject the department's *decision* as a violation of the California Constitution's mandate that all the state's water be conserved; and (3) to enforce CEQA by ordering Los Angeles to reject its environmentally harmful pumping program and accept the less damaging alternative of water conservation in Los Angeles.

To these claims the city responded (1) that its EIR fulfilled the requirements of the court's 1973 order; (2) that its EIR incorporated the findings of more than fifty public meetings and consultations with valley officials and citizens; and (3) that the groundwater pumping would benefit the valley by providing it with a greater supply of water than would be possible from only surface supplies. As to Inyo's constitutional claim that Los Angeles conserve water, the department argued that Inyo county could not press such claim because it owned no water rights competing with those of Los Angeles; moreover, conservation in Los Angeles lacked relevance to a groundwater pumping program designed to benefit water users in the Owens Valley.

DROUGHT OF 1976–1977 INTENSIFIES THE CONFLICT

Before it could resolve these claims, however, the court of appeal became the vortex of even more intense conflict between county and city—conflict produced by the severe California drought of 1976–77. By its August 1976 order setting the rate of 149 cfs, the court of appeal seemed to force Los Angeles to react. During the relatively dry 1976 water year, when surface supplies in Owens Valley were low, the department filled the aqueduct by pumping at rates sometimes exceeding 200 cfs. Cut back in August to a 149-cfs rate, the city turned to its other sources of water—the Colorado River and the California Water Project.

But as 1976 ended with even less precipitation than 1975, amid predictions that 1977 could produce the worst drought in California's history, even southern California's vast water supply system became overtaxed. By year's end 1976, as reservoirs dwindled, most northern California communities had adopted water conservation measures saving 25 to 60 percent. Because the California Water Project could not meet all its municipal requirements and leave any significant supplies for Central Valley agriculture, the State

Department of Water Resources obtained an important agreement from the Metropolitan Water District (MWD). (MWD serves a large part of southern California and at times sells water to the DWP.) MWD agreed to forego most of its 1977 importation of northern California water and to rely exclusively on its Colorado River supply.

Nonetheless, officials in the southland contended that with only moderate ten percent conservation effort, all needs could be met. Los Angeles' problem, then, was not a shortage of water but a matter of economics. Colorado River water from MWD generally cost Los Angeles more than groundwater from the Owens Valley.

Los Angeles asks the court to allow pumping at a maximum rate of 315 cfs.— In late February 1977 the department cited these facts to the court in support of its motion to pump at a maximum rate of 315 cfs. In further support of its positions, the department submitted unsworn statements that it had solicited from Owens Valley ranchers, whom the department had led to believe would receive irrigation supplies only if the pumping rate was increased.

Pointing out that the drought had produced greater distress in Inyo than Los Angeles, the county responded by urging the court to reject the department's claim in light of Los Angeles' failure to adopt a single water conservation ordinance. The county also criticized the department for misrepresenting the ranchers' position and presented a sworn statement from the president of the Inyo Cattlemen's Association that the department had failed to disclose to the ranchers that the court's August 1976 order guaranteed them their customary supply of water.

In an extraordinary preliminary memo, court replies that until Los Angeles conserves water, its request to extract additional Owens Valley groundwater is not likely to be granted.—The court's response to these claims spoke to all Californians and to all times. Issuing a preliminary memorandum on March 24, but four days after hearing argument, the justices wrote that Los Angeles' failure to adopt an effective conservation program, standing alone, would compel denial of DWP's motion to increase the pumping rate:

> In relation to the state's current water crisis, the effort at voluntary conservation is inadequate to justify the requested relief. The California Constitution abjures the waste of water and seeks its conservation in the interest of the state's entire population. When the state's water resources dwindle, the constitutional demands grow more stringent and compelling, to the end that scarcity and personal sacrifice be shared as widely as possible among the state's inhabitants.

Moreover, the court did not find impressive Los Angeles' argument that it should increase its Owens Valley extraction in order to save the higher purchase cost of Colorado River water:

> Unless and until the municipal government of Los Angeles installs and implements methods which are predictably capable of achieving substantial water

savings and demonstrates a need for water rather than rate preservation, its motion for leave to extract additional underground water from Owens Valley is not likely to achieve success.

Although the court had before and has since published lengthy decisions sustaining the county's claim under CEQA, its brief four page memorandum of March 24, 1977, may likely endure as its most significant teaching. In the midst of the worst drought in our history, the court said that shortage required the sharing of resources throughout the state. Sharing became not a gesture but a *constitutional duty;* the state is but one ship in which all its citizens are equal passengers. If one region or city does not face hardships as great as those in other parts of the state, it must if possible restrict its own use of resources to alleviate the greater hardship of other Californians.

Equally important, the court's ruling suggested that before new resources could be extracted, the alternative of conservation must first be implemented—a highly significant rule that not only spoke to the conditions of the 1977 drought, but that also speaks to all future developers of natural resources. Before completing its review of the department's EIR, the court would further clarify this valuable rule—but not before having to face yet another critical conflict between county and city.

As noted above, in August 1976 the court ordered DWP not to reduce its supply of water to Owens Valley users below that customarily maintained since May 1975. In the valley's view, this order required the normal supply of irrigation water to begin on April 1 as customary. The department, on the other hand, in its public statements indicated that *if* allowed to pump at the maximum rate of 315 cfs, it would then "be able" to supply irrigation water at *half* the 1975 rate. April 1, 1977 passed, and neither county nor ranchers received assurances when the irrigation season would commence or how much water would be available. The next day, when the Board of Supervisors received the department's request for permission to increase pumping, the Board urged the department not to threaten contempt of court by failing to supply the normal amount of irrigation water. By April 11 the department had provided no response, except for a press statement that it was confused as to whether the court meant for water to be supplied at the 1975 or 1976 rate. In the valley, a department official stated that *no* irrigation water would be released without further order from the court. The county then asked the court to order irrigation forthwith. Only after this motion was filed, did the department announce that on April 15 it would begin supplying irrigation water—but at half the normal rate.

Again the court acted with unprecedented dispatch. The county's motion was filed on April 13, the department's response on the 21st. The court heard oral argument on Friday, April 22, and issued its decision the following Monday. It ordered the department at once to provide irrigation water during the 1977 season at 75 percent of the normal full supply.

Although the county had asked for the full supply in 1977—to compensate for the 50 percent cutback the prior year and the poor condition of the pasture lands—county and ranchers welcomed the relief that the court provided. The court's order of a 25 percent cutback in 1977 conformed to the water conservation goal that Governor Edmund G. Brown, Jr., had requested of all Californians and that the county had demanded of Los Angeles. Even more importantly, the court's action proved to the ranchers and other citizens of Inyo that the department would fail in its effort to play "water politics." For the moment the department was frustrated in its attempt to manipulate the irrigation supply as a dividing wedge between the ranchers and other citizens of Inyo.

1977: COURT RULINGS VINDICATE INYO'S CLAIMS

With the interim pumping rate and irrigation supply disputes momentarily resolved, county and city awaited the court's judgment on the lawfulness of the EIR and on the city's decision to expand its long-range groundwater extraction. On June 27 the answer came: virtually total vindication of Inyo's claims.

EIR must include pumping for aqueduct export.—By its decision of that date (*County of Inyo* v. *City of Los Angeles* (1977) 71 Cal. App. 3d 185) the court of appeal held that DWP's EIR was legally inadequate and refused to certify the department's compliance with CEQA. With forceful and precise language, the court traced the tortuous history of DWP's EIR preparation. Characterizing DWP's misinterpretation of the project to exclude groundwater for export as "serious," "wishful" and "egregious," the court pointed to its consequences. Not only had Los Angeles evaded an assessment of the project's impact on Inyo, but it had also concealed from the citizens of Los Angeles as well as Inyo the true nature of the groundwater pumping proposal and its impact on the people and environment of both communities.

CEQA requires Los Angeles to select the alternative least damaging to the environment.—Responding to the county's claim that DWP had failed to consider the constitutionally mandated alternative of water conservation in Los Angeles, the court wrote:

> The underlying policy and express provisions of CEQA limit the approving agency's power to authorize an environmentally harmful proposal when an economically feasible alternative is available. Notably, the Los Angeles EIR omits another alternative, one freighted with costs other than dollars. The omitted alternative is a tangible, foreseeably effective plan for achieving distinctly articulated water conservation goals within the Los Angeles service area. It is doubtful whether an EIR can fulfill CEQA's demands without proposing so obvious an alternative.

In this brief passage the court charted again a new course for county and city and all others to follow. Not only must conservation be examined as the alternative preferred by the California Constitution; but also the substantive provisions of CEQA, as interpreted by the legislature and Supreme Court, *required* selection of the conservation alternative if conservation (as contrasted to extraction) would result in less damage to the environment. Never before had a court so ruled.

The court concluded its opinion with an admonition to the city: it should not await the compulsion of further judicial decrees to fulfill its legal duties— duties not necessarily limited to preparing a valid EIR on Owens Valley groundwater pumping. In addition to the duties of conservation and of rejecting harmful projects in the face of less damaging alternatives, the court cited the advice of California Deputy Attorney General Larry King that DWP would most faithfully fulfill the law by preparing a comprehensive EIR on *all* of its water gathering activities, which would enable the city each year to select from its many sources the conservation and extraction pattern that minimized harm to the environment.

CITING DROUGHT AND DWP'S WATER CONSERVATION PROGRAM, COURT GRANTS CITY'S PETITION TO PUMP 315 CFS UNTIL MARCH 1978

The court's landmark ruling was but two days old, however, when the city boldly petitioned the court anew for permission to pump groundwater at a maximum rate of 315 cfs. This time the department came to court better prepared. In response to the court's March 24 memorandum, the city had instituted a mandatory conservation program calling for 10 percent reduction in water use; actual savings were in excess of 15 percent. Of at least equal significance, the city's motion was supported by the Metropolitan Water District. MWD claimed that its other consumers in southern California would be harmed if Los Angeles exercised its lawful right to purchase more MWD (Colorado River) water. Basically the city argued that since the drought was so severe that all water supplies and groundwater basins in the state were being drawn down to their limits, the Owens Valley groundwater basin should not be excepted.

The county objected to these arguments. Even though the city had for the first time in its history implemented a mandatory water conservation plan, its performance did not match that of northern California urban centers, or even the 25 percent cutback which the court had ordered in Owens Valley. Moreover, argued Inyo, MWD should not complain until it had achieved 25 percent savings in its entire service area. The county also stressed again that it had suffered from man-made as well as natural drought, because of the pumping since 1970. Finally, the county urged that the 149-cfs rate be maintained to provide DWP an incentive to complete an adequate EIR and comply with the law.

A tense courtroom heard these arguments on July 21. The justices, normally inquisitive and lively at oral argument, spoke little. But one day later their decision came: provided that DWP pump only from deep wells and that the city maintain 15 percent conservation, the pumping rate until March 1978 would be doubled to 315 cfs.

The city greeted this news with elation. City Attorney Pines in a press release hailed his efforts successfully protecting the city's rights; later he cited the July pumping order as proof that his office had achieved victory in its litigation against Inyo County. Other southern California communities also expressed relief; the City of San Diego put aside plans for implementing mandatory water conservation.

The people of Inyo were stunned. How could they have prevailed totally in their legal claims a month before, only now to have the fruits of that victory denied? Why should Los Angeles take all Owens Valley water, while saving only 15 percent, when Owens Valley was expected to and willing to save 25 percent? What purpose did it serve to challenge Los Angeles in court and win on the merits, if *in extremis* the city to the south and its neighbors could prove that "might still makes right?"

The county nonetheless took this defeat with dignity. According to some, Inyo could accept defeat easily because she had become conditioned by years of the city's feudal bondage. But other people in the valley—especially Inyo's Board of Supervisors—saw the need to do better and to work harder. The county engaged a professional hydrologist, to overcome the DWP's monopoly on expert knowledge of the groundwater supply, and then looked beyond the courtroom to find a long-term resolution of its dispute against the city.

STATE SUPREME COURT DENIES CITY'S PETITION THAT IT REVIEW COURT OF APPEAL'S DECISIONS

However, the last and greatest judicial victory of 1977 belonged to Inyo alone. Frustrated in its efforts to implement a groundwater program free of the county's objection and judicial supervision, the city doubled its legal forces and in early August petitioned the California Supreme Court to review the court of appeal's decisions. Not only did DWP argue that the court should have accepted its EIR as adequate. It also claimed that *all* of the court's decisions since 1973—including its decision to exercise original juris-diction, its ruling that the city must prepare an EIR, and its restraints on groundwater pumping—had been in error. The city and its supporters, in-cluding the Metropolitan Water District and the *Los Angeles Times,* firmly believed that the Supreme Court would release them from the court of appeal, which in their view had become "an adversary contestant dueling with Los Angeles to restrict export from Owens Valley and to reallocate its water rights."

The county responded to these charges and then awaited the decision. If the Supreme Court accepted Los Angeles' petitions, Inyo's five-year effort to secure justice from the courts would be cast into doubt for the months or years that would be required for the Supreme Court to render a new decision of its own. If the court denied the petitions, however, Inyo's positions—and the propriety of the court of appeal's forward-looking mandates—would be vindicated.

On October 6 the word came, ironically from Los Angeles. While sitting in that city, the Supreme Court by unanimous vote and without elaboration denied Los Angeles' petitions. The next day's *Los Angeles Times* headlined, "Owens Valley Wins Major Water Battle over L.A."

WHAT LIES AHEAD FOR VALLEY AND CITY?

For the people of Inyo, and the people of Los Angeles, the Supreme Court's decision came at the right time. For even as the two were battling in the summer of 1977, the California Department of Water Resources and the Attorney General were bringing county and city to the conference table to explore the possibilities of cooperative management of the water resources in the Owens Valley for the mutual benefit of both parties. The county gratefully accepted this invitation, hoping to secure a voluntary plan that would produce not only an EIR, but also a water management plan that would protect its environment and still fairly provide both Los Angeles and Inyo with water. DWP, while also accepting the invitation of the state, withheld any commitments until the Supreme Court completed review of the case.

With the high court's final word received and with both sides standing to benefit from cooperation rather than confrontation, county and city have continued to meet. Many difficult problems remain. Hopefully they will be ameliorated as the county becomes a more active participant in the evaluation of hydrologic data and the decisions that flow from such evaluation. In the end, the success of this effort will depend upon both county and city accepting the wisdom that Justice Friedman imparted in the court of appeal's 1976 decision: "Neither party can have what it wants or needs; rather the needs of both must be recognized and balanced."

Nor should resolution of the groundwater dispute halt further cooperative efforts in the valley. Other problems of long standing must also be addressed, with all concerned recognizing not only the lawful prerogative of the city as owner of land and water rights, but also recognizing the need to restrain the absentee landlord's actual and potential abuse of power in preventing Inyo citizens from determining their own future. Among the problems today, in the valley's tourist-oriented economy, business people need more security than the five-year lease to which DWP currently restricts its town properties. The city will earn much good will when it forthrightly offers these properties for sale or longer lease, in a spirit of accommodating the existing economy rather than withholding one more implement of suzerainty. Similarly, ranch leases can and should be written to give each lessee security and a firm commitment of water, while still protecting the city from the creation of competing water rights or claims. Finally, in supplying domestic water to the towns, cooperation rather than conflict should prevail. If the department were to charge valley customers a fair rate for valley water, and if it recognized the need for independent Public Utilities Commission review of its valley rates, then the people of the valley would welcome additional measures to prevent waste of water.

During the past decade the Owens Valley has served as the battleground from which have emerged experiences and rules of law to which others—in the West, the nation, and the world—will look for guidance in the coming years of increasing shortages and sharpened conflicts. Let all who read this recent history recognize, however, that Inyo's greatest achievement and the court's greatest reward lie not in the protection of Inyo's inanimate resources, but rather in the renaissance of self-respect and self-determination in her *people*. Ahead of us waits the next and greater question: whether genuine cooperation—between the powerful and the few, between the urban center and the rural valley, between the consumer of vast resources and the dwellers on the land from which those resources come—will also emerge from America's Deepest Valley.

Water to the City

THE ISSUES RAISED BY INYO County's lawsuit against Los Angeles' pumping of groundwater from under its lands in Inyo County for beneficial use in Owens Valley and Los Angeles extend beyond environment, energy and economics.

GROUNDWATER IN THE DEEPEST VALLEY: IS IT A QUESTION OF USER OR USE?

These broader issues can be focused by asking, "Is it a question of user or use?" The answer is based on our lifestyle preference, the money we are willing to commit to achieve that, and our willingness to make sacrifices. The answer will reflect society's view toward the development of renewable natural resources, such as water, and nonrenewable resources, such as oil.

A word about writing style: the arguments made against the city's activities in Owens Valley frequently appear in a style relying heavily on adjectives which color fact and create varying shades of meaning. That style has a strong emotional tone which is important to keep in mind.

OWNERSHIP OF WATER

One facet of the "user or use" question is ownership of water. The right to *use* water can be obtained by any person, agency, city, etc., if certain laws and administrative regulations are followed.

Los Angeles' rights to water in the Owens Valley were developed according to those laws and regulations. In 1905 the city posted a notice of its intention to use 1000 cubic feet per second (cfs) of Owens River in Los Angeles and filed a copy with the Inyo County Recorder. In 1934 the city applied to the State Water Rights Board for permission to divert 200 cfs from streams tributary to Mono Lake for use in Los Angeles. A permit was issued in 1940 and a license, which confirms the amount of reasonable beneficial use, was issued by the State Water Resources Control Board in 1974.

Rights to use groundwater are based on the ownership of property overlying a basin. When conflicts arise between pumpers, they settle among themselves or in court since the legislature has not established laws providing for the acquisition of rights through the permit process as it did for surface water.

Paul H. Lane, author of this chapter, is Chief Engineer of Water Works and Assistant Manager of the Los Angeles Department of Water and Power. Mr. Lane lived in Owens Valley in the early 1930s near Keeler where he attended school and from 1961 to 1966 near Big Pine. He was a member of the Big Pine School Board. His Department career began in 1949 and he has been involved with the Owens-Mono operations since 1961. He has a fond appreciation for Owens Valley.

The City of Los Angeles owns 240,000 acres in Inyo County, most overlying the Owens Valley groundwater basin. As a result of conflicts between pumpers in the Bishop area 50 years ago (the *Hillside* case), the city does not pump groundwater from a certain area in and around Bishop for export. There have been no other conflicts between pumpers in Owens Valley that have resulted in a limitation on the city's pumping for local use or export.

THE SECOND LOS ANGELES AQUEDUCT

Groundwater was one water source for the second aqueduct which was approved by Los Angeles in 1963 to increase export to 666 cfs. The other sources were to be streams in the Mono Basin and savings achieved by increased efficiency in irrigating the city's Owens Valley lands.

With the second aqueduct, the use of the Owens Valley groundwater basin was expanded. Historically, the city had relied upon the underground as a storage reservoir to maintain the supply to the city. Pumping rates as high as 188 cfs occurred during droughts in the early 1930s and 1960s. The new use to be made of

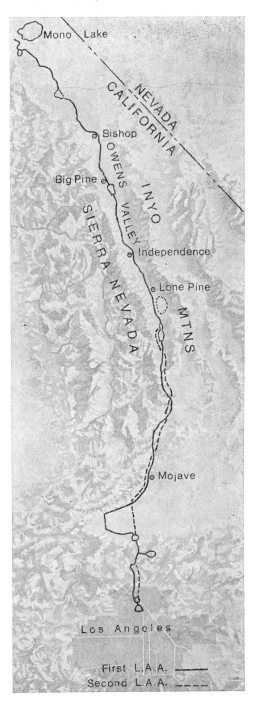

Los Angeles Aqueduct System

the basin was to salvage some of the water wasting to the atmosphere because of high groundwater levels. The 1968 Inyo County General Plan discusses the water salvage development potential in Owens Valley:

> By establishing a ground water operation it would be possible to control the levels of the ground water table in such a way as to prevent loss of water consumed by evaporation and transpiration. A mechanism could be established to maintain quantities of water required in conjunction with surface storage supplies to maintain a full flow of the Los Angeles aqueduct system; plus to maintain the water levels necessary to control evaporation and transpiration. (Page 25)

The concept of salvage relates to the *reasonable* beneficial use of water as distinct from beneficial use. Although the Supreme Court in *Hillside* found that subirrigation resulting from high groundwater levels was a beneficial use, the use was not *reasonable,* considering the facts of that case.

The projected pumping rates for the second aqueduct varied from a maximum of 250 cfs in the driest years to zero in the wettest. The average would be 89 cfs. Because the proposed pumping would be less than the average inflow to the groundwater basin (400 cfs), there would be no continual lowering of water levels as in the San Joaquin Valley, where pumping exceeds average inflow.

Need.—There were four reasons for building a second Los Angeles aqueduct. First, the Supreme Court in *Arizona* v. *California* issued a decision in 1963 that established the amounts of water that Arizona, California and Nevada could divert from the Colorado River. Ultimately, when Arizona completed an aqueduct to utilize its share, the Metropolitan Water District of Southern California (MWD) would lose approximately half of its flow in the Colorado River aqueduct. The Central Arizona Project is now under construction and should be completed by 1985. Parenthetically, MWD's rights are being jeopardized by another claim—that of the Navajo Indians.

Second, the city needed another aqueduct to beneficially use all the Mono Basin water permitted by the State Water Rights Board. If this water was not used, the city would lose part of its filing. Had that happened, water supplies to southern California would have had to be increased from the State Water Project.

The amount of water contracted for by MWD from the State Water Project is based on Los Angeles obtaining 666 cfs from the second aqueduct. Parenthetically, the State Water Project is also in jeopardy. Facilities in existence are sufficient to deliver one-half the water to which the state is obligated.

Third, the quality of Mono Basin streams and Owens Valley groundwater would be superior to that of the Colorado River and State Project waters.

Fourth, water from the second aqueduct was projected to cost $25 per acre-foot. Water from the MWD, which cost $29 at the time the second

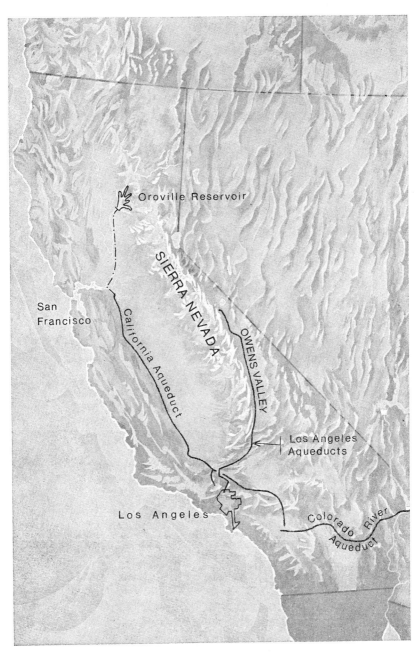

Aqueducts serving Los Angeles or Southern California: the State's California Aqueduct brings water from the Feather River; MWD's Colorado River Aqueduct from the Colorado River; and the Los Angeles Aqueduct from the Owens River and Mono Basin.

aqueduct was approved, was projected to cost $75 in the early 1970s. The rate effective July 1, 1978, is $95. Los Angeles Aqueduct water, excluding any credit for generation of electricity, cost less than $40 per acre-foot.

Water use in the Owens Valley.—Before the second aqueduct project, water for irrigation of 30,000 acres of the city's lands had been available on a feast or famine basis. When there was more surface water than needed to fill the aqueduct, city lands were irrigated. In dry years there was no irrigation and wells were turned on to maintain export to Los Angeles. Irrigation was cut off during five years between 1948 and 1970 and reduced during two.

A part of the second aqueduct project would replace the hit-or-miss irrigation method. The best 15,000 acres of the intermittently irrigated 30,000 acres were to be selected and supplied water year-in and year-out by pumping groundwater. Thus, even though the average acreage would be less, the firm supply combined with the higher productivity lands would result in net improvement for ranch lessees. No plans were made for use of water on city lands other than irrigation of 15,000 acres and use by livestock.

Construction.—The estimated cost of the second aqueduct was to be approximately $100 million. Because the city's pumping during the 1930s and 1960s was at rates near those planned with the Second Aqueduct, only two percent of the construction cost was for new wells. The aqueduct, begun in 1964, was completed and placed in service on June 26, 1970.

Inyo's study of second aqueduct.—Inyo County knew about the water sources and operation of the second aqueduct project. Their knowledge came from meetings with the city, a 1964 report by Stoddard and Karrer, consulting engineers who had been hired by Inyo to review the city's project, and a 1966 report by Los Angeles made in response to a resolution introduced by Senator William Symons (Inyo). This latter report described aqueduct system operations and local water use, both historically and forecasted with operation of the second aqueduct.

A WATER AND LAND USE PLAN

In September 1967, Inyo County petitioned the state to prepare a "comprehensive watershed protection plan" for the Owens River Basin and to prohibit increased export until the plan was adopted. Discussions on such a plan occurred off and on until November 1971, when representatives from the county, state and city agreed that DWP would prepare a water and land use plan. A detailed water study would be published first. That would be summarized and combined with the land use element to complete the second document. Public meetings were held in spring 1972 to obtain input. A draft of the water report was completed in October 1972 and given to the county and DWR (State Department of Water Resources) for comments. The projected maximum and average pumping rates in the report were 376 cfs and 147 cfs, respectively. The average rate represents a 65 percent increase over the rate approved in 1963 for the second aqueduct.

Why the increased pumping?—Several changes occurred between 1963 and October 1972 that required increased groundwater pumping. One thing didn't change—the average export to Los Angeles: it has always been 666 cfs.

What did change? The amount of land to be irrigated. In the negotiations with lessees to select 15,000 acres of the most productive land to be irrigated on a year-in and year-out basis using groundwater, DWP agreed to approximately 19,000 acres. The supply for this greater acreage would have to come from groundwater.

Also, DWP had planned to construct windmills, pipelines and troughs to supply water for livestock as part of the second aqueduct project. Those plans were not implemented. Instead, most stockwater continued to be diverted through unlined canals and ditches, a method of supply that required more groundwater pumping.

Another need resulted from DWP's participation in the Interagency Committee on Owens Valley Land and Wildlife (formed in 1970). The committee has established several recreation/wildlife areas that use water, such as the Buckley Ponds Wildlife Habitat Enhancement Project near Bishop.

Further, DFG was planning to expand operations at fish hatcheries and rearing ponds in the Owens Valley beyond the levels that could be supported by natural spring flow. Pumping would be necessary, and even though much of that water would flow through the hatcheries and contribute to the aqueduct system, the average pumping would increase because the wells would have to be operated during wet years.

THE EIR

Inyo County's November 1972 lawsuit seeking an EIR on increased pumping for export came as a surprise. Not only had the second aqueduct been in full operation before the California Environmental Quality Act (CEQA) took effect on November 23, 1970, but it had been operating for more than two years prior to the lawsuit.

DWP prepared the EIR mandated by the Third District Appellate Court's June 5, 1973 decision on a project defined as increasing pumping above the rate of 89 cfs for use in Owens Valley. This was based on the court's separation of increased pumping from the second aqueduct.

Consultants were retained. In January 1974 DWP formed the Owens Valley Groundwater EIR Advisory Committee of 17 residents of the Owens Valley having a diversity of interests. In mid-1974 Inyo County hired two consultants to assist them in review of the EIR's hydrology, flora and fauna. The draft EIR was completed in August 1974, one month after the date approved by the superior court in October 1973. A revised draft was published in January 1975 that included a discussion of alternatives calling for reduction in export from the Owens Valley.

After public meetings and technical workshops in Owens Valley, comments on the draft were evaluated. Consultants did additional work and more data was collected. The final EIR was released in May 1976. It contained detailed responses to comments made by members of the advisory committee and categorical responses to comments of others. The recommended project had been modified. Copies of the final EIR were given to the state for comments. None were received during the normal review period provided by CEQA's guidelines. The final EIR was approved by the Los Angeles Board of Water and Power Commissioners July 15, 1976.

Inyo objected to adequacy of the EIR, citing incorrect project definition and inadequate environmental assessments. On June 27, 1977, the appellate court found the project defined incorrectly, finding that the construction of the second aqueduct was separate from its operation and that all increased pumping above the long-term historic average should be considered rather than just the increment resulting after the passage of CEQA in 1970. About the city's environmental assessments, the court said:

> The project concept does not vitally affect the "impact" sections of the Report. The forecasts of environmental consequences in the Owens Valley are premised upon a long-term pumping rate of 140 cfs, which approximates the "project" as conceived in this Court's decision of June 1973. Thus, the informative quality of the EIR's environmental forecast is not affected by the ill-conceived initial project description.
>
> Inyo County strongly criticizes the environmental impact sections of the EIR, charging that the report understates the harm to flora and fauna of the Owens Valley and fails to describe air pollution potentialities. Courts are not equipped to select among the conflicting opinions of warring experts. It is not the function of the Court to determine the accuracy of the report's environmental forecasts. Reasonable foreseeability is enough.

On February 27, 1978, the court, in denying $85,000 of attorney fees to Inyo County's special counsel Mr. Rossmann, noted, "Its [Inyo County's] resistance to the environmental impact report was not impelled by the report's deficiencies but by its own litigational interests." *

OWENS VALLEY ENVIRONMENT

A representative of the Sierra Club stated, "We recognize that Los Angeles is probably the savior of the Valley . . . our goal is to preserve the Valley as it is now." (*National Geographic*, January 1976, page 123). Living in Owens Valley is a life apart from the pollution, congestion and other urban problems familiar to us all.

Air quality.—Air quality is among the best in the state, with visibilities of 50 miles, 80 percent of the time. Infrequent dust storms, less than two per year based on visibility records at the Bishop airport from 1959 to 1975, arise from all parts of the valley. An article in the April 1876 Inyo newspaper notes such a storm.

---

* This observation is, as of May 1978, not final and is subject to voiding and reversal by the California Supreme Court.—Ed.

The air basin implementation plan approved in 1971 states that a monitoring program for particulate will begin when funds become available. Not until 1978 did an approved sampling program begin, the last basin in California to start such a program. The delay in monitoring is testimony to the absence of a problem.

Other evidence came in 1976 when the Inyo County Planning Commission acted on Lake Minerals Corporation's proposal to expand by 8,000 acres the salt recovery operations on Owens Lake. Information from the China Lake Naval Weapons Center indicated that the salt recovery operations at the lake were the single most important source of dust during wind storms. The commission approved the expansion of the salt recovery operations with a negative declaration (no significant impact) based on a one-page initial study which did not mention dust.

Vegetation and groundwater.—Groundwater is within 10 feet of the floor of Owens Valley in most areas. As a result, water evaporates from the soil and plants. Evaporation from the soil is not beneficial. The use by plants may be beneficial. Whether it is a reasonable beneficial use depends on the value of the water and uses the water would otherwise serve. Groundwater pumped by DWP would be taken away from some plants and used by people and business in Los Angeles and for ranching, recreation and support of wildlife habitats in Owens Valley.

DWP's pumping is from lower zones in the groundwater basin. These are separated from the shallow zone, which the plants draw from, by zones of clay. The result is that fluctuations in the shallow zone caused by deep pumping take 5 to 10 years or more. The vegetation changes that ultimately would take place were described in the EIR.

DWP expanded its monitoring of water levels and vegetation in 1975. After three years, vegetation appears to be most affected by the amount and seasonal occurrence of rainfall and the patterns of livestock grazing. Shallow water levels declined two feet or less over most of the valley floor during that period.

REASONABLE WATER USE

Los Angeles.—The per capita use of water in Los Angeles was relatively stable from 1958 to 1978 at roughly 175 gallons per person per day (gpcd). Per capita use is all water used in the city (residential, commercial, industrial and governmental) divided by total city population. This figure of 175 gallons per capita per day is about average for the South Coastal Hydrologic Study Area, which extends from Ventura County to the Mexican border (DWR *Bulletin 198*, page 16). On a statewide basis, this per capita use is the lowest; the statewide study area average is 340 gpcd.

One reason for the city's relatively low per capita use is that the city began metering in 1903. People pay for all the water they use. Beginning in

December 1977, all residents started paying for water at the same rate, regardless of the amount of use. The same is true for commerce and industry.

The city has a voluntary conservation program which began before and continues after the mandatory provisions in effect during the 1977 drought. Kits to reduce water use in showers and toilets have been made available free to the entire city, and more than 600,000 kits have been given out. Hundreds of thousands of information brochures and educational materials have been given to citizens and schools. There is an active speakers bureau. Programs also assist industry, and DWP has crews assigned to detecting leaks. An ordinance prohibits hosing off sidewalks and driveways, untimely repair of leaks, serving water in restaurants unless requested, and the use of nonrecycling fountains.

Owens Valley.—Per capita use in Owens Valley ranged from more than 500 gpcd to more than 1,400 gpcd (DWR, *The California Drought 1977— An Update February 15, 1977,* page 149). This does not include any agricultural use. There were no meters in Owens Valley until 1976 and residential use is unmetered in 1978.

Irrigation is predominantly flood irrigation of uncultivated land; less than one-ninth of the acreage is sprinklered. The average use is four acre-feet per acre. In contrast, Water Code Section 1004 specifies that 2.5 feet per acre is considered beneficial for uncultivated land. Water is delivered through unlined canals and ditches; most other farming areas use pipes or concrete canals.

WATER RESOURCE DECISIONS

I think of water resource decisions in terms of the three Es: environment, energy and economics. Balance is important. The following is a list of primary considerations in each category for the use of groundwater from the Owens Valley basin.

Environment.—In Owens Valley, the issues are aesthetics, air quality, vegetation and wildlife. In Los Angeles, the issue is air quality because the oil that would have to be burned to produce the same amount of electricity as produced by water flowing through power plants along the aqueduct would add to air pollution in the Los Angeles area.

Energy.—Water from Owens Valley flows by gravity to Los Angeles and produces electricity at hydroelectric power plants enroute. An alternate supply from the Colorado River or State Aqueducts has to be moved over mountains using pumping plants that consume energy.

Economics.—In Owens Valley, economics is related to recreation and ranching enterprises that depend on water. In Los Angeles, economics is related to the cost of alternate supplies from the Colorado River and State Aqueducts.

SOMETHING OTHER THAN GROUNDWATER?

The October 10, 1977 *Wall Street Journal* discussed Owens Valley groundwater and Inyo's goal in terms of control of destiny. I have heard that issue repeatedly and I believe it has prolonged and exacerbated whatever real controversy has existed or exists between the city and Inyo over water, whether surface or groundwater.

IT IS A QUESTION OF USER

I believe the answer to the opening question is: it is a question of user. The competition for resources is such that it can be no other way. To allow a resource to be unused may be beneficial but not reasonable. The State Constitution mandates that the state's water resources be put to use to the fullest extent possible. To this end, the needs for water should be reasonable and the resource development program represent a balance between the three Es—environment, energy and economics. I believe there is such a balanced program for Owens Valley groundwater and that the city will preserve Owens Valley as one of California's scenic treasures because that goal is compatible with protection of the city's water supply.

New information

SINCE THE TYPE for our original nine chapters was first set, in 1962, some roads and trails have been rerouted and new information has never ceased flowing in. The following items bring the text up to date (1978). We urge you to mark all these changes in the margins of your book and on maps. Each year is sure to bring additional changes; for the latest information, check with the "Sources of Information" listed below.

Alabama Hills p. 24.—Recognizing its dramatic scenery and high value for public recreation, the BLM has designated the Alabama Hills "Recreation Land." Camping is permitted, but bring your own wood and water.

Bighorn Sheep Zoological Areas pp. 84–86, 155.—To try to halt the severe decline of the Sierra bighorn, two areas where the sheep have priority over other uses have been established along the Sierra crest west of Lone Pine and Independence. Travel through the areas is limited to the Shepherd, Baxter and Sawmill Pass trails.

Birds.—Chukars *seldom* compete with native quail for food and habitat, p. 156. The white pelican is a protected bird, p. 158.

Bishop Creek canyon p. 57.—Six miles of high-speed road have replaced the old narrow road of the lower canyon. To see the geological features described in the text, take the *old* Bishop Creek road. About 5 miles west of Bishop, where the new road swings off to the right, follow the old road that heads into the canyon and follows the creek.

The bristlecone pine pp. 50–53.—Self-guiding trails, interpretive signs and handsome displays. The road is two-lane blacktop to Schulman Grove; to the Patriarch, it is graded and narrow; beyond, it is very rocky and rough. Be sure to start out with a full gas tank and a supply of water.

Grandview Campground. A dry camp—bring wood as well as water.

Sierra Viewpoint. Magnificent panoramic views in every direction.

White Mountain Research Station. The navy completed its projects and no longer supports the station. Astronomical research may assume major importance. Low-altitude facilities are now near Bishop.

Schulman Grove Visitor Center. Picnic tables, exhibits, ranger talks. You can never truly know the bristlecone unless you experience the Methusaleh Walk. Nowhere else in the world can you walk such a trail in as strange a forest—a dead-living forest of silver-gray skeletons and scraggly living trees. Bare branches tufted at the ends with stubby green needles. Twisted black and gray roots clinging to the white dolomite as it crumbles into sand. No ground cover, a few dwarfed plants, no sound of water, seldom a bird—a silent forest, with little to distract you from the bristlecone.

Pinus longaeva, p. 127, is the scientific name for these bristlecone. In 1970 Dana K. Bailey, after intensive study, determined that these and other Great Basin bristlecone differ enough from those in the Rocky Mountains that they should be classified as a separate species.

California Electric Power facilities, p. 57, were acquired by Southern California Edison.

Campgrounds p. 17.—Three different agencies—the BLM, U. S. Forest Service and Inyo County—provide campgrounds. The Interagency Visitor Center near Lone Pine (see below) has information on *all* of them.

Cottonwood Creek and Lakes pp. 23, 32, 78–81.—Extension of the Carroll Creek Road, now called the Horseshoe Meadow Road, in 1967 brought far-reaching changes to the Cottonwood basin. Four of the thirteen lakes, long famous for their golden trout, have been closed to fishing—a sad example of people wanting to "open up the wilderness," only to find that wilderness disappears in the very process of opening it up.

The Cottonwood Lakes are the primary source in all the world for golden trout eggs. Prior to 1967, the 10½-mile trail from lower Cottonwood Creek kept fishing pressure in balance with the fish population; goldens were plentiful and fishermen often caught their limits. But in 1967, the Horseshoe Meadow Road made it possible to reach the lakes by hiking only five easy miles instead of ten very steep ones. Faced with the probability that crowds of fishermen might fish out the lakes in a single season, even before the road was completed the State Fish and Game Commission closed Lakes 1, 2, 3, 4 and their tributaries to all fishing. Lakes 5, 6 and all the lakes of the South Fork chain remain open.

In general, the Sierra's small lakes and streams can maintain their fish populations naturally *only as long as* they are not fished by too many people. When new roads and easy trails bring crowds, the waters either must be closed—as at Cottonwood—or they must be planted with hatchery catchables. One by one, waters with wild trout have disappeared. Planted regularly with catchables, those same waters lose all the thrill and variety that made them special and become just like dozens of other roadside waters.

Trails. Inquire at the Interagency Visitor Center near Lone Pine about campgrounds, road conditions and trail mileages. The hikes on pp. 78–81 now begin near the end of the Horseshoe Meadow Road (about 9700) instead of at lower Cottonwood Creek (5300). Subtract at least 6½ miles from all our old trail mileages and delete paragraph 4 on p. 78. Most of the other trail descriptions still apply. Horseshoe Meadow and Trail (Mulkey) Pass are now easy hikes; Cottonwood and South Fork Lakes, moderate. Golden Trout Camp has recently been operated as a boys' camp. The Stevens sawmill burned in 1965.

Earth movements p. 100.—The station at Tioga Pass is *four* inches higher than it was 17 years ago, not two and one-half inches.

Fish of the Owens River p. 162.—Because of the relatively low temperature of the Owens River, it is doubtful that channel catfish will ever become abundant. Ecologically, the river is better suited for black bass than for channel catfish. The 15-mile stretch between Pleasant Valley Dam and Five Bridges is managed for wild trout only and no stocking occurs there.

Highway 6 now begins at Bishop and leads east over Montgomery Pass into Nevada. The highway between Olancha and Bishop is now simply Highway 395. South of China Lake, what used to be Highway 6 is now Highway 14. Change all maps and especially lines 3 to 5 on p. 19.

Horn pp. 113–114.—The correct word is not *matterhorn,* but *horn.*

Independence p. 41.—See corrected map below for historic buildings and the new location of the Eastern California Museum. The museum and Little Pine Village have extensive collections on exhibit: Paiute-Shoshone baskets and other artifacts, tools and early farming equipment. Displays focus on Camp Independence, 1862–1877; Cerro Gordo; the Japanese Relocation Camp at Manzanar, World War II; rocks, minerals and fossils. To subscribe to the museum bulletin, write Box 206, Independence, CA 93526.

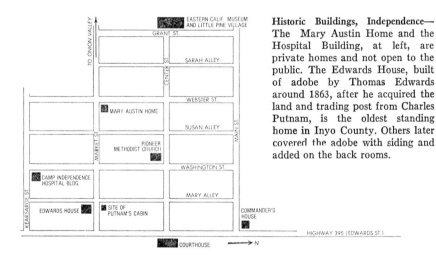

Historic Buildings, Independence— The Mary Austin Home and the Hospital Building, at left, are private homes and not open to the public. The Edwards House, built of adobe by Thomas Edwards around 1863, after he acquired the land and trading post from Charles Putnam, is the oldest standing home in Inyo County. Others later covered the adobe with siding and added on the back rooms.

Indian Wells Valley p. 18.—N.O.T.S. renamed Naval Weapons Center.

Interagency Visitor Center, Lone Pine p. 28.—Important source of all kinds of visitor information. See below "Sources of Information."

Inyo dolomite, p. 25, was used in the terrazzo flooring of the Los Angeles International Airport.

The John Muir Wilderness Area, p. 97, encompasses the former High Sierra Primitive Area.

Laws Railroad Museum and Historical Site pp. 62–63.—Centered around the 1883 depot and yards of the Carson & Colorado narrow-gauge railroad, the museum complex also includes a historic Catholic church and several Old-West-style buildings that served as movie props in the Paramount film "Nevada Smith." Collections include Indian artifacts, bottles, musical instruments and farm equipment. Contemporary local art is often on exhibit. In summer, open daily; in winter, usually on weekends. The Bishop Museum &

Historical Society welcomes your membership to support the restoration program: Box 363, Bishop, CA 93514.

Maps.—The best single map of the area by far is the Forest Visitors Map published in 1972 by the Inyo National Forest. Scale, ½ inch = 1 mile; 30 x 40 inches, 4-color. Available at ranger stations.

Mazourka Canyon Road p. 35.—Cars need *above-average* clearance.

Ninemile Canyon p. 19.—Lines 7 and 8 should read: "About 10 miles north of the Highway 14-395 junction, the Ninemile Canyon road . . . "

Off-road vehicles.—Inquire at the "Sources of Information" listed below for maps showing what areas are open for racing and cross-country.

Olancha Sand Dunes p. 26.—The dunes are open to off-road vehicles and to organized racing.

Owens Valley geology p. 102.—The diagram should be titled "Generalized geologic structure of Owens Valley."

Paiutes p. 170.—The Owens Valley Paiute-Shoshone Cultural Center, in Bishop 1½ miles west of Highway 395 on Line Street, is under construction. Inquire locally when it will open to the public. Conceived by the Tribal Elders, the project is directed by the Owens Valley Paiute-Shoshone Indian Bands Board of Trustees.

Palisades sketch, p. 51, is labeled incorrectly. Middle Palisade is just to the right of Birch Mountain, Mount Sill just to the left of North Palisade. Palisade Glacier extends farther to the right.

Pine Creek Mine p. 60.—Union Carbide Corporation owns the mine.

Redrock Canyon p. 17.—Lines 7–9 should read: "Just before entering the canyon, if you look on the hillside to the right, you can see pale lavender sediments ending abruptly at the fault against hard brown rock." The present word order implies that the sediments lie along the fault, which they do *not*.

Trails and Wilderness Permits pp. 68–99.—To hike trails within the John Muir Wilderness—that is, most of the trails described—you need a wilderness permit. Permits are free and available at Inyo National Forest ranger stations in Lone Pine and Bishop and at the seasonal entrance stations. Hiking is limited on some trails, unlimited on others. Inquire about limitations on the trail you want to travel as far in advance as possible, lest you arrive at the roadend packed and ready to take off, only to find the day's quota is full. Since camping places along the Mount Whitney trail are scarce, reservations are necessary during most of the summer. Within a broad policy of accomodating as many people as possible without destroying the very wilderness qualities they come for, back country limitations vary from place to place and are likely to change. They may include: a reservation system; limits on group size and length of stay; daily quotas; where wood is scarce, prohibitions on wood fires; where forage is scarce, limits on grazing; where meadows and lakeshores are hard packed from trampling, closure to all camping and grazing until plants return.

Pacific Crest Trail. New sections of the trail were constructed in the 1970s, too recently to show on many maps. Inquire locally.

Tule elk p. 151.—The controversy was resolved by agreement on the number of elk, distributed among five herds. Hunts are no longer permitted; surplus elk are removed to other locations. A knoll about 8 miles south of Big Pine is one of the best viewpoints to see the elk.

Volcanic Tableland p. 118.—The ash flows are 700,000 years old.

SOURCES OF INFORMATION

Some of the information on pages 55, 67 and 69 is no longer correct. Addresses have changed; some back-country camps are no longer in business.

Interagency Visitor Center. South of Lone Pine at the junction of Highway 395 and State Route 136. The one center where you can obtain information on facilities provided by *all* federal, state and local agencies serving Owens Valley. Established in 1977 by the twelve agencies responsible for land and resource management. Viewpoint of Mount Whitney, outdoor and indoor exhibits, large selection of books and maps. Latest information on campgrounds, weather and trail conditions. Box 889, Lone Pine, CA 93545.

Inyo National Forest. Wilderness permits, maps, information. Lone Pine District Ranger, Lone Pine; White Mountain District Ranger, 798 North Main Street, Bishop.

Bureau of Land Management, 873 North Main Street, Bishop. Brochures, maps, information.

California Department of Fish and Game, Bishop. Maps and information.

Eastern High Sierra Packers Assoc., Box 147, Bishop, CA 93514. Guided trips; horses, mules, burros. Write for list of pack stations.

Palisade School of Mountaineering, Box 694, Bishop, CA 93514. Winter: ski mountaineering, guided alpine ski tours. Summer: instruction in mountaineering, rock climbing, ice and snow climbing; seminar on mountain medicine; guided climbs.

Accomodations and services. Bishop Chamber of Commerce and Visitor Center, City Park, Bishop. Lone Pine Chamber of Commerce, 104 North Main Street, Lone Pine.

NEW BOOKS

Trail guides, road guides, new books on the Sierra, on history and natural history roll off the presses at such a rate it is hard to keep up with them. Write these publishers for their lists of new titles:

Chalfant Press, P O Box 787, Bishop, CA 93514. Local history.

Sierra Club Books, 530 Bush Street, San Francisco, CA 94108. Backpacking, mountaineering, climbing and trail guides.

University of California Press, 2223 Fulton Street, Berkeley, CA 94720. California Natural History Guides, see especially: *Geology of the Sierra Nevada* by Mary Hill; *Sierra*

Wildflowers by Theodore Niehaus; *Native Trees of the Sierra Nevada* by Peterson & Peterson; *Introduction to California Plant Life* by Robert Ornduff.

Wilderness Press, 2440 Bancroft Way, Berkeley, CA 94704. Backpacking and trail guides blessed with excellent maps.

Department of Fish and Game, 1416 Ninth Street, Sacramento, CA 95814.

La Siesta Press, Box 406, Glendale, CA 91209. Road and trail guides.

Selected Reading

Among recent books, the following are highly recommended. You will find most of these for sale in Owens Valley. The Interagency Visitor Center at Lone Pine, the museums at Independence and Laws, the Ranger Station in Bishop and the bookstores stock a wide variety of local and regional books.

DAVIDSON, CAPT. J. W. *The Expedition of Capt. J. W. Davidson from Fort Tejon to the Owens Valley in 1859.* Edited by Philip J. Wilke and Harry W. Lawton. Socorro, New Mexico, P O Box 1366: Ballena Press, 1976. Owens Valley and its native Indians as Captain Davidson saw them in 1859.

DEDECKER, MARY. *Mines of the Eastern Sierra.* Glendale: La Siesta Press, 1966. True stories of the booms and busts.

HOUSTON, JEANNE WAKATSUKI AND JAMES D. HOUSTON. *Farewell to Manzanar.* San Francisco: San Francisco Book Co., 1974. Effect of World War II internment at Manzanar on the Wakatsuki family and friends.

KAHRL, WILLIAM. "The Politics of California Water: Owens Valley and the Los Angeles Aqueduct, 1900–1927." *California Historical Quarterly,* Volume LV, Spring and Summer, 1976.

LIKES, ROBERT C. AND GLENN R. DAY. *From this Mountain—Cerro Gordo.* Bishop: Chalfant Press, 1975. History of the famous silver mines.

NADEAU, REMI. *City-Makers.* Trans-Anglo Books, 1965. Silver from Cerro Gordo and the Panamints, and other important events in the early history of El Pueblo de Los Angeles.

———. *The Water Seekers.* Revised edition. Bishop: Chalfant Press, 1974. Back in print, the fast-paced story of the Los Angeles Aqueduct.

WOOD, RICHARD COKE. *Owens Valley as I Knew It: The Owens Valley and The Los Angeles Controversy.* Bishop: Chalfant Press, 1973. Coke Wood—"Mr. California" and Director of the Pacific Center for Western Historical Studies—writes from personal experience; he lived in Owens Valley 1918–1934.

INDEX

Mail Orders

for publications on the Eastern Sierra by Genny Smith Books

Deepest Valley: A Guide to Owens Valley, Its Roadsides and Mountain Trails, revised edition 1978, edited by Genny Smith. Paper only.

Mammoth Lakes Sierra, fourth edition 1976, edited by Genny Smith. Companion book to Deepest Valley. Authoritative guide to the superbly beautiful fifty-mile portion of the eastern Sierra slope north of Owens Valley. Roadsides, trails, geologic story, climates, trees, wildflowers, mammals, fish, birds and history. Sixty-eight photographs, many illustrations and maps, 192 pages, paper only.

Historic Owens Valley Postcards 1859–1899, edited by Genny Smith. Each set consists of eight different historic photographs printed on oversize postcards. Photographs and text together provide a mini-history of Owens Valley. Packaged handsomely, an attractive gift.

Battle for Owens Valley Groundwater, 1970– A reprint of the new chapters in the 1978 edition of Deepest Valley. Critical issues of the Inyo County lawsuit to limit groundwater pumping for the Los Angeles Aqueduct. Implications for water use throughout the West. 28 pages.

Write for prices and mail order information
Chalfant Press
PO Box 787, Bishop, California 93514

Chalfant Press supplies retail orders only.
Dealers: Order from William Kaufmann, Inc., One First Street, Los Altos, Ca., 94022.

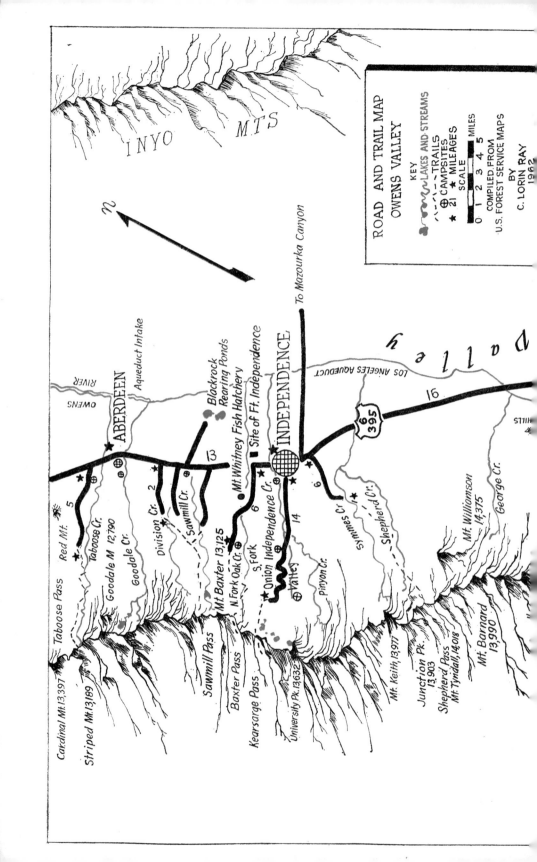

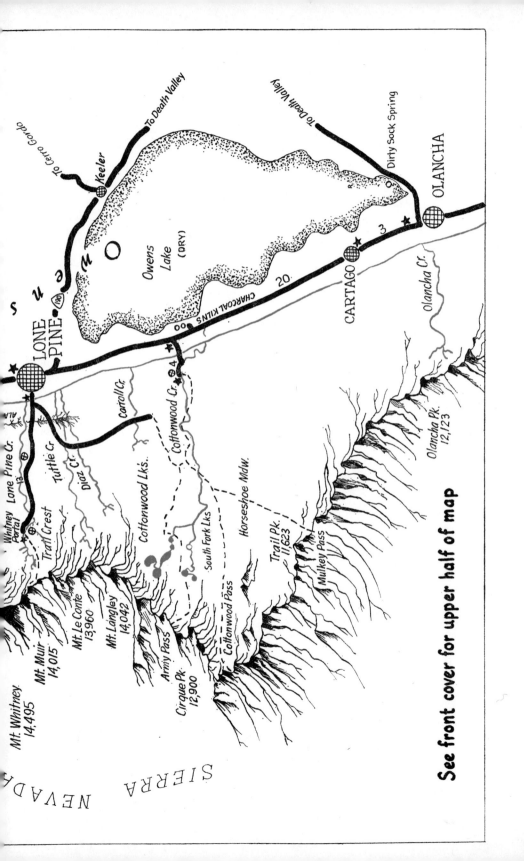

See front cover for upper half of map